Severed Ties and Silenced Voices

Separation and Social Adaptation
in Two Swedish Immigrant Families

D1227451

Severed Ties and Silenced Voices

Separation and Social Adaptation
in Two Swedish Immigrant Families

Roger McKnight

Every thing passes like a flash of lightning;
the good and the evil last so short a time,
that they are hardly worth our being rejoic'd,
or grieved at them.

QueenKristina
(1626-1689)

Nordic Studies Press
Chicago

Severed Ties and Silenced Voices
Separation and Social Adaptation
in Two Swedish Immigrant Families

by Roger McKnight

© Nordic Studies Press 2008

Nordic Studies Press
5226 N. Sawyer
Chicago, IL 60625
USA

www.nordicstudiespress.com

ISBN 0-9772714-2-0

Cover design and typeset by Double Click Design
Printed in the United States by ABC Printing Company
Chicago, IL

Contents

Preface 1

Introduction 3

Chapter I: The Emigrants' Dilemma 9

Chapter II: The Värmland Background 15

Chapter III: Anders Johannesson: The Halland Beginnings 29

Chapter IV: Settling In: Kansas Lake 43

Chapter V: Lars and Caroline at Kansas Lake 57

Chapter VI: Conflict 65

Chapter VII: Missing Lars 77

Chapter VIII: New Problems 83

Chapter IX: Finding Lars 89

Chapter X: Early Trial Reports 97

Chapter XI: On Trial 101

Chapter XII: The Verdict 115

Chapter XIII: The Response 127

Chapter XIV: At Stillwater Prison 133

Chapter XV: Caroline: A Riddle 147

Chapter XVI: Veinge Revisited 161

Chapter XVII: In a New World 169

Chapter XVIII: Facing Freedom 175

Chapter XIX: Caroline in Wisconsin: Reinventing Her History 181

Chapter XX: Returning Home 191

Chapter XXI: Moving On 199

Chapter XXII: A New Life 203

Chapter XXIII: The Waning Years 209

Chapter XXIV: The Pioneer Past 215

Chapter XXV: The Legacy 227

Postscript 231

Endnotes 237

Bibliography 270

Photos and Illustrations 283

Preface

In Dr. McKnight's study of alienation, passion, murder, small town justice, and aftermath, he introduces us to the complexities of the immigrants' experiences across time and space. Drawing upon his extensive research, a deep understanding of immigration history, and a sensitivity to the possible feelings of people in the past, he opens new doors in Swedish-American history. Rarely, have historians ventured into the darker sides of this field, which has long been dominated by studies of pioneer leaders, early settlements, church fathers, cultural and organizational leaders, and successful immigrants. I was once told by a prominent historian that studying the working class Swedish neighborhoods of Minneapolis was inappropriate and we ought forget that part of history. A similar comment surely would have been made about Dr. McKnight's work. However, history is about all of the past – or at least all those parts we can reconstruct from the sources. To know that some immigrants failed, committed horrible crimes, and spent much of their lives in prison or that people intentionally disappeared and left families and later generations with mysteries unsolved and often unsolvable is to understand the past with far greater depth. This is what this book will help any reader to do.

Byron Nordstrom
Professor of History
Gustavus Adolphus College

Introduction

Moving to a new culture and starting over can lead to great personal fulfillment. It may also be a journey fraught with peril. <u>Severed Ties and Silenced Voices</u> is a documented account of one such perilous journey. It deals with three Swedish immigrants, their families, and their search for a better life in America. Their story depicts the common wish for material improvement and social betterment. It also reveals many of the harsh realities of the immigrant experience.

Like newcomers in any setting, the Swedes in this story carried with them a set of learned behavior patterns, which to a large degree dictated their actions in their new homeland. They faced the problem of being separated from their birthright and losing loved ones and friends. The uneasy task of gaining acceptance in their new culture was an added difficulty. How the immigrants responded to those problems was crucial in determining the course of their lives. Studying the nature of their responses is a key component to <u>Severed Ties and Silenced Voices</u>.

The immigrants left numerous relatives behind in Sweden and took others with them to America. In that context, the broader aim of this text is to study the social background of rural nineteenth-century

Sweden, which the figures in this story called home. The first specific purpose is to illustrate the lasting impact their homeland experiences had on the three immigrants. The second intent is to study the trials that the Swedes faced in America and the long-term personal effects of those trials.

The text follows the immigrants and their families from 1833 to the mid twentieth century. Of prime chronological importance are their early years in Sweden, the contours of their lives in America, and the succession of challenges they faced in Sweden and the United States alike. The narrative describes the natural, societal, and personal forces that influenced the life-changing decisions they were forced to make.

The narrative is a social history of many aspects of their times, but it also deals with the psychology of the individuals and the mental and spiritual price they paid in pulling up roots and settling in some of the last untamed areas of the Upper Midwest. Along the way, the immigrants experienced alienation, violence, and abandonment. Many of their actions were shrouded in mystery. In that connection, their story suggests an important question: Were the numerous difficulties they encountered largely ones of their own making or mainly the result of conditions beyond their control? Several social themes relevant to the nineteenth century follow from that question. They are: the impact of government oppression in Sweden; the role of women in Swedish and American society; the problems of domestic abuse; the place of ethnic groups in America; the role of church leaders in molding public attitudes; and the relative importance of tradition in preserving community history.

In short, <u>Severed Ties and Silenced Voices</u> is an unromanticized and true story of the move from Sweden to America, as seen through the eyes of several humble people who lived it. This account of poor and illiterate immigrants illustrates the difficulties of leaving one's native culture behind and making oneself over in a new land. In addition, the text takes up the questions: Was it possible to keep familial connections alive between the Old World and the New? Or was the passage across the Atlantic the great definitive and permanent divider of families?

Writing this text has been an experience in serendipity. It originated in a research project on crime and incarceration among Swedish Americans in Minnesota. That project led to the accidental discovery of documents concerning the immigrants of this story in the archives of the Minnesota Historical Society. Those documents caused the author to wonder: Who were those three immigrants exactly? And how did their lives come to be recorded, if they themselves could not read or write? Finding the answers to those questions entailed a long search via individual contact persons and research institutions spread across Sweden and the Midwest.

Several archives and individuals in Sweden deserve special thanks for their assistance. Included are the following: Håkan Håkansson and Birgitta Wiman of the Halland Genealogical Society in Halmstad. Their help was indispensable. The insights of Nils Alexandersson, Nils and Asta Berg, and Evelyn Hardenmark were also helpful.

The staff members at Svenska Emigrantinstitutet (The House of Emigrants) in Växjö showed endless patience and understanding. Johan Goddijn and Bo Björklund were especially accommodating. Researcher Carl-Johan Ivarsson, of Säffle, supplied valuable information and personal guidance about the immigrants' origins in Värmland.

In Minnesota the following institutions have offered kind and useful assistance: The Watonwan County Historical Society; The Blue Earth County Historical Society; and the Recorder's Office at the Watonwan County Courthouse in St. James. In Wisconsin the Register of Deeds at the Douglas County Courthouse, in Superior, provided valuable documents. I would also like to thank researcher Gay McClellan in Minnesota.

None of the details for this work would have been remotely possible without the help of four individuals. They are Carol Bratland of St. James, Minnesota, the great-great granddaughter of Lars and Caroline Johnson; Pat Henke of Fall Creek, Wisconsin, the great-granddaughter of Andrew and Caroline Johnson; Judy Klee of Temecula, California, the great-great granddaughter of Charles J. Johnson; and Donna Bieg of Tucson, Arizona, the great-great granddaughter of Andrew Johnson and Johanna Persdotter. To them I owe a special note of thanks for their encouragement, tireless help, and enthusiasm. Special thanks as well to my wife Barb for her many insightful comments on the lives of the immigrant Swedes.

Preparing this text has meant dealing with many older Swedish writings and numerous nineteenth and early twentieth-century American courtroom papers and legal documents. The orthography, syntax, and dating of those records are often irregular and difficult to decipher. To make them more readily accessible to readers, I have translated the Swedish texts and normalized the questionable English constructions when necessary. Most of the quotations from the Swedish sources may be found in their original Swedish form in the Endnotes. I take sole responsibility for the accuracy of the translations and the presentation of information from the source materials.

Nineteenth-century Scandinavians and Americans lived in an era relatively close to us in time, but their assumptions and sensibilities could differ from our own in striking ways. Getting to know the individuals in this story has deepened my understanding of society and human nature, with their many constants and variables. I wish my readers the same invaluable experience and food for thought in studying the immigrants' lives.

Roger McKnight
Gustavus Adolphus College

Chapter I
The Emigrants' Dilemma

This is the story of three immigrants and their families. They were Lars Fredrik, Karolina, and Anders, humble farm people from nineteenth-century Sweden. In the prime of their lives, they sailed to America, leaving behind generations of tradition and numerous family members. As with most of the poor, their names appear in no history books and they were unable to write their own tale of life in Europe and the United States. Still, the events of their lives serve to illuminate the age in which they lived, from the early 1800s to the start of the twentieth century. Their experiences point to timeless themes of alienation, adaptation, and survival in the midst of imposing societal and personal problems. To gain an understanding of their story and how they fit into the social fabric of the time, it is necessary to piece together the lives of the three immigrants from their beginnings and to study the makeup of the communities they came from.

Lars Fredrik, Karolina, and Anders's long exodus from Sweden to America had its origins in the poverty of their homeland. It continued with the choices they made in the face of that poverty. For generations, Swedish commoners had struggled against deprivation and starvation. The three emigrants' families were no exception to that rule. In truth, the Sweden of the early nineteenth century was one of the most impoverished nations in all of Europe. The rich were few but very rich; the poor were legion and greatly exploited. Foodstuffs and the necessities of life were scarce, and those that existed were unequally distributed. Sweden's social and governmental system was in a tattered state that the nation's leaders had few prospects of repairing. By the middle of the century, Lars Fredrik, Karolina, and Anders themselves were among those in the most difficult straits. They owned little and endured much.

In terms of upward mobility, Lars Fredrik, Karolina, and Anders faced an impossible gridlock as they were growing up in the Sweden of the 1830s and 1840s. Social stratification contributed largely to their poverty. Sweden was a monarchy lacking in democracy. The king governed with the legislature but had absolute veto power on vital issues. Besides the king, the dominant force was the Four Estates, a privileged caste of clergy, nobles, burghers, and freehold farmers that dated back to the Middle Ages. Though they accounted for only one-sixth or less of the population, they controlled over ninety percent of the nation's wealth. The remaining segments of the populace consisted of poor farmers, the great mass of agricultural workers, and the urban poor, who had no political representation and possessed less than ten percent of the wealth. Over eighty-five percent of Swedes made their living in agriculture. Lars Fredrik, Karolina, Anders and their families belonged to that impoverished farming majority.[1]

Social stratification was nowhere more evident than in the rural districts. At the top of the hierarchy were the landowning farmers, some of whom possessed immense wealth.[2] However, the most common group of landowners consisted of homesteaders (*hemmansägare*). Those men, of whom Anders's father was a representative, owned smaller farms. Below the landowners came the tenant farmers or crofters (*torpare*). They rented land, tilled the soil, and paid part of their rent by sharing a percentage of their crops with the landowners. At the bottom of the social ladder were settled but destitute families of beggars (*tiggare*), who traveled the byways of their parishes seeking food and clothing and asking for alms.

Common to all those groups, except for the very highest echelons of landowners, was their greater or lesser degree of need. Lars Fredrik's,

Karolina's, and Anders's parents were among those who existed on the margins of the Swedish economy. A historian summarized their situation: "Simply put, there were too many people and not enough land or jobs in the agricultural sector. In addition, the working conditions of the rural poor were horrible, and farming in parts of Sweden at times was a futile endeavor, usually because of poor soil."[3] With travel limited and work scarce, the poor had little choice before 1850 but to stay on the land and manage with meager resources.

Swedes made attempts to provide for those unable to carry on with the demanding farm labor. Highly relevant to the families of Lars Fredrik, Karolina, and Anders was the practice of assigning aging agricultural workers to so-called *undantag* status. This word played an important role in the lives of farm people.[4] It designated a plot of land separated from the productive acres of a farm and inhabited by those who were the oldest residents or the ones least able to carry on any longer with gainful farm labor. Sons who took over the family farm or outsiders who purchased a farm gave the *undantag* to their aging parents or to the retiring landholders as a form of retirement insurance. The transfer was made as a written contract, which allowed the older farmers to live as extra boarders in the main farmhouse along with the new owners, or in a special cottage set off on the edges of the productive farmland.[5] Many of Sweden's rural inhabitants were relegated to just such marginal housing arrangements.

Not all the troubles facing the working classes were imposed on them from above. Alcohol abuse had long plagued the commoners, and the areas where Lars Fredrik, Karolina, and Anders grew up were typical in that respect. Alcoholism became most widespread during what historian Franklin Scott described as "the drunken decades" of the early 1800s. When Lars Fredrik, Karolina, and Anders were born, distilling liquor from potatoes was cheap and easily done. Yearly consumption of hard liquor was nearly eleven liters per capita. Added to that figure was the drinking of beer and wine.[6] In certain areas of Sweden the average life span for working-class men sank to as low as forty-five years by 1850, with alcohol contributing significantly to the dreadful statistic.

Land policies in Sweden brought about various changes in patterns of living. Most notable was a series of resettlement acts, which broke up the farm villages and placed families on isolated separate

11

holdings spread across the countryside. Those holdings had, in turn, been divided and subdivided by landowners' heirs as the result of a population explosion. In Sweden as a whole, the population grew by one percent a year throughout the first half of the 1800s. That led to an increase of 1.1 million inhabitants by 1850.[7]

By the mid-1860s making a living by farming had become difficult even on holdings that once were the most productive. An added pressure came in the form of crop failure. Nearly every generation of Swedes experienced at least one period of serious want due to harsh weather conditions. The most calamitous of those crises came in the 1860s, when Lars Fredrik, Karolina, and Anders reached their twenties and began raising families of their own. Crops were ruined for three years in a row between 1866 and 1868. The Great Famine of those years spared no parts of Sweden. As Swedish historian Lars Ljungmark remarked: "Crop failures had nearly catastrophic consequences in rural areas caught between explosive population growth and sluggish land development."[8]

Class hierarchy and humiliating social mores worsened already miserable conditions for the poor. Discrimination by the Swedish government toward the poorer classes was endemic. Non-compliant men, such as Lars Fredrik's father, suffered greatly from the censure of officials. Worst off, however, were women of the poorer classes. A series of laws, going as far back as the Protestant Reformation of the 1500s, defined all women as minors. Those laws stipulated that women could only follow professions and trades, inherit property, or marry if they had the permission and guiding hand of a male guardian. Only widows were exempt from those strictures. For working-class women there was little choice but to find a husband to depend on or to seek employment in the most menial of positions, most often as serving girls or milkmaids.[9]

Exerting the greatest stranglehold on the customs of the common people was the State Church, or the Church of Sweden. Religious services not held under the auspices of the Lutheran clergy were illegal. Terms for conducting and attending services were spelled out by an ordinance from 1726 called the Conventicle Decree.[10] The act declared that Swedish commoners who gathered for private religious purposes without an ordained clergyman present were liable to stiff fines, imprisonment, or even exile from Sweden. This was clearly a maneuver to limit the active participation of laymen in congregational activities and decision-making. It also helped the State to reinforce its right to determine religious doctrine for the nation. Terms of the Conventicle Decree still held sway during Lars Fredrik, Karolina, and Anders's early years, and the act was not abolished until 1858. Even then, the Church of Sweden continued to exert pressure on parishioners, especially by insisting on mandatory church attendance.

Other bothersome intrusions came in the form of obligatory reports by the Church of Sweden clergy on the home life of all their parishioners. Those were the inconvenient Household Examinations, which catalogued congregation members' knowledge of the catechism, as well as any extraordinary personal traits or individual activities. Supplementing those papers were the church ledgers recording individual or family movements in or out of the parishes. The ledgers included information on parishioners who were relocating within Sweden or emigrating to foreign countries. In short, religious freedom was nonexistent in nineteenth-century Sweden.[11]

Despite those restrictions, the Sweden of Lars Fredrik, Karolina, and Anders's youth was not wholly static. Some changes began even before mid-century. One important development was in education. For generations the working poor had largely been illiterate, but in 1842 the Universal Education Act, mandated by the central government, went into effect.[12] The ordinance guaranteed all Swedish children the right to a sixth-grade education. They were taught general skills, but the main thrust was an attempt to eliminate illiteracy.

After 1850 change became more common. In 1865-1866 an important act of parliamentary reform abolished the Four Estates, and during the second half of the century commoners gained increased representation. The place of women also improved, a fact that aided Karolina when she made plans to emigrate. Women were declared to reach their majority at age twenty-five, and divorce laws were redefined to allow both sexes to sue for divorce and inherit property equally. Parallel to those developments was the growth of a more mobile society. Mechanization, steamship lines, railways, telegraph systems, and increasing literacy among the commoners created new possibilities in transportation and communication. One observer in the nineteenth century found rural Swedes woefully unaware of political affairs and issues outside their work, but they were keenly aware of their own poverty and the new-found social and technological opportunities at their disposal.[13]

In the 1860s those advances enabled the Swedish commoners to start a mass migration of previously unknown proportions. For the poor, the choice was simple: to stay at home and risk starvation or pack up and leave. Even those Swedes who found themselves on the lowest rungs of the social ladder began looking for ways to escape their plight. Famine may have lurked around the corner of every farmer's cottage, but a means of avoiding it was now at hand. It was under such conditions that Lars Fredrik, the oldest of the three Swedes, and his wife Karolina first turned their thoughts to hopes of gaining a better life in America. Once their minds were made up, the move followed quickly.

Chapter II
The Värmland Background

Lars Fredrik and Karolina were natives of Värmland, in west-central Sweden. He was born Lars Fredrik Johannesson Holm in 1831, and his wife, born in 1842, bore the Swedish name Karolina Andersdotter. The province they called home was poor but diverse. It was far from the centers of power in Stockholm and close to the Norwegian border. The landscape featured mountains, extensive forestlands, and countless lakes. Lars Fredrik and Karolina grew up near Lake Vänern, Sweden's largest body of freshwater. Their homes were located on the slopes above Harefjorden, a lake that empties into Vänern. Those two lakes dominated the landscape. Their calm, glistening surface could give way to storms and turbulent water, providing scenes that were surely etched in the couple's memories from childhood.

The countryside was dotted with small farmsteads, which housed large families of freeholders. The soil was poor and could hardly have supported big households if not for a mixed economy of cash crops, animal husbandry, handcrafts, and lumbering. Yet farmers persistently opened up new tracts for agriculture, and the people of Värmland were noted for their innovative small-scale farming techniques.

Unlike most rural Swedes, Värmlanders were mobile. Workers defied difficult road conditions and traveled widely to find seasonal employment in sawmills and to do carpentry work or labor in the fields digging root crops. Adaptability was a key component in their search for work.[1]

The people of Värmland were as varied as the landscape. There were settled Swedish families in the few trading centers, a mixture of Norwegians and Swedes in the areas closest to Norway, and sizable settlements of Finns. This last group consisted of descendants of Finnish farmers and foresters brought to Sweden in the seventeenth century when Finland formed part of the Swedish empire. The Finns settled in some of the more distant parts of Värmland and became known as Forest Finns. They added to the scattering of original and memorable characters who lived all across Värmland but especially in the vast tracts of forest to the north.[2]

Most nineteenth-century Värmlanders were poorly fed, ill housed, uneducated, and accustomed to hardship. Lars Fredrik Johannesson Holm's family was typical in all those respects. Lars Fredrik grew up at Sterserudstorp in Bro parish, a self-contained farm village that was unaffected by resettlement policies. (Figure 1) The area he was born in consisted of subdivided holdings, and the population explosion caused much overcrowding. The family had lived in the area since at least the beginning of the nineteenth century. His parents fell into poverty in the early years of their marriage, when they still had under-age children. As a result, Lars Fredrik's father owned a small *undantag* cottage on the most marginal of farmland. The struggle to make ends meet continued to be a critical issue for the family well into the 1860s, and the difficulties left their mark on Lars Fredrik's early life.

His family's poverty was extreme, even by the standards of that age. As the years mounted, dysfunctional behavior and unstable personality traits worsened the situation. Lars Fredrik's father, Johannes Olof Holm, was regularly listed in the Bro parish church records with negative attributes attached to his name. Lars Fredrik's mother, Ingrid Larsdotter, had seven children, four sons and three daughters. One of the sons later moved to the Stockholm area, but the other siblings remained in Värmland as adults.

The Holm cabin at Sterserudstorp was small and crowded, but family living went on, even if the course of life was seldom smooth.

At the root of the problem was Johannes Olof's behavior. In 1838, Lars Fredrik's father was first warned by the Bro parish pastor for practicing a form of verbal magic known as signeri. Later on Johannes Olof Holm was again reported for the same deviant behavior, this time to the higher authorities in the Church of Sweden. The church record for 1841-1845 stated the following about Johannes Olof: "Reported for making threats by practicing Signeri. Warned October 3, 1838, by N. H. [the pastor] forthwith to cease and desist."[3]

In contrast to forms of magic that entailed direct interaction with the devil (and known as diabolism), signeri involved the use of incantations or hexes intended to invoke supernatural powers to intercede in human affairs, either as a way to benefit people or to call down evil forces on them. The practice traced its origins as far back as the Viking Age, a thousand years earlier, and had continued with the coming of Christianity in the Middle Ages. Its use was then permitted only among the clergy and was intended for beneficial purposes. By the nineteenth century signeri was associated in Sweden mainly with local healers, who used verses or home remedies to facilitate cures or ward off illnesses.[4] Such healers were popular among the poor, who were either distrustful of (or unable to pay for) the services of licensed medical doctors located in towns and cities, distant from isolated farmsteads.

For parishioners who lived off the beaten track, sympathetic and knowledgeable neighbors were the most reliable caregivers. Even with such healers troubles could arise, however. Those who were short tempered or easily offended were known to turn the tables on the trusting public, or even their own neighbors, and wish injury on people they felt had dealt badly with them. Those who exhibited such erratic behavior could be labeled as misfits. At other times signeri was used by the underprivileged as a tool for issuing threats against the governing classes. This use of verbal magic is what one modern scholar has referred to as "the games of the powerless," that is, a ploy by the poor and disenfranchised to gain revenge against those they perceived as their oppressors. In rural areas the perceived oppressors were landowning farmers, law enforcement officers, or clergymen in the Church of Sweden. In Värmland signeri was most often associated in the public mind with the Forest Finns.[5] Johannes Olof Holm was likely influenced by traditions of verbal magic brought to his district from outside the province or from other parts of Värmland, including the Finnish settlements.

In isolated areas the use of signeri persisted well into the modern era. Johannes Olof Holm was one of those who continued practicing it. His actions were taken seriously and they spoke to the clergy of anger at the community and of non-Christian beliefs. The enduring image of Johannes Olof Holm is that of an embittered and troubled man. Alone with his thoughts in his family's forest cabin and incensed at his ever increasing poverty, he hurled insults at the secular and ecclesiastical figures who invaded his home with lengthening lists of ordinances, reminders of taxes, and demands for piety.

Johannes Olof had personal cause for his anger. He came from a large family whose position in Värmland society at one time spoke of solid values and social responsibility. His grandfather was a church sexton and his father a church warden and county assessor.[6] Most likely because of drink, Johannes Olof was the first in his family who slid into poverty, whereupon he took up the marginal farmstead at Sterserudstorp. The considerable steps he took down the ladder of social prestige were enough to bring out the frustration and anger in him, which led to his threats of verbal magic against the established community. The easiest targets were those above him, some of whom were his own father's former associates. His threats against those people left Johannes Olof's family in an even more vulnerable position than their poverty alone would have entailed. The result was that his tendency toward a passive downward spiral, both socially and economically, became mixed with outward shows of aggressive posturing in public and domestic instability or violence in the home.

The warnings from the Lutheran clergy remained as black marks on Johannes Olof's record for the rest of his life. Decade after decade the minister's remarks in the Household Examination book repeated the details of his various transgressions. The censure against Johannes Olof recurred throughout his son Lars Fredrik's formative years and even up to the point of his emigration to America. Officials across the district would have remained aware of its harsh wording and judged the family accordingly.

To make matters worse, Lars Fredrik himself also bore the mental scars of official rejection. In 1850, when he was only nineteen, his name was stricken from the Swedish central government tax records.[7]

A single word explained the action. It stated that Lars Fredrik was a "dwarf" (*dvärg*). The government's assertion was that Lars Fredrik was too small and physically unfit to do the work of an able-bodied man. He was therefore freed (or, perhaps more aptly, forbidden) from paying taxes to the Swedish government on whatever income he might scrape together. This declaration hindered Lars Fredrik from obtaining gainful employment, and it stood against him as a badge of dishonor. In 1852, furthermore, at the age of twenty-one, Lars Fredrik was called up for military service. He reported to the army for duty but was cashiered because of his dwarf status. Laconically, the discharge papers summarized the action in the following way: "Dwarf, discharged from military duty."[8]

It is questionable whether Lars Fredrik was a dwarf in any medical sense. Descriptions of him said only that he boasted of a thick shock of blond hair, sported a beard, and was an unusually small man. He bore deep mental scars as a result of his short stature. The army discharge can only have increased his feelings of inadequacy. Shamed in the full light of public view, he returned home to Sterserudstorp in 1852, further rejected by the Swedish authorities. It was a blatant challenge to his masculinity. From that point on, Lars Fredrik carried strong feelings of persecution and a "small man's complex." He overcompensated for his social exclusion by acting the aggressive, sharp-tongued bully, ill at ease in company and full of spite for his neighbors. Beyond all doubt, his outward shows of hostility concealed the fears and insecurity he felt inside. As the years mounted, his conduct carried the growing hallmarks of mental instability, and he was forced ever further into the periphery of community life.

Given his marginal state in the early 1850s, it must have come as something of a surprise to the community when he married Karolina ten years later. She was the second oldest child of Anders Nilsson, a lifelong resident of Värmland, and Greta Stina Olofsdotter, his wife. A man of many interests, Karolina's father had enjoyed a certain responsible standing and a good name in local Värmland society in his early years. He held several different positions ranging from farming to small business, all of which lent a shimmer of success and responsible behavior to his name.

Through her early years, Karolina's family worked to maintain that show of respectability, but troubles were ever present and began to increase. Her mother and father appear to have had little in common. Greta Stina came from landed money, while Anders Nilsson's parents were of less wealth. Anders started out in farming. He later worked as a tailor and a clockmaker. Despite those titles, Anders Nilsson's life was plagued with difficulties. He faltered as a farmer and there are doubts about his clockmaking skills, since no examples of his handmade clocks have survived to the present. Even in his youth he had experienced trouble. In 1833 he was convicted in district court for leaving a loaded gun in an unlocked room, where a maidservant was mortally wounded. Sweden's Göta Court of Appeals later acquitted him of any wrongdoing, and so he remained a free man. Afterwards, however, he was always a target of suspicion for irresponsibility.[9]

Anders Nilsson moved his wife and children from residence to residence. Between 1836 and 1848 the family lived at five different addresses in Värmland. Later Anders built the farm Sjöhaget (Lake Forest) at the settlement of Djupviken. After his wife's death in 1861, he sold most of that property and settled at a small home called Fridhem (Peaceful Home), which is where he continued with clockmaking and also saw his fortunes decline even further.

During the 1840s and 1850s the Nilsson's family life had been relatively stable, despite the frequent moves and rumblings of discontent. Karolina attended school for a few years while they were in Djupviken, but not long enough to attain any true literacy. This was mainly due to her having begun school in the early years of Universal Education reforms in Sweden. Though the education act of 1842 granted all children the right to six years of schooling, real opportunities for children of poor families were so few that six months of total lifetime instruction was often the truer attainment. Not all school districts enforced attendance requirements nor were all parents willing to let their children go to school. A shortage of trained teachers also presented a barrier to good instruction.

In those early schools, boys were taught to read and write, while girls were taught only to read. Thus the ability to read and write was far from true for all commoners, regardless of what the government intended. Years later Karolina herself commented: "I can read a little in Swedish. Cannot write."[10] That sad fact was hardly surprising given the difficult school situation in her area. The schoolhouse there was built in 1839, but no pupils reported for classes until the Universal Education Act went into effect three years later, the same year Karolina was born. The Djupviken school building remained tiny, measuring barely seven by eleven yards. Classes were in session only ten weeks a year, mainly during the summer months. In the lower grades, which Karolina began in the late 1840s, pupils were taught reading, writing, and arithmetic. They sat in rows on benches without back supports and were taught to write by forming letters of the alphabet in sandboxes. Average attendance never amounted to more than fifty percent of the eligible pupils.[11] Karolina is likely to have attended classes only sporadically.

Karolina stayed at her parents' home until she was twenty, by which time her father's affairs had begun to deteriorate seriously. Sometime in the late 1850s or in 1860, she met Lars Fredrik and they became engaged. The Kila pastor, who later married them, commented on her in 1861. He wrote that she and Lars Fredrik had their banns read for the first time in the Kila parish church on December 6, 1861.[12] That signaled the start of the Christmas season. It spoke of future happiness, but the couple had problems fulfilling that promise. Married on June 12, 1862 (when she was twenty and he thirty-one), they first lived at Lars Fredrik's family home. The first two children in their family, Anna Charlotta and Julia Maria, were born there in 1863 and 1865.[13]

The years 1860 to 1868 were a period of trial and tribulation. Even before she married, Karolina surely faced enormous pressure. First was the puzzle of how to deal with her father. Anders Nilsson was impecunious, a problem made worse by alcoholism. His drinking habits and poor work ethic accounted for most of his severest financial losses. Before Karolina's mother died, her own father, Olof Andersson, took steps to assure that none of Greta Stina's inheritance fell into her husband Anders Nilsson's hands. A well-to-do landowner, Olof Andersson knew his son-in-law all too well. In this connection, a Swedish researcher has written of Anders Nilsson:

> *We know that his father-in-law Olof Andersson*
> *rewrote his will so all the inheritance from Karolina's*
> *mother would go straight to her children because Anders*
> *Nilsson had squandered all the money and estate that he*
> *had inherited from his own father.*[14]

Anders Nilsson's reputation of not being able to care for money was thus well known. That trait followed him to the bitter end. He not only lacked money to help Karolina find a suitable husband but he himself continued living in poverty until he died penniless in 1896, leaving behind only an anvil, a few miscellaneous household items, and an impoverished second wife.[15]

In the early 1860s Karolina faced the prospect of contending with her father after her mother was gone. While she was still alive, Greta Stina's nurturing ways and the support of her own father must have functioned for Karolina as welcome buffers against Anders, who likely began insisting that his daughters leave home so that he could avoid having to support them. In fact, Karolina appears to have started looking for a way to leave her father even before her mother died. And so Karolina met and married Lars Fredrik and got caught in the middle — between her father's profligacy in Djupviken and Lars Fredrik and his father's strange ways at Sterserudstorp.

Karolina's second dilemma was how to deal with her new husband after 1862. Lars Fredrik was socially and occupationally handicapped. All his attempts at work were desultory. Without a job, he could eke out only the barest of livings for his growing family. Finally, he took to begging. In making that move, he was not alone. Begging had for centuries been common among the landless and unemployed, and the practice was widely tolerated by the Swedish public. It became especially noticeable during the famine years of the 1860s, just when Lars Fredrik and Karolina were starting out together. Faced with the problem of growing numbers of beggars on the roadways, Swedish authorities made attempts to eliminate the practice. In 1847, for instance, the custom was formally forbidden across the land by Swedish law.[16] Nonetheless it persisted throughout the nineteenth and into the early twentieth centuries.

Begging became so common that it reached the point of being an accepted means of making a living among the very poorest classes. Each Swedish parish had the understood responsibility of determining areas in which it was permissible to beg and for specifying the order in which each beggar was to visit farms in his parish. Those mandates were the so-called beggars' passes issued by local law officers or church officials. Some parishes went so far as to issue begging badges, which beggars wore on their coats. They functioned as a sign that specific individuals had been granted permission to beg and that the parish farmers were obligated to give them alms. On occasion Swedish farmers even set aside special beggars' benches on their farms, which beggars were required to sit on while waiting for handouts of food, grain, or clothing.[17]

Most beggars were starving, hard-pressed persons seeking a means of survival. Lars Fredrik fit that category precisely. He wandered the countryside because of real need. Yet he brought no honor to his family. In a society that defined power in terms of physical strength and material possessions, Lars Fredrik was on the outside looking in. Already declared physically unfit, he carried on with activities that reinforced his standing as an outsider. He was hemmed in between the conflicting mandates to accept his jobless status and still try to maintain his self-respect as the head of his family. In turn, Karolina, too, was caught in a trap. She had left her family home and was faced with the difficult transition to life at Sterserudstorp. At Lars Fredrik's parents' home, the poverty was even greater than at her father's farmstead.

The family of Johannes Olof Holm would have had few friends and none with any standing in the community. In that socially isolated setting, it was easy for Lars Fredrik to begin taking out his frustrations on his young wife. In the early years he surely had a psychological advantage over Karolina because of the age difference. Their marriage was soon further complicated by arguments and domestic abuse. Lars Fredrik's years of living on the margins gave rise to his violent tendencies and Karolina was on the receiving end. Karolina described the nature of their life together:

> *Lars Fredrik and I quarreled sometimes. We quarreled about everything, he did not work on the farm much. I have had trouble with him about other men and every man with whom he has seen me talking. He thought I did not work enough, and we have quarreled about this, he has often struck me. We used to fight, pull hair and have a general rough and tumble fight. My husband was not on friendly terms with any of his neighbors.* [18]

Those abusive habits appeared early in their marriage and continued unabated throughout the 1860s.

As the decade drew to a close, Lars Fredrik and Karolina's existence was marked by a combination of personal and family difficulties and exacerbated by systemic government oppression. When talk of

23

emigration arose, both could welcome the chance to start anew. For her part, Karolina could look back and try to understand what had led her to her troubled position. The unwritten law in her society was that people married within their own social class, and families could attempt to establish courtships between young, single persons who promised to be compatible partners. However, in the final result young women were allowed to follow their own wishes in choosing spouses, or to take steps toward breaking off engagements if they and their fiancés proved incompatible.[19] Karolina must have had better offers of marriage early on. At the very least, she surely met other men with more to offer than Lars Fredrik. In addition, it would have been obvious to her, perhaps painfully so, that Lars Fredrik's social status was lower even than her own. She chose him nonetheless. Later she had reason to wonder why. It seems unfathomable that she was romantically attached to him. Neither was she pregnant when they got married.

Certainly Lars Fredrik had little, if anything, to offer her materially, and the possibility that he possessed a boyish charm as a young man, which observers failed to discern, is remote. The only hint as to her initial meeting with Lars Fredrik lay in the fact that his mother was a native of Karolina's Kila parish and may have established a connection between the two families, who lived on opposite sides of Harefjorden. (Figure 8) In short, Karolina surely married Lars Fredrik for reasons other than true love, most likely for the practical reasons that her father pressured her to leave home and she needed a male guardian. Even before leaving Sweden, she had reasons to regret that decision. For Lars Fredrik, the memory of being shunted aside by the Swedish authorities was indelibly imprinted on his psyche. He had every reason to wish to shed his outcast state and be treated as a social equal in a new setting.

The crucial spark that convinced the Johannesson Holms to leave for America was the recruitment work of several Midwestern states and private business concerns in America. The governments of Wisconsin and Minnesota launched emigration campaigns in Europe, which sought farmers to populate the uninhabited areas of those states. Salaried representatives of the Wisconsin and Minnesota governments or private enterprises were sent to northern Europe on recruitment trips. Agents moved about among the common people describing the attractions of the Midwest.

The earliest well-known emigration agent to Sweden was Hans Mattson, who had his origins in Skåne, in deep southern Sweden. Mattson himself immigrated to Minnesota in 1851 and established himself as a leading farmer, politician, and newspaper editor. He returned to Sweden in 1868 as the commissioner of the Board of Immigration for the State of Minnesota and as a promoter of private railroad interests. Hans Mattson traveled extensively in southern Sweden during 1868 speaking warmly of the opportunities in America. The Minnesota historian Theodore Blegen described Mattson as a modern-day Marco Polo, who returned to his impoverished homeland with tales of fabulous, far-off lands. The result was that "people flocked from their houses to the roads and streets in order to catch a glimpse of the returned traveler."[20]   Mattson himself wrote later: "I found myself besieged [in Sweden] by people who wished to accompany me back to America in the spring."[21]   He sent one steamship fully loaded with Swedish emigrants to America, and then personally accompanied another party of Swedes to the United States a few weeks later. Franklin Scott summarized Mattson's trip in factual terms: "His first recruiting trip to Sweden fell in the period of hard times in the late 1860s, and he brought back 800 immigrants."[22]

Mattson's major recruiting trip outside of southern Sweden in 1868 was a longer trip to Värmland.[23] News of America reached residents of Bro and Kila parishes in the wake of Mattson's visit. Beyond all doubt Lars Fredrik and Karolina's decision to leave Sweden was one of the outcomes. After hearing the recruiter's descriptions in person or from relatives and friends, they were surely convinced to take the decisive step. Karolina used part of the inheritance money from her mother to pay an emigration agent for transportation from Kristiania (Oslo), Norway, direct to Madison, Wisconsin. The family left Kila for Kristiania on April 11, 1868.[24] They surely looked back, wondering if it was their last glimpse of the old home area.

Between Sterserudstorp and Kila and the Norwegian capital lay uneven terrain. The journey demanded a measured and unhurried pace. (Figure 2) In Lars Fredrik and Karolina's company were their two daughters, Karolina's older sister Anna Maria Andersdotter, her husband Adam Peter Jonasson, and that couple's children. Lars Fredrik was thirty-seven and Karolina twenty-six. They were joining in the beginning of the historic mass emigration caused largely by the Great Famine of the 1860s. During the decade between 1861 and 1870, as many as four out of every 1,000 inhabitants left Värmland. The most remarkable upsurge began in 1868, when a total of 1,461 persons emigrated from Värmland and headed for the United States. That figure was a noticeable increase from the pre-famine year of 1864, when only 162 Värmlanders moved overseas. By the end of the century, over 89,000 Swedes had left the province dreaming of a better life in America.[25]

Though Lars Fredrik and Karolina had much of a distressing nature to leave behind in Värmland, their goals in America were less well explained. Karolina herself was surely tired of her husband and may have been looking for an escape hatch in America. Her only recorded statement, however, was more concrete. She said she wished to own land of her own in the United States and make it productive.[26] She and Lars Fredrik also had in mind the optimistic stories of Hans Mattson, which exerted an irresistible psychological pull from the American side.

The group waited for nearly three weeks in Norway. Finally, on May 8 they departed Kristiania for Hull, England, and sailed from Liverpool in mid-May, 1868.[27]

Later family traditions told of the Johannesson Holm and Jonasson party being placed aboard a sailing ship in Liverpool rather than a steamer. The Atlantic liner had been overbooked, an indication that the volume of emigrant traffic was heavy from all of northern Europe during those famine years. Hindered by storms, the sailing ship was blown back toward Europe over and over again, resulting in a torturous trans-Atlantic passage of eleven weeks. Lars Fredrik and Karolina's younger daughter Julia Maria perished at some point between Norway and the American Midwest. The family never mentioned her name again after they departed from Norway, leading to the assumption she was buried at sea.[28]

The Johannesson Holms and Jonassons reached Madison, Wisconsin, in the summer of 1868. Karolina's sister and her family stayed in Madison, but Lars Fredrik and Karolina paused there only briefly. In the last part of that summer, Karolina took a while off to relax in Madison. She and Anna Maria realized the dream of owning land by buying four acres on the outskirts of Madison, and Karolina stopped to have her photograph taken in a downtown photographer's shop.[29]

Soon thereafter she and Lars Fredrik hurried on westward. They followed the construction of the railroads across southern Wisconsin and Minnesota. Whether they came to the Midwest specifically because of railroad expansion, or if they only happened to arrive in Wisconsin just as the lines were being built there is a puzzle. Once again, the key to an answer was likely Hans Mattson. Mattson saw to it that news of railroad construction spread quickly among Swedes traveling west of Chicago. Lars Fredrik and Karolina fit that description. They joined with hundreds of other immigrants pushing on across the Upper Midwest.

For the next three years they continued the westward march. In the fall of 1868, they reached the Mississippi River at La Crosse, Wisconsin, and crossed over into Minnesota. Then they passed by Waseca and Mankato in southern Minnesota. In 1870 several rail lines were converging there. Soon the lines extended farther to the southwest. Following in that direction, Lars Fredrik and Karolina reached the Minnesota prairies in 1871. They found a plot of land and settled near the wooded banks of Kansas Lake in Watonwan County. There on the Minnesota flatlands, Lars Fredrik Johannesson Holm came to be known to Americans as Lars Johnson, and Karolina took the name of Caroline Johnson. In the spring of 1871, the Watonwan County Recorder's Office described Lars simply as "a farmer."[30]

The journey from Värmland had been long and arduous. Along the way the couple first lost a daughter at sea, then parted company with Caroline's sister and brother-and-in-law in Wisconsin, and now found themselves faced with the prospect of creating a new life on the treeless prairies of Minnesota. They were a quarter of the way around the globe from home. Along the way they had met countless other Scandinavians. One of those was Anders, the third immigrant of the story. Lars and Caroline had, in fact, met Anders at least twice on the way across Wisconsin and Minnesota. On both occasions they talked and interacted with him and his family and then moved on. As the 1870s began, the ever-expanding path of the railroads led all three of the newcomers on the same course across the emerging farmlands of western Minnesota.

Chapter III
Anders Johannesson:
The Halland Beginnings

Like so many others, Anders was a refugee from the Great Famine of the 1860s. He had come to America with high hopes of carrying on with the farming life he knew in Sweden, and he was prepared to work to attain that goal. During the late 1860s, he moved farther and farther westward across the Midwest, doing manual labor, looking for land, and planning for the future. At the same time, he found that simply moving to America and casting off the Swedish past was not an option. Not unlike Lars and Caroline, Anders had a significant history behind him in Sweden, which occupied his thoughts during his early years in America.

Anders's beginnings traced back to western Sweden, albeit far to the south of the Johannesson Holms' Värmland. His story began on New Year's Day of 1833 in the Swedish province of Halland, just across the straits from Denmark. (Figure 5) On that day a wedding ceremony took place at the picturesque church in the parish of Breared. (Figure 4) Married then were eighteen-year-old Johannes Jönsson, a farmhand, and nineteen-year-old Kjerstin Håkansdotter, a serving girl. [1]

Eight years later Johannes and Kjerstin became Anders's parents.

As a result, a detailed look at their personal history is in order. Kjerstin Håkansdotter was born on January 29, 1813, at Breared, while Johannes Jönsson was born nearby on May 12, 1814. Breared was located on an ages-old highway leading from the south-central Swedish highlands to the shipping ports on the southwest coast. Before he died in 1829, Kjerstin's father had owned a farm called Attavara, located on the banks of a lake by the same name.[2] (Figure 6)   After marrying Kjerstin, Johannes Jönsson took over the Attavara farm.[3]   In 1833 Johannes and Kjerstin set up as farmers and started a family.

Their prospects were modest. The area they lived in was among the poorer districts of Halland. In contrast to the richer coastal areas near the port city of Halmstad, the inland regions surrounding Breared's church were hilly and heavily forested, with fields of heather intersticed. A chary highland climate made raising crops an uncertain enterprise. Earning a living commonly involved a mixed economy of animal husbandry, fishing in nearby lakes, and gathering heather for sale in Halmstad. Though precarious, farm life there had supported Johannes's and Kjerstin's families from as far back as the mid-eighteenth century.

The Attavara farm was on the waterfront. The lake offered an ample supply of fresh water, fishing, and cooling relief from the summer heat. (Figure 3) Yet even there a bad harvest or extreme weather could bring on severe hardship, or even famine and starvation. From 1833 to 1843, the Jönssons escaped such catastrophes. In the beginning they ran their farm uneventfully and profitably.

At Attavara, Johannes and Kjerstin had three children. In 1833 their first son, Håkan Johannesson, was born, followed in 1841 by a second boy, Anders Johannesson. In 1837 Kjerstin gave birth to a daughter, Botilla.[4]   This girl's life was later cut short when she died in a drowning accident. It happened when Botilla was only seven. Parish records gave the first bit of information: "25 April 1844 drowned; 12 May was buried the girl Botilla from Skaftaberget."[5]   The pain of the first daughter's death was made worse by the fact that she was buried on her father Johannes's thirtieth birthday (May 12, 1844).

Various bits of evidence spoke of troubles later on at Attavara. Johannes Jönsson's youth was a disadvantage for farming. Without his father-in-law's guiding hand, Johannes was most likely ill prepared to manage a farmstead efficiently over the long haul. Attavara was not large. Nevertheless for varying lengths of time from 1838 to 1842, no fewer than fifteen persons called Attavara home. Five farmhands lived and worked there for longer or shorter stints. Beginning in 1841, furthermore, Johannes's parents and one of Kjerstin's relatives lived at the farm in an *undantag* setting. Two others living for a time in a cottage at Attavara were a local widow and her daughter. For the better part of one year, Kjerstin's brother also stayed at Attavara.[6] The household was hard pressed to house so many persons, but Johannes and Kjerstin were of an open disposition and willing to help the needy, both young and old.

The year 1840 placed a further burden on their finances. Johannes and Kjerstin renovated the farmhouse then, but the improvements almost certainly exceeded their ability to pay for them. By 1842 they began selling sections of land, and in November, 1843, they left Attavara for good.[7] The fact that the farm housed so many persons and underwent renovation indicated not only that the Jönssons were noted for hospitality but also that their ability to manage the holding wisely and efficiently had declined by the end of their first decade of married life.

In addition to the problem of overextending themselves financially is the suggestion that Johannes was a less than robust farmer. That possibility was suggested by details from his later life. In his mid-fifties Johannes complained of failing eyesight and stayed in bed much of the time while his grown sons did the farm work. At the same time his neighbors agreed to cultivate some of his land for him.[8] Possibly Johannes began suffering from disabilities even in his early years of marriage. By age twenty-nine, at any rate, his problems were serious enough that he prepared to give up his farm and move farther south in Halland.

The Jönssons left Attavara quietly. At the end of 1843, they arrived at the parish of Veinge, also in the inland districts of Halland. (Figure 7) Though their new home was only fifteen miles from Attavara, the move called for careful logistic considerations. The narrow, primitive road heading south wound through hilly and heavily forested land until, near Veinge, it eventually opened out onto flatter countryside. There the Jönssons found land more suitable for crops. Still, even there stands of dense forest surrounded the cultivated fields. Johannes and Kjerstin set up housekeeping in Veinge at a settlement known as

Göstorp. It consisted of a row of six subdivided farmsteads.

The Jönssons settled on the sixth holding in the row, that is, Göstorp #6. Their individual farm was commonly referred to as Skaftaberget.[9] There at the base of a sloping, tree-lined outcropping, they lived for nearly a quarter of a century, from 1843 to the late 1860s. The new farm offered better farming than Attavara, but the lakeside life was missing. At Göstorp they found what for all the world seemed like a permanent home. At that farm three of their children grew to adulthood, while four others died in childhood.

Johannes's fortunes varied during those years. In the 1840s he worked as a tenant farmer. By 1860 he saved enough money to buy the Göstorp property.[10] At Göstorp four daughters were born to Johannes and Kjerstin. A custom in northern Europe was to name newborns after their deceased older siblings, and the Jönssons followed that tradition consistently. The first girl born at Göstorp was named Bothilda, in remembrance of the drowned first daughter, Botilla, from Attavara. Born in 1845, Bothilda lived only three years, six months, and twenty-three days before succumbing in 1849 to congestion of the lungs, as a complication of tuberculosis.

In 1848 came two more daughters — twin girls. The first was named Petronilla. Her sister was stillborn. Petronilla was christened on July 5, the same day her sister was buried. Never given a name, the dead child was referred to simply as "the stillborn girlchild/twin — from Skaftaberget."[11] Following Petronilla and her twin sister in 1850 came another sister, named Johanna. She died one month later, of what the death record bluntly described as a stroke.[12] Petronilla was the family's only girl who survived childhood. She grew up with two brothers. Håkan was fifteen years older and Anders seven years older than she. In short, Johannes and Kjerstin fit the unhappy category that one historian of nineteenth-century Swedish domestic life has termed "high-risk families" (*riskfamiljer*). In an age marked by soaring childhood death rates, such unlucky families suffered an even higher frequency of childhood mortality than others. The reasons were a combination of genetics, disease, primitive health care practices, frequent accidents, and unpredicted personal tragedies.[13]

In the midst of those family tragedies, life in Veinge moved along for the survivors. At Göstorp, Håkan and Anders spent their formative years. The boys worked on their parents' farm and avoided school nearly entirely. By the time they were grown, they were still unable to read or write Swedish. They had to find others to compose letters on their behalf or read aloud to them all the mail they received. That was not surprising given the fact that school life and its benefits were as conspicuously lacking in Veinge as at Karolina's Djupviken in Värmland. Veinge's first school opened in 1832. During the 1840s children in the school's lower levels learned spelling, reading, and geography. They were taught to write by forming the letters of dictated words, first in a sandbox and then on a slate tablet.

The original purpose of the Veinge school was to teach children to live "a Christian life" *(ett kristet liv)*, but this idea was met with criticism from local farmers, who demanded that their children help out on the farms instead. Boys were needed in summertime to care for cattle and in the fall for harvesting. One writer summarized the tone of the local opposition in the following way: "School would get in the way of work, and in order to survive people had to work."[14] It was this attitude that deprived Håkan and Anders of a basic education.

In the 1840s and 1850s both boys were confirmed in the Church of Sweden. At age twenty, Håkan left his father's farm in 1853 to work at a neighboring farmstead but returned to Skaftaberget as early as 1854. Eight years later, at twenty-one, Anders also took a step away from home. He moved in 1862, only to return the same year. The exact reasons for the sons' hasty returns are missing, but it is safe to assume the jobs they moved to were temporary or the work unsatisfactory. Unlike other youths in their social class, they did not hire out as farmhands for longer periods but stuck close to their parents. Anders stayed at home after 1862 and was available for the heavy work at Göstorp. Håkan, who was now thirty, left Skaftaberget again, this time to become a tenant farmer at another Göstorp holding.[15]

The sons were on their way to establishing themselves in Veinge. By the end of 1862, in fact, both Håkan and Anders had married and become fathers. The older brother was the first to wed. On May 5, 1862, Håkan married the family girl Hanna Andersdotter, from the nearby farm Göstorp #4. There Hanna had grown up with her father, a tenant farmer, her mother, and her sister Svenborg, whom the Veinge pastor described as "feeble minded." Hanna was two years older than her husband Håkan. Their first child was born in 1862, ten days before their wedding. They named her Botilda, in honor of

Håkan's two deceased sisters of the same name.[16]

By the end of 1862, Håkan and Hanna were keeping house together. Håkan moved only two farms down the road from his parents' home to Hanna's father's farm, where he took over as the tenant. In 1864 a second daughter, Anna Johanna, was born. By the mid-1860s the family moved to the neighboring farmstead Göstorp #3, where Håkan continued as a tenant farmer.[17]

It would be an understatement to say that Håkan's was not a promising position. Tenant farmers were overworked, chronically poor, and constantly subject to starvation and disease. In the damp climate and poorly heated dwellings, respiratory diseases devastated their families. Though they broke new acreage for the landowners who granted them their plots, tenant farmers were almost always denied the chances of gaining ownership of that land. When one new plot was broken, the landowners took over control and the tenant farmers were expected to move on to other sections of the property and open them up to cultivation, thus ensuring the tenant farmers' continued backbreaking labor and unending poverty. An historian of Veinge parish summarized the process: "When the tenant farmer's plot was placed under cultivation and the newly opened fields began yielding harvests, the tenant farmer had to move on deeper into the forests."[18] That pattern could repeat itself over and over again. Another Swedish writer has described the plight of such men: "The tenant farmer was our country's pioneer, constantly at work, always poor, exploited to an extreme by the landowner."[19]

Living conditions were basic. A typical tenant farmer's cottage contained an open fireplace and a cobblestone floor. The diet consisted of potatoes or mackerel, porridge, and milk. A luxury such as coffee was used only on Sundays.[20] When the tenant farmer grew old and unable to work, he and his wife were assigned to an *undantag* retirement cottage, where they were left to live in continued poverty. Such were Håkan Johannesson's discouraging long-term prospects during the mid-1860s when he entered his thirties as a married man and family breadwinner. Staying at Göstorp would have reduced his chances of advancement to nil.[21]

Anders's wedding followed close on the heels of Håkan's. On October 11, 1862, he wed Johanna Persdotter, a serving woman from the nearby farm of Göstorp #5. Born in 1831, Johanna was nearly ten-and-a-half years older than Anders. In her youth she lived in Veinge with her mother, who later remarried. Johanna's stepfather was a former seaman. Victims of consumption, both Johanna's mother and stepfather died within two months of each other in early 1860, reducing her family to just herself and two sisters in Veinge.[22]

Johanna married Anders only three days before she gave birth to their first child. Given the age difference, Anders's parents probably did not arrange their courtship. The relationship resulted, in all likelihood, from a chance meeting at a village dance or began in the course of their daily farm work. The further result was Johanna's pregnancy, after which Anders agreed to marry her. As was the case with Håkan and Hanna, there was no notice of an engagement, which would have led to the couple's formal cohabitation and an expected pregnancy. As a result, it is not certain what the couple's living arrangement was prior to marriage, though Anders was likely still living at home with his parents. The rural Halland they knew was, to all appearances, a tolerant area that lacked strict social controls in reference to premarital sexual unions. Among the farming populace in many Halland parishes, for example, nearly half of the new brides were pregnant at the time of their weddings in church. Hanna and Johanna fit that pattern. In addition, neither Håkan and Hanna nor Anders and Johanna seem to have felt any extreme family or church pressure to marry as soon as Hanna and Johanna discovered they were pregnant. Instead both couples waited until only days before their children were born to have a church wedding.[23]

At one point, just after 1862, Anders and Johanna were living as non-paying lodgers (*inhyses*) in his parents' home at Skaftaberget. This situation indicated, on one hand, that Anders was unable to pay for a place for his own family to live. On the other hand, staying at his father's enabled him to avoid the hopeless lot of a tenant farmer, which his brother Håkan bravely bore up under. By 1865 Anders joined his father as the co-owner of the Skaftaberget farm.[24]

It was not a great mystery why the honor of taking over the family farm was given to Anders rather than his older brother. Clearly Anders was the apple of his parents' eye. That became a minor sore point between Håkan and Anders. Through the years there were instances when Håkan found it necessary to pick up the slack after his younger brother. There may have been other extenuating circumstances behind those apparent inconsistencies in family affairs as well. Hard liquor flowed freely in Veinge at the time, and it is not impossible that alcohol use held Håkan back in his father's eyes.[25]

Though Anders's position at his parents' farm was, on the surface, better than Håkan's tenant farmer status, his and Johanna's life was not free of problems. Their first child, named Nils Peter, died after living barely a year. During the following years two more sons were born to them. The second son, also named Nils Peter, arrived in 1864, followed in 1866 by the third, Per August. Throughout the 1860s and 1870s, Nils Peter and Per August remained on farms in southern Sweden, first as children at home and then as part of the rural working class.[26]

Studying the Jönssons' family life up to the mid-1860s, we can only judge them as common members of the agrarian poor. They were hardworking, practical people with strong family ties and little, or no, formal education. They remained more loyal to the bonds within their own kinship group and more cognizant of the aims of the local farming community and their Halland background than of the larger goals of the Swedish nation. They had not traveled beyond the borders of their native Halland. Indeed they seem never to have ventured outside the boundaries of the parishes they lived in. Like the Johannesson Holms in Värmland, the Jönssons were desperately poor and almost totally at the mercy of the rugged landscape and harsh climate. They were, at the same time, members of a social class inured to hardship and suffering after centuries of backbreaking labor. Only that fact made the frequent pregnancies, the deaths of children, the constant toil, the meager supplies, and the lack of educational opportunities bearable.

A strict division of labor governed their lives. The women worked in the house, cleaning, baking, preparing meals, tending to children, weaving and mending clothes, fetching water, and doing the milking. The men plowed, sowed crops, repaired machinery and tools, cared for animals, and worked the forests. At haymaking and harvest time both sexes worked together. Such was the unswerving routine, which was broken only by church services, holidays, weddings, and village dances. The life they knew sustained them, but only barely. Though the central government and the Church of Sweden defined their official habits and holidays on a formal level, they could take greater comfort in the solidarity of the farming community and their time-honored folkways.

Nothing in the harshness of the Jönssons' experience could have fully prepared them, however, for the Great Famine of the 1860s. The devastations of that period exceeded earlier crop failures. By all accounts, 1866 and 1867 were the worst years. Preceded by several seasons of poor harvests, 1867 especially came to be known as "the year of great need" (*det stora svagåret*). In the summers the fields suffered from long periods of drought, only to be inundated by heavy rains at harvest time, thus destroying whatever meager crops were ready to be gathered. In countless families starvation became a fact of life. The extent to which the catastrophe affected the inner districts of Halland was summarized from first-hand observation by the parish pastor at Breared, who wrote in 1868:

> *No change has happened in the parish this year. No*
> *strange natural occurrences have taken place during*
> *the year. For most people nearly complete crop failure,*
> *for others total failure, for both sowing of crops and making*
> *hay, due to the unusual heat and drought during the summer.*[27]

Complicating those problems were late springs and unusually early frosts. While Halland suffered searing heat, other areas of Sweden had freezing temperatures as early as July and August. The result of that momentous calamity was widespread want, hopelessness, and abandoned farmsteads.[28]

Failed harvests marked a turning point in the Jönssons' lives. In the middle of the 1860s, Håkan lost his position as a tenant farmer. He moved his family back to his parents' farm, just as Anders had done earlier.[29] For a short time Johannes Jönsson and his two sons were reunited as farmers (*brukare*) at Göstorp #6.[30] It is not certain when the idea of leaving for America took root in their family, but they were clearly considering it long before Hans Mattson's 1868 recruitment tour began. Anders was the first to take action. By the mid-1860s he had already grown restless and bad harvests did not help his situation or improve his mood.

At the same time that the famine brought the family members back under the same roof, it also sundered them. After a series of heart-wrenching decisions, the Jönssons left Göstorp. Johannes Jönsson and Anders failed to make a go of the farm and were forced to sell off their personal belongings at an auction in 1866.[31]   Then Johannes sold the farm to another farmer in early 1867. Otherwise the family's activities provided a tempting but frustratingly inconclusive picture of their movements in Halland between 1865 and 1868. Sometime during that period they left Sweden. Unlike the Johannessson Holms in Värmland, they abandoned the country without receiving official permission from the Veinge clergy. Therefore their movements are clouded to view.[32]

In one year alone Johannes, Håkan, and Anders were among forty parishioners who disappeared without a trace from Veinge parish, an indication of the desperation people were experiencing and also of their loss of faith in the Swedish government's will or ability to help them. Johannes and Anders were first described as former farm owners and finally as being without a permanent home, a result of their having sold their farm.[33]

The Jönssons went west to America, but when they all left and what route they took remained unclear. Anders departed for America as early as the spring of 1866, even before the worst of the famine began. His wife said later that he left for the United States "against her wishes" but with the strong hope of "gaining a better life" there for himself and his family.[34]   Swedish records said only that Håkan left for America in 1867, and the same notations indicated that Johannes, Kjerstin, Anders, Håkan, and Petronilla all departed from Veinge in secret (*utan bevis*).[35]   Most probably, Anders left first, in 1866, and was followed the next year by Johannes, Kjerstin, Håkan, and Petronilla.[36] In 1867 both parents were well past fifty. Håkan was thirty-four and Anders twenty-six. Only Petronilla, at eighteen, was free of worries about spouse and children.

On a psychological level their departure was suggestive of an extremely in-grown family relationship. The common image of emigration in that era was of a younger man and his wife and their small children leaving the aged parents and grandparents behind. They embarked on the hopeful journey to America, never to see the older generation again. Yet Håkan and Anders chose the opposite course. They left their wives and young children behind and took the aging parents with them. They maintained those close, but puzzling, loyalties to the immediate family to the very end of their lives.

The likelihood is that all five family members passed through the harbor at Copenhagen, where Danish officials were traditionally lax about checking the accuracy of travel documents. Emigrants wishing to conceal their identity or place of origin in Sweden could "buy an overcoat" (*köpa rock*) on the black market in Copenhagen. In the pocket of that coat were falsified travel papers, which allowed for safe passage to America. Surely the Jönssons used the overcoat method or some other clandestine, less-than-legal means of departing from Scandinavia. From there they embarked on the great Atlantic crossing.

There were compelling reasons why the family would pull up stakes and start on a journey to a new continent when the parents were already well past mid-life. However, their exact thoughts on the matter were not recorded. They either met the challenge with the grim countenances of those who had failed as farmers — and for the second time — or they welcomed the change as a new lease on life. Surely they had higher expectations of the New World than of the Old.

Left in their wake at Göstorp were six persons. They were Håkan's wife Hanna and the couple's two daughters as well as Anders's wife Johanna and their two sons. As with so much else in their lives, they did not explain the dynamics of their situation. Perhaps Hanna Andersdotter and Johanna Persdotter chose not to emigrate, for purely personal reasons. Hanna may have stayed in Sweden to care for her mentally challenged sister Svenborg. Without a family member to assume responsibility for her, Svenborg would have been abandoned to her fate once her parents died. Johanna, on the other hand, was pregnant in 1866 and expecting the birth of her and Anders's third child. If she hesitated to cross the Atlantic for that reason, she was wise. Pregnant women fared badly on the long and storm-tossed voyages. Deaths of mothers and new-borns at sea were commonplace.[37] In addition, Johanna still had a close relationship with her two sisters in Veinge.[38]

In her situation, Johanna may well have preferred the known hardships at home to the uncertainties of life abroad. The second possibility is that, with money in short supply in Sweden, Håkan and Anders promised to send for their families after getting settled in the United States. Support for that idea is that Anders later mailed money to Johanna for the support of their sons and promised to send for his family once he got his feet on the ground in America.[39]   Whatever arrangements they made, Håkan and Anders bade farewell to their Swedish spouses when they sailed from Europe, uncertain when, or if, they would meet again. In Veinge, Hanna Andersdotter and Johanna Persdotter then joined the long line of married women the Swedes came to know as "America widows." Like many of their peers, Hanna and Johanna waited in poverty at home for news and money to arrive from their husbands in the New World.[40] That which once was a close-knit, apparently inseparable family unit was now split asunder on two different continents.

The Jönsson family also turned their backs on Sweden. Their departure from home was sudden. Still, it fit a pattern of emigration typical of small Swedish landholders stricken by overpopulation, diminished harvests, large debts, and the threat of starvation. Such hardships were as severe in Halland as in Värmland. Between 1850 and 1925, 62,000 Hallanders emigrated legally. That amounted to approximately five out of every 1,000 inhabitants, one of the highest figures in that respect for all of Sweden. Even so, in 1866 only seventy Hallanders were reported as legally emigrating from the entire province. That number was a significant increase, however, over 1864 and 1865, when just seven and fifteen persons officially left Halland for America. By 1867 and 1868, the numbers of emigrants from Halland rose to 135 and 415 respectively.[41] Those figures indicated the swiftness with which the famine spread and how quickly the dream of a better life in America took hold. The Jönssons of Veinge were among those strongly affected by America fever.

The Jönssons were as silent about their arrival in America as about their departure from Europe. If they landed in New York City, they would have taken a boat through the Great Lakes to the Midwest. Failing that, they traveled westward by train from the East Coast. Of the two routes, going by boat was the cheaper. In either case, they stopped in a major city — Milwaukee or Chicago — on their way. They then headed west. Johannes Jönsson later stated that they crossed Wisconsin.[42] By the end of the 1860s, the Jönssons reached the American heartland and stopped at the Mississippi River.

They reached the Mississippi at the same time as the Johannesson Holms. Both family groups went by ferryboat over to the river town of Winona, Minnesota, arriving there in 1868. In Winona they found an energetic young city, known as the Gateway to the West in

Minnesota. Steamboats plied the river, a railroad bridge over the Mississippi was planned, and rail lines led in and out of the area. In the hustle and bustle of that river setting, the two Swedish family groups — the Johannesson Holms and the Jönssons — met in late 1868 and recognized each other as fellow countrymen. Later they came in contact again. Only one thing was clear from those meetings. The two families did not see eye to eye. Lars Fredrik's contentious side and his jealousy of other men remained with him, and he made a strong negative impression on all of the Jönssons.

Chapter IV
Settling In: Kansas Lake

Swedes and Norwegians were among the first farmers in Minnesota. They began arriving in the eastern parts of the territory in the mid-1850s. Their numbers increased steadily in the early 1860s. After the Civil War their movement into the state reached mass proportions. They joined pioneers from across Europe in staking claims in the heavily wooded eastern and southern counties. This settlement was "river-oriented" and relied on steamboat traffic for communication with centers back east. The Euro Americans stayed near waterways and built communities such as Stillwater and Winona, which were remindful of older river towns in the Ohio and Mississippi River valleys.

Settlement stopped short of the prairies in western Minnesota. European immigrants, accustomed to farming in their wooded homelands, were at first reluctant to move onto the treeless areas. As a result, southwestern Minnesota was among the last parts of the state settled by Europeans. In terms of farming conditions and standard of living, the southwestern part of the state remained a rugged frontier area into the early 1880s.[1] In the late 1860s railroads put an end to the era of the riverboat and pointed the way westward. Extending out from eastern Minnesota, rail lines opened up communications with the prairie lands to the west. Only a decade after the introduction of the railroad in Minnesota, rail lines had reached, and in many cases given rise to, the agricultural settlements across the state. The two formed a symbiotic relationship. The rail companies served the farming populace, and the farmers, in turn, sought out the lines of railroad construction and settled near them.[2]

Work on the railroad was grueling. Crew stations set up at ten-mile intervals to link the sections of the expanding lines. In summer and winter, men performed heavy labor for eleven to twelve hours daily, on meager rations of beans and coffee and wages ranging from $1.25 to $2.00 a day. Most sections gangs were housed in converted boxcars, known as "bunk cars." Life there was harsh. Fatigue, sickness, lice, and vermin became commonplace irritants. Nevertheless between 1865 and 1870, approximately 2,000 miles of rail lines were laid in Minnesota, all with the help of European immigrant workers laboring under such difficult conditions.

The Jönssons, as well as the Johannesson Holms, arrived in southeastern Minnesota, then, at just the most propitious time for railroad development. The years immediately following the Civil War and just before their arrival in the area saw the beginning of the great boom in railroad construction. The Chicago & Northwestern and the Galena and Chicago Union railroads reached out across northern Illinois and into southern Wisconsin. "Railroad fever had reached epidemic proportions," in the words of railroad historian John C. Luecke. The companies made preparations to extend from Chicago and Milwaukee to Madison, Wisconsin, and then even farther westward. Luecke has written: "The Chicago & Northwestern progressed on a generally east-west axis across northern Illinois and through the wooded region of Wisconsin. 1870 brought the rails of the C&NW to the shores of the Mississippi River, this time at La Crosse. Ahead lay Minnesota."[3]

Anders and Håkan Johannesson followed those lines and worked as common laborers, but in La Crosse temporary problems arose. The Chicago & Northwestern tracks ended there, and the company waited for a bridge to be built over to Winona. Job opportunities for men like Anders and Håkan were on hold. On the Minnesota side, however, another rail line already existed. It was the Winona & St. Peter

Company, a hometown line that had slowly inched its way westward across southern Minnesota throughout the 1860s. It reached Waseca and then headed farther west toward Mankato in the late 1860s.

Anders and Håkan left Winona in 1868, joined the Winona & St. Peter line, and found work on its western terminus. In the fall, the work of extending the line from there to Mankato began. By December of 1868, a force of 200 workmen neared Janesville, halfway between Waseca and Mankato, and in the summer of 1869 the rails reached Mankato. Anders and Håkan were among those who helped complete the last miles of that stretch. The City of Mankato formally announced direct passenger connections with Winona in 1870.[4] By then, only the open prairie to the west of Mankato remained to be crossed.

Once it reached Mankato, the Winona & St. Peter line continued on farther north, but another company, the St. Paul & Sioux City, reached Mankato from St. Paul and Minneapolis. By 1869, St. Paul & Sioux City Railroad Company engineers had surveyed the land, established the railroad right-of-way, and laid out trails to the west and south from Mankato, toward the spot where St. James would later be built as a center for the rail company's shops. By the end of the 1860s, the federal government had also surveyed the new area, including Watonwan County. In time, the Kansas Lake country, south of St. James, would become available to Nordic immigrants hungry for land. In the summer of 1869, Anders and his brother left the railroad at Mankato and traveled the twenty miles westward to Madelia, where they bought land at Kansas Lake. Covering the distance on foot, they arrived in Watonwan County a year ahead of the railroad itself. (Figure 9)

They were not unusual in using that mode of transport. One of the early pastors of the Swedish settlement at Sveadahl, in Watonwan County, remembered that all the earliest Scandinavian pioneers walked to the site of their first land claims. The pastor described the process in romanticized terms but with an eye out for the difficulties:

> *The Homestead era — what a time! What experiences! Who could ever forget those times? One sees long lines of newly-arrived Swedes wandering the path on foot from Mankato via Lake Crystal and Madelia out to their townships — or in the vicinity of them — to search out the 80 acres that they were to get free of charge here in the new land from Uncle Sam and — from God. The three days and nights, which every bachelor had to spend in his homestead-shanty every sixth month, of course they carried the memory of*

> *that for a lifetime. And then the sodhuts, or cellars, that most*
> *families were forced to call home during their earliest years.*[5]

Like other Scandinavians, Anders followed the railroad line's preliminary surveyed footpath. It was a three or four day trip from Mankato, if conditions were good. From Madelia, he hiked across the virgin grasslands ever farther westward. On the final leg of his trek, he walked to Kansas Lake to take up his farmland. A settler had to beat his own path, crossing streams and barriers wherever suitable. Anders and his family after him would have carried their possessions with them, just as other settlers did. It was not unusual for an individual to travel by foot for ten, fifteen, or even fifty miles at a stretch, oftentimes covering the distance with a bag of grain and various household necessities strapped on his back.[6]

Hazards abounded. Before 1869 the only way to reach Mankato was by hired carts. Drivers of those conveyances carried goods, women, and children. They forced the men to walk behind them, however. Most newcomers, even those who later used the railroad, were hungry and virtually penniless by the time they reached Mankato. It was the lack of cash that caused whole families to continue on westward by foot, rather than with hired carts. The result was extreme fatigue, which led to accidents and some deaths. Overnight stopping places were under the stars on the open prairie or, rarely, in the huts of the few homesteaders beyond Mankato.[7]

The land Anders purchased was United States government Homestead acreage.[8] He and his parents took possession of it on July 22, 1869. Anders and his father also took out United States naturalization papers in 1869.[9] The eighty acres Håkan bought were adjacent to Anders and his parents' farm. The family's choice of land near Kansas Lake clearly traced back to the parents' and Håkan's memories of Lake Attavara. Lacking wells on the prairie, they needed a reliable supply of water. The lake also offered them good fishing. Anders and Håkan began clearing the fields and building their houses, thereby satisfying the government residency requirements.

After the troubles in Sweden and the railroad drudgery in America, the Jönssons at last had a home again. In Watonwan County the English-speaking community soon Anglicized Anders's and Håkan's names to Andrew and Hogan Johnson, and their parents became known as John and Christine Johnson.[10] They lived half a mile from the lakefront. Their only means of traveling to town during their first years was on foot or by oxcart. As the Johnsons busily settled in at Kansas Lake, Petronilla left there. She adopted the new name of Petronella or Nellie Johnson and hired out as a domestic. By the mid-1870s she was serving as a housekeeper for a Swedish family in nearby Nicollet County.[11]

Andrew and Hogan were still living in transition. From their base at Kansas Lake, they spent parts of 1869 and 1870 working on the railroad from Mankato out to Watonwan County. They were part of a crew of 150 men who graded the railroad path and laid the tracks from Mankato to St. James. Other workers helped plat and build the town of St. James itself. During the fall of 1870, the railroad company brought in a crew of carpenters to construct buildings. Soon the town had two hotels, nine retail stores, and three saloons. Not long after that, churches began appearing. As the St. James Herald wrote later (February 14, 1873): "In from 6 to 8 weeks a respectable sized town was built up where during the summer previous scarcely a house could be seen on the whole prairie."[12]

The first passenger train to Watonwan County was a special run carrying railroad officials from St. Paul by way of Mankato. It arrived in November of 1870. Soon thereafter regular passenger service commenced. Daily trains had been running on the line for barely four months, therefore, when Lars and Caroline arrived at the St. James depot in early 1871. Unnoticed at first, they quickly covered the seven miles out to Kansas Lake and joined the other Scandinavian settlers in the vicinity.

After the spring of 1871, 1,000 men continued the rail construction on the long prairie stretch leading from St. James toward distant Sioux City, the next settled town. By the fall of that year, they had laid another fifty-six miles of track to the southwest of St. James.[13] There Andrew and Hogan could earn extra cash even nearer to home. In fact, throughout the early 1870s the settlers in Watonwan County were frequently called out to work on the rail lines.

"Work on the road," as they called it, did not always run smoothly. Around 1870 construction of the St. Paul & Sioux City line outward from St. James stalled because of the company's indecision whether to extend the line straight south to Iowa or southwest to Sioux City. In the end, the company decided to run lines in both directions. That intervening period of discussion about where and what to build left many of the Scandinavian section crews idle in Watonwan County. Some took advantage of the down time and staked out claims on the county's remaining vacant land, an influx that added to the number of settlers in the area.

By 1871 Swedish immigrants had established farmsteads all around Kansas Lake. Barely a mile to the east, at nearby Long Lake, was a sizable Norwegian colony. That created a tight-knit Scandinavian community life that made the use of English a virtual non-necessity. By speaking Norwegian and Swedish, settlers could perform all the daily transactions of work, family, and church life. Only in dealing with the American governmental infrastructure or merchants in town did they need any English.

The Scandinavians were taking part in a historic movement onto the last major farming frontier of Minnesota. In the rush of their lives, Andrew and his family had little time, however, to consider the historical value of their adventure. Life on the Minnesota prairie was at least as demanding as the harsh conditions in rural Sweden. Kansas Lake was small and the prairie vast. From their homes, the Swedes viewed only a pristine lake surrounded by underbrush and mile upon mile of untamed, treeless expanse. Indeed only a handful of Europeans had been intrepid enough to precede the railroad onto the Watonwan prairie. First on the scene had been scattered families of rugged Norwegians, who during the 1850s and early 1860s carved out their farms far from the nearest trading centers and learned to tolerate the enormous isolation. In those years a round-trip venture to Mankato, forty-five miles away, took five to seven days by oxcart.[14]

As late as 1860, less than ten years before the Johnsons arrived in Watonwan County, the territory between Madelia and Sioux City was still essentially devoid of Euro Americans. The only existing trail leading west toward Sioux City was blazed by a lone man. He was Jens Torson, a Norwegian pioneer from near Madelia. Through the 1850s and into the early 1860s, Torson carried the United States mail on his back "across [the] trackless waste almost the entire distance without a single settlement" from Mankato to the Missouri River. He traveled in all seasons, going by foot or horseback in summer and on skis in winter. Torson's only shelter consisted of a few crude huts spaced out along the way.[15]

One St. Paul & Sioux City rail official gave an indication of how empty the area was in Torson's day. In 1871 the railroad's chief engineer Judson Bishop and his technical crew surveyed the area from St. James to Sioux City and established a right-of-way for the company. Bishop described the vast territory as "naked prairie, almost as destitute of trees as of human inhabitants." Along the entire route across southwestern Minnesota, he found only four cabins, two occupied by homesteaders and two by trappers. Bishop noted the speed with which that situation changed. After staying just a week in Sioux City, he and his troupe returned to St. James by the same route they had just carved out, only to find that their wagon tracks had already been worn down to a well-traveled road. Settlers coming in from the east had followed his path and staked out claims along it while he was still in Sioux City. He also noted that the killing off of herds of elk and the destruction of packs of wolves and other wildlife soon followed and continued unabated from then on.[16]

Through the years this line of rapid settlement and its parallel decimation of the environment continued. With surveying teams and homesteaders came landscape transformation. The land the Swedes lived on at Kansas Lake was not exempt, as the chronicles of Watonwan County newspapers testified. Beginning in the 1860s fish and animals of record size and numbers were captured, marveled at, and then destroyed. At the same time as the elk herds disappeared, wolf packs were also systemically eradicated and the stocks of fish in lakes and rivers depleted.

The reduction of the number of wolves on the prairie was recorded regularly and always with a sense of accomplishment. Though it happened years after Andrew and his family arrived in Watonwan County, The Madelia Times could report on one wolf attack (November 5, 1886): "The wolves kill quite a number of Juno Lyon's sheep." The St. James Journal showed that settlers were quick to take action against such attacks. One instance came on May 6, 1888, when the St. James editor wrote: "John Coleman of South Branch brought in five young wolves last Saturday, and received a $15.00 bounty." More land became accessible for crops and cattle, but bio-diversity suffered. While livestock and cultivated acres multiplied, native flora and fauna disappeared.

Even if they lived in an era that preceded modern-day environmental concerns, the Swedes and Norwegians in Long Lake township, such as Andrew and his family, could not have been blind to the changes taking place in the landscape and the role they were playing in those changes.[17] Whether they saw the transformation as positive or negative, they were caught on the horns of a dilemma. In order to survive, they must hunt and fish and take part in the land rush, clear the fields, and then plant. The only alternative was life-long social instability and rootlessness in America.

Being without a home in a new land suggested an alienation that was potentially worse than the disenfranchisement they had experienced back in Europe. Knowing that, Andrew exchanged his proletarian status for that of a settled farmer. Still, he and the other Swedes were hardly living in the lap of luxury. Their labor was unremitting. The newcomers required decades to get the knack of farming the prairie. As a result, they wasted resources. Part of the problem lay in knowing what crops to plant. For Scandinavians, barley, rye, and wheat were the most familiar and most productive back home, but their success with those crops was mixed in Minnesota, with its different soil and more extreme seasonal climate shifts. Farming the prairie was a process of trial and error, which could lead to frustration or fatalism. Many abandoned their farmsteads even before they were fully developed.[18]

Putting up the right kinds of houses also presented a problem. Luckily, the Swedes and Norwegians had the solution. Unlike the Yankees, Germans, or Irish, who preferred houses open to the prairie but exposed to wind and rain, the Scandinavians understood what northern winters were like. Just as they had done at home, they built their dwellings, the so-called "earth cabins" (*jordstugor*), into hillsides and made them of rough timber with sod piled against it. As one Swede in Watonwan County recalled: "[Sod] a foot thick for walls, one window with four eight-by-ten-inch panes of glass and one door. This constituted the pioneer's palace, which was usually about ten by twelve by six [feet]." The floor was of hard, shoveled clay.[19]

A member of the West Sveadahl congregation near Kansas Lake inventoried the Nordic settlers' typical quarters of that era:

> *The little dark hole in the ground (sodhouse) served as the*
> *farmhouse; the hay stack as the barnyard; the bundles of hay as*
> *fuel both in the winter and the summer; the dog served as a "fence"*

> *to keep both the owner's and the neighbors' cattle in the right fields:*
> *the ox, if a person was lucky enough to own one or a team of them,*
> *served both as an "automobile" and a "tractor."*[20]

The Swedes used bales of hay, dried prairie grass, and husked corncobs or corn stalks for their home fires in Watonwan County. The Swedish-American women were clever at binding those materials into whisks or bundles, which they regularly fed into the flames. Such fuel produced good heat but also a nearly unbearably bad smell and smoky conditions inside the house.[21] All the Johnsons at Kansas Lake lived in just such houses. At one point, Caroline told of piling corn stalks in the upper room of her and Lars's house during the autumn as a store of fuel for the upcoming winter.[22]

From 1869 to 1872, Andrew struggled to make a go of his and his parents' Kansas Lake farm under just such basic, even primitive, conditions. By sheer dint of persistence, he and his brother cleared the brush from their land and planted a few acres of potatoes, wheat, and some corn in 1870. By 1872 Andrew had thirty acres in cultivation. He also had cattle and two oxen, while Hogan bought a reaper, a mower, and other farm implements in St. James. Andrew kept working on his house, which resembled the "earth cabins" of the homeland Scandinavians, but even after three or four years the dwelling was still of a terribly humble sort that even the most destitute in Sweden would have blanched at the sight of.[23] Andrew described his and his parents' living quarters:

> *My house was a very poor one. It contained only one room —*
> *Father and Mother lived with me all the time — we had only two*
> *beds in the room — The door was on the east side of the house.*
> *There was only one door in the house and this was near one end*
> *of the house. The beds set opposite each other — one on one*
> *side of the house and the other on the other side of the house.*[24]

His neighbor Caroline later described Andrew's house as having only one room, where "all occupied the same room for all purposes."[25] The interior of his dwelling bore unmistakable resemblances to the tenant farmers' huts back in Sweden. Since he was sending money home to Johanna in Sweden, Andrew surely had limited resources for improving his dwelling at Kansas Lake.

In such cramped conditions the family would have been forced to improvise. Dried hay could be used for rugs on the dirt floor and the table could be made to fold against the wall to allow for more space.

They could use traditional Scandinavian-style trundle beds, with compartments that the family pulled out like drawers to accommodate additional persons. They could also fashion benches out of split logs, as was done in rural Sweden. With such homemade arrangements, the only purchased furnishing Andrew and his parents would need was an iron stove, with an oven for baking.[26]

Other Swedes arrived at the lake at the same time as Andrew and his family. Near neighbors were Charles J. Johnson and his parents. Like Andrew's folks, Charles's father and mother were also known, confusingly enough, as John and Christine Johnson. They were former tenant farmers from Dalsland, who came to America in 1857 when the father was already fifty-five and Charles only five. To the north of Kansas Lake lived Peter and Catherine Olson, also from Dalsland. They had been common farmhands when they left Sweden in 1866.[27] At the south end of the lake resided the family of Charles Westman, from Småland, and directly north of the lakeshore lived Henrick Henricksson and family, from Skåne.

In a combination of admiration and sympathy, some later residents spoke of the poverty of those first Kansas Lake settlers as being beyond description and impossible for succeeding generations to fathom. According to that view, their faith was also at its ebb, as they huddled in their cabins far distant from the nearest ecclesiastical centers, nearly devoid of hope and desperately homesick. The pioneers themselves failed to see their spiritual life in such light. They took quick, decisive steps to found their own church. In 1871, thirty-seven men banded together to start the Kansas Lake Swedish Lutheran Church. Included among the founding members were Hogan and his father. Visiting pastor Mikael Sandell held the church's first religious service in August of 1871 in the home of Henrick Henricksson.

On his second visit to Kansas Lake in 1871, Pastor Sandell presided over the official organization of the congregation. A tiny log meetinghouse on the east bank of the lake served as the church building until members voted to move the church to acres owned by Andrew and Hogan's father, who sold them the land and reached an agreement that congregation members would open more of his land to cultivation. (Figure 25) That church building was planned to be ready by January of 1872, but whether it actually stood at that location at so early a date is not certain.[28] Despite its severe limitations, the Kansas

Lake settlement was a transplanted Swedish colony that could look to the future. It had land, a tax base, a visiting pastor, and a steady influx of new settlers.

The Scandinavians had spiritual sustenance and the desire for material comfort. Nevertheless barriers existed between them and the American mainstream. The English-speaking Establishment in the trading and rail centers at Madelia and St. James was separated from Watonwan County's Scandinavians by differences in language and culture. The divide was considerable, even if glimpses of it did not begin appearing in print in Watonwan County until the 1880s. After that, there were enough published indications to show the division had long existed. One instance occurred in 1882 when a Norwegian American, George Knudson, won the county's Republican Party nomination for State Senator over George P. Johnston, an Anglophone candidate. Johnston's supporters argued that Knudson won the nomination because Scandinavians in Watonwan County ignored the political issues and voted for him along ethnic lines alone. A considerable debate on the issue followed in the Madelia and St. James newspapers.

Another example of the cultural gap came in the form of a comment from the Scandinavian side. On May 10, 1884, two anonymous residents of Long Lake township sent in a news report to <u>The St. James Journal</u>. The contributors gave information on happenings at Kansas Lake. They also explained why similar reports came in so seldom from their township. Residents there were avid readers of the newspaper, but they were not so good at writing. They concluded: "We are rather poor writers, especially in the English language." Lacking proper schooling in formal English, most Scandinavian Americans remained silent about topics touching the larger society and observed the English-language community from a distance.

Even in a rail center such as St. James this division of ethnic groups persisted. In that age of machines and diverse ethnic groups, a true melting pot might have developed in the town and railroad setting. Yet such was not the case. Entertainments and lectures by visiting performers, scholars, and ministers were aimed at specific constituencies. In the late 1870s, St. James began supporting an English-language Literature Society, while the Scandinavian Club in town sponsored debate teams, public meetings, talks, and dances exclusively for Scandinavian Americans. In the 1880s St. James, with a population of barely more than 700, featured German Lutheran, Norwegian Lutheran, and Swedish Lutheran churches, in addition to Episcopalian, Methodist, Baptist, Presbyterian, and Catholic congregations for the town's English speakers.

By the late 1880s many Scandinavians, by their own estimate, had made considerable progress with English. Others were not so sure. On January 6, 1888, The Madelia Times published a parody of Scandinavian-American customs and speech. The text suggested that Scandinavian political candidates were not fit to send to the Minnesota legislature because of their "green[horn] and absurd ways." The Madelia article attributed those failings partly to the Scandinavians' drinking propensities, "from which they cannot be extricated." To make matters worse, the text was written in a phonetic script that made fun of the immigrants' heavily accented English.

The Scandinavian Debating Society of Watonwan County responded by calling the Madelia editor's ideas taunting insinuations (The St. James Journal, January 7, 1888). The Madelia paper published an apology. At that point the argument died down and life went on. It was clear from those and other examples, however, that the Scandinavian-American groups to a large degree lived their own lives and kept their own customs. They were in contact with the English-speaking culture but not entirely accepted by it. Neither group completely understood the cultural norms of the other.[29]

The original Kansas Lake settlers were silent about the mental effects their new living space and America's cultural diversity had on them. Not until the 1890s did the children of that first generation find time to reflect on their parents' initial disorientation. Looking back on the first twenty-five years of his congregation, Kansas Lake pastor P. J. Eckman wrote in 1897:

> *The results of all our inquiries seem to indicate that the*
> *movement of the Swedes here [to Kansas Lake] took place in*
> *the years 1868 and [18]70. How things looked and what*
> *conditions were like at that time is easier to imagine than*
> *describe. If the elders [in that group] who are still living and now*
> *have grown old and gray-haired had the chance to tell us about it,*
> *we would most likely break down in tears or be obliged to smile*
> *at them as hopeless liars. They would be able to tell about poverty,*
> *misery, and hardship, how upon their arrival here they were all*
> *strangers in a strange land, homeless, without a roof over their*

> *heads, without food and money and almost to the point of being*
> *bereft of their faith in the Lord.*[30]

The immigrants surely found the woodless prairies of the Midwest and the individualist Yankee culture unlike anything they could have imagined in their homeland.

Other descendants spoke out in reference to the settlers' connection with the Church of Sweden. They recalled the immigrants' persistent reliance on Old World methods and stated: "Even in a strange land, thousands of miles from their home, without the guidance of an ordained minister, these men were guided by patterns of thought and action established by the Church [of Sweden]."[31]   That observation overlooked the fact that they fell back on the traditions of a church whose paternalism for generations had stood in the way of freedom of expression and worship for Swedish commonfolk.

The immigrant culture the Swedish newcomers relied on offered a sense of community and comfort, but it also left them outside the American mainstream. That was particularly true for those who did not know English or knew it imperfectly. For such individuals there was little choice but to restrict their social and spiritual lives to the narrow confines of the ethnic community. For Andrew and his family this situation was a source of concern. After seven years in America, Andrew still knew little English. In the early 1870s he had to rely on his neighbor Charles Johnson to translate for him when he went to St. James to discuss business and legal matters. Charles explained that Andrew "could speak some English at the time but not very much."[32]

Likewise, Hogan and his parents seem never to have learned English, or if they did they spoke it with a heavy accent. In confusion, officials in St. James rendered their last name in numerous ways, such as "Johnson," "Jonson," "Jensin," and "Jenson," and failed ever to get a true handle on their first names.[33] Mirrored in the many misspellings were scores of frustrating conversations between the immigrants and the record-keepers and storeowners in town. To those born in America, the newcomers' speech must have appeared quaint and curious, or even impossible to understand. Patience with the situation was necessary to save the day on countless occasions.

The physical surroundings and cultural aspects in Andrew's new home area were troublesome. The landscape was unfamiliar and took time to adapt to, while American culture presented barriers to assimilation. Nevertheless, between 1869 and 1871, Andrew's family had a new lease on life. They owned virgin farmland and had only to make it productive. That inspired hope. Sadly, that feeling of peace proved short-lived, as clouds gathered on the horizon. After Lars and Caroline had lived at Kansas Lake for a few months, it became necessary to interact with them as neighbors. In time, contacts between the families grew more and more complex. The catalyst was Lars. His unpredictable personality and actions held the key to understanding the interaction between the two farms in the early 1870s.

Chapter V
Lars and Caroline at Kansas Lake

Lars and Caroline traveled to St. James on the same railroad line that Andrew and his brother helped to lay. Before St. James, the couple stayed for two years between Waseca and Mankato. They had a house and kept boarders on the railroad, most likely engineers, workers' families, and a few company inspectors. There Lars, Caroline, and Andrew had met for the second time, somewhere around 1869. From that point on, the two families offered varying accounts of their contacts with each other.

Lars and Caroline's daughter Annie, who was only six at the time, later recalled a scene from her family's residence around the time of the second encounter in the Waseca area. According to Annie, Andrew and Lars were involved in a heated argument and Andrew threw an ax at Lars. Annie commented:

> She [Caroline] told me not to say Andrew throwed the ax
> at father — I know he did throw an ax at father. This was
> when we were on the railroad keeping boarders down below
> Mankato and before we came to Kansas Lake to live. I was
> standing in the door and saw him throw the ax — This was

2 or 3 years before we came to live in this [Watonwan]
county.[1]

Andrew later denied the ax-throwing incident, but he did not contest the statement that he met Lars at that time or that there was friction between the two men. He maintained instead that the tension only started developing in earnest later at Kansas Lake.[2]

Lars and Andrew's disagreement carried over from their railroading days. Nevertheless, in 1871 Lars made the apparently irrational decision to move his family to a farmstead barely a quarter mile from his antagonist Andrew's farm at Kansas Lake. Lars and Caroline arrived there sometime in February or early March of 1871. Their farm was located just to the southwest of Kansas Lake itself. Andrew's homestead lay to the west of Lars and Caroline's and just west and south of Charles Johnson and his parents' farm.[3] The well-trodden footpaths leading from farm to farm and circling the lake allowed for frequent contact among all the settlers near or along the waterfront.

In one sense, Lars and Caroline's choice of a spot to settle was only logical, since both spouses were born and raised near Lake Vänern. Close to the banks of Kansas Lake, they, like Andrew and his family, might feel spiritually at home. In addition, on the railroad across Wisconsin and Minnesota they had had contact with Andrew and other Swedes who preceded them to Watonwan County. Lars and Caroline must have chosen the Kansas Lake farm after meeting those fellow countrymen and hearing of the options open farther west in Minnesota. Likewise, they could not have failed to know about the railroad companies' active settlement promotions.

By 1871 Lars and Caroline had three children. In addition to Annie, a daughter named Isabel was born in Wisconsin in 1869 and a son John Albert was born at Kansas Lake in early March of 1871.[4] At Kansas Lake the family cultivated wheat, corn, and barley while keeping cattle. By 1872 they had planted sixteen acres. Naturally, the couple had found no house waiting for them at Kansas Lake, but Lars well understood that spending a Minnesota winter in a temporary lean-to was not an option for anyone wishing to avoid death by freezing. So — with the encouragement and help of neighbors — he surely cast off his slothfulness in the spring and summer of 1871 and built their house himself. It was made of wood and sod and consisted of two rooms. The entire family shared a single bed in one of those rooms, with the girls sleeping at the foot of the bed and the parents and their son at the head. To conserve heat in the winter, they slept in the cellar room, which was dug into the side of a rise in the ground and contained only one half-window that let in barely enough light to see by. In the summer they used the upper room, where grain and corn stalks were stored in the winter.[5]

Though conditions were harsh, Lars and Caroline, to all outward appearances, lived relatively comfortably in comparison with the other settlers. Lars and Caroline's storeroom contained foodstuffs. They owned chickens and four cows, which were said to be valued at $50.00 a head.[6] Other settlers later contradicted that assessment, however, by reporting that Lars often left his family in dire poverty, while he wandered the Minnesota countryside begging.

Along with all the other Swedes at Kansas Lake, Lars and Caroline were looking for a fresh start. In doing so, they sought an environment with the potential for successful agriculture. Like other settlers, they had a practiced eye for good countryside. In their view, the major advantage in Minnesota was that the prairie, thankfully, was free of stones, which had plagued farmers in Sweden for centuries. The big disadvantage was fire. By pioneer times, prairie fires had burned most of the trees in Watonwan County, leaving the banks of Kansas Lake as one of the few spots with small woods and a feeling of relative security.[7]

During the first years of their settlement, nature was at rest. The fires stayed away. In 1871, however, it did not take the immigrants long to discover that the fiercest blast blowing their way came from Lars. He burst into their midst in the most non-conciliatory and undiplomatic of Swedish ways. As early as his first spring at Kansas Lake, he turned contentious and accusatory. He argued with neighbors over whose equipment was whose and where their cattle should graze. He showed his violent side in the way he treated animals. Settlers saw him abusing livestock and some felt he might kill them. Andrew described Lars as the only man in the township who would do harm to farm animals. He explained that Lars "would run after cattle with a pitchfork." Later on, Lars began threatening to shoot livestock.[8] He also borrowed tools from other farmers and returned them in disrepair. By 1872 Lars had begun publicly accusing his neighbors of dishonest dealings. In short, his supposed desire to improve his lot and be considered an equal partner with other men in America had come to naught.

Meeting Lars in the early 1870s, the Swedish settlers formed first impressions of him, which remained with them long afterward. They began putting labels on him, just as Swedes in Värmland had done. Hogan noted at once how small Lars was. Both he and Charles Johnson reported that the Swedes called him "Little Lars," thus corroborating comments from the clergy in Värmland about Lars's dwarf-like appearance. In fact, that was the only name many people in Watonwan County knew him by. The St. James Herald (March 28, 1873) reflected the common use of the term when it reported on a mysterious man at Kansas Lake known only as "Little Lars."[9]

Charles Johnson got to know Lars in the summer of 1871 concerning various dealings about their farms. Charles concentrated on studying Lars's mental state and reached the conclusion that his neighbor was mentally ill. Three years later Charles thought back on his initial meeting with the newcomer and concluded that his first impression still applied. Charles stated: "I did not hear much against Lars [from others in advance]. I thought he was insane the first time I saw him."[10] In 1872 that feeling prompted Charles to speak with H. S. Willson, the Watonwan County probate court judge, about Lars. Charles explained: "I told Willson myself that Lars Johnson was in my opinion insane."[11] Charles's father shared that feeling. On different occasions, the elder Johnson commented: "Lars was a vicious man and a bad neighbor"; "we all said Lars was too ugly [mean] for a woman to live with"; "we were speaking of little petty quarrels that Lars had with his neighbors generally — I said at this time that Lars was a bad man."[12]

It took little more to convince others. While Lars stayed at home, he insisted his wife hire out for manual labor with nearby farmers. Caroline worked the harvest fields with neighbors in 1871 and 1872. The problem was that all of those farmers were men, which heightened Lars's jealousy. Her neighbors treated her fairly, however. Andrew and others paid her $2.00 a day for harvesting, putting up hay, spreading manure, and doing similar jobs. She was making a going wage in that respect, since the accepted pay was $3.00 a day for harvesting and $1.50 for other chores.[13]

One day in September of 1872, Andrew met Caroline in St. James.

He paid her $7.00 in back wages and waited while she shopped at a general merchandise store owned by a Norwegian named Gilbur Texley. Even before the day was over, Lars caught wind of their meeting, no doubt from neighbors who had seen them in town, and flew into a rage. Only half clad, he ran about the Kansas Lake settlement hurling threats and waving a gun. One farmer reported that Lars arrived at his house "with barely a rag on him" yelling and threatening to shoot people, including Andrew. Later that day Caroline assured Lars her meeting with Andrew was unplanned and resulted only in a business transaction, but she was unable to avoid a serious fight with Lars that night about the matter.[14]

Others gave a fuller version of what had happened that day. Andrew said he took a load of wheat to market in town and met Caroline by accident. After her shopping, he drove her back to Kansas Lake and left her off at the home of Peter and Catherine Olson, who had children the same age as Caroline's daughter Annie. As Andrew drove on home, Caroline ran up the lane to the Olsons' house eager to see Catherine and visit with Annie, who was working for the Olsons. Catherine Olson later told of the fleeting but poignant moment when Caroline showed her daughter the goods she had purchased at Texley's and chatted with the Olsons. Innocent as it all sounded, Lars still felt Andrew had committed an insult to his rights as a husband by being seen in public with Caroline. Lars spread that news around the settlement.[15]

After that experience, Lars's behavior worsened. To keep Caroline from meeting other men, he forbade her doing hired farm work. People saw him beating Caroline and heard him accusing her of chasing after Andrew. At other times he aimed his wrath in the opposite direction. Andrew's father said Lars "went around the neighborhood telling that Andrew was running after his wife."[16] Concern continued to grow. Neighbors talked incessantly about Lars's anti-social habits. Much of that talk took place among the Swedish men when they were called out to work on the road. Andrew remembered those discussions: "That Lars was insane and ought to be in the Insane Asylum had been talked of all the summer before our going to Madelia [in 1872], by the neighbors."[17]

At the same time, Caroline was getting advice and thinking of suing for divorce. She said: "Charles Johnson and his father told me

I ought to get a divorce from Lars, that he was too ugly [mean] to live with."[18] Caroline explained her own reasons in concise terms: "I thought he [Lars] was crazy and all who knew him thought he was crazy." She added: "I wanted to get a divorce because I did not want to live with Lars any longer."[19]

Matters calmed at times in 1871 and again early in 1872, after Lars went off on various of his begging tours. Sandwiched between those journeys were periods when relations between the two families became civil and tensions relaxed. Andrew and his parents lent implements to Lars. Those included a beetle for pounding holes, which Lars brought back in disrepair. At another point, according to daughter Annie, Andrew bought some clothes from Lars and was seen wearing them.[20] In such cases, the need to share scarce goods on the prairie could override personal conflicts. Yet there was a breaking point. Once the tensions reached a serious point, they quickly escalated out of control and offers of help became more guarded or stopped altogether.

The dangerous stage began in 1872. As the fall neared, Lars approached another Kansas Lake immigrant and church member, A. P. Wennerborg, and asked about obtaining a better weapon. Though a peaceable man, Wennerborg lent Lars a gun "with powder" ("a large rifle," as Caroline described it).[21] From then on, most residents feared that Lars was out to do them harm. Hogan had no doubts about the matter. He stated that Lars intended to shoot his neighbors. According to Hogan, Lars once approached Andrew while he was threshing grain and threatened to shoot him on the spot. Hogan added: "I think he would shoot anyone, he borrowed a gun for this purpose so I heard the neighbors say."[22] Charles's father remembered that time, too. He stated emphatically: "We all talked to the effect that it was not safe for Lars to be running around with a loaded gun."[23] Lars's threats were clearly a throwback to his father's use of signeri and feelings of persecution. However, Lars's irate comments were not issued as incantations or hexes against people at Kansas Lake, in the mode of his father, but as outbursts directed pointedly at the community pressure he felt closing in on him from all sides.

Lars felt especially threatened by individuals who wanted him separated from Caroline. He reacted strongly at the time neighbors were trying to serve divorce papers against him. Lars surely feared he would be run out of his home in the event of a divorce. Naturally enough, he also resented attempts to have him declared mentally ill. Being called insane was threatening enough. Being committed to an asylum in a new country with a language he did not understand was doubly frightening. Such fears only increased his unpredictability. No one expressed the general feeling of disapproval about Lars more clearly than Dr. Hiram Neill of St. James. He received reports of Lars's unusual behavior immediately after the time when Andrew and Caroline met at Texley's store and decided to investigate. Dr. Neill said: "I enquired of his [Lars's] history and found he had been a beggar and entirely worthless."[24]

Just as his father could seclude himself in his cottage and rail against intrusions, Lars lazed in his prairie farmhouse and variously commanded, or refused to allow, his younger wife to go out to the fields to work. Alone with his thoughts, he fretted over the measures he knew, or imagined, his neighbors were planning against him. Neither was he shy about voicing his suspicions and anger. He made the rounds of the settlement spelling out his feelings. As 1872 wore on, local residents had more and more reason to fear Lars's talk was not filled with empty threats. Abusing Caroline and brandishing a gun clearly stood out as portents of further violence. Another fit of jealously or bad temper could bring disaster down on the Kansas Lake Swedes. The realization of those fears could damage and change lives throughout the community.

Chapter VI
Conflict

The fall of 1872 was mild. Warm, dry days and brisk nights made for a good harvest. During that halcyon time, daily life on the Kansas Lake farms went on as usual. Andrew bought a pair of oxen and kept working on his farm buildings. He was also bringing in his crops. At one point he went into town and co-signed a note for Hogan to buy the reaper and mower from the local implement dealer. Meanwhile Caroline tended to the animals and the fields at her farm. Annie fed the chickens at home and did chores at the Olsons' house. All through the autumn Lars kept telling people he planned to start off on another of his begging trips.

Beneath that calm surface, tensions were building. As farmers began harvesting, Caroline defied Lars and went out to work for them again, while Lars whiled away his time, or, as Caroline put it: "At this time Lars was home doing nothing."[1] Some days Caroline had the ten-year-old Annie with her to help out alongside the adults. When not working for Andrew, Caroline took employment with Hogan and another Swede named John Peter Johnson. Those days were filled with heavy and steady work, but stories about Andrew and Caroline started circulating in the area. It was whispered they were carrying on a love affair in the farm fields. No one could verify that assertion. Still the topic was not dropped. Even Annie was asked about it, but she said she saw nothing out of the ordinary.[2]

Even if they were not having physical relations, Caroline was increasingly drawn to Andrew. In his humble way, he cut a dashing figure in their frontier setting. He had light brown hair, blue eyes, and a fair complexion. At 5' 8" he stood just above the average height for men in his environment.[3] There were similarities in Andrew's and Caroline's lives that brought them together as well. They were only one year apart in age, and while still very young both, in the same year, had wed spouses a decade or more older than they. Now they may well have been searching for new avenues of affection.

Andrew had the earmarks of a gregarious nature and a mental caretaker for others. Caroline, in turn, was a frequent visitor to Andrew's house, where she talked with him and confided in his parents.[4] That further angered Lars. Caroline said: "Lars did not tell me that I must not go to Andrew's house," but he ordered her to stop working in the fields along with Andrew. Caroline added: "Andrew did not come to our house much. Lars did not want Andrew or any one else to come there."[5] Through all this time neither Lars nor Caroline made it clear whether they knew Andrew was married in Sweden. If they did know or wondered, that was guaranteed to add fuel to Lars's anger.

Regardless of how much she knew about Andrew's past, Caroline's visits at her neighbors' farm were surely more for moral assurance than to plan trysts with Andrew. Andrew's mother had a liking for the younger woman and seems to have taken her under her wing. The two women could discuss Caroline's children, Lars's bad habits, and Caroline's sense of isolation. Even there, however, wild stories flourished. People saw ulterior motives behind her visits at Andrew and his parents' home. Caroline had to deny that she went to Andrew's to plot Lars's undoing. Caroline stated: "I had no understanding with Andrew that if I could get a divorce I would marry him." Later she and Andrew's mother strongly denied the suggestion that Caroline urged Andrew to kill Lars so that she and Andrew could get married.[6]

Despite those denials, Caroline's mind was surely a battleground of warring emotions. Her growing feelings of affection for Andrew collided with her ever-dwindling patience with Lars and the struggle to keep their farm going. Time and again she turned back to Charles Johnson and his father for advice. The two men mediated between her and Lars. Charles objected to Lars's mistreatment of Caroline. John and Charles Johnson repeated their advice that Caroline should seek a divorce.[7] At first she was interested, but afoot in the community were other serious objections to Lars. Foremost were the persistent and growing concerns about his mental health.

In 1872 neighbors started talking once more about swearing out a warrant to have Lars committed. Chief among the concerns was Lars's habit of going off begging and leaving his family for long stretches. That the Watonwan County community at large considered Lars mentally ill and negligent of his family was reflected in the daily and weekly press. The Swedish-American newspaper <u>Svenska Nybyggaren</u> (The Swedish Pioneer), in St. Paul, later wrote a series of weekly notices on news from outstate Minnesota in which it mentioned Lars's strange behavior and discussed community attitudes about him. It described Lars (April 17, 1873, and June 5, 1873) as "the half-crazy one" and as suffering from "mental deficiency."[8]

The newspaper also reported (April 7, 1873) that Lars "was at times insane and in that condition he was in the habit of undertaking long begging trips to the neighboring townships and counties and his wife and children often suffered dire hardships." It added (April 17, 1873) that "Caroline and the children suffered shortages of everything."[9] In truth, what the family most needed was for Lars to stay home, help out with the heavy farm work, and cooperate with his fellow settlers. Instead he talked about leaving. Hogan observed this: "The last time I spoke to him [Lars] he talked as if he intended to go away. This was during October 1872. He said he intended to go down in the settlement to beg. He did this all the previous winter."[10]

Nearly every mention of Lars during the 1870s, by Americans and Swedes alike, referred to his begging. The Americans had good reasons for suspecting him for what, in their eyes, was such a degrading practice. When the topic came up, the Americans consistently uttered denigrating comments about it. At the very best, they spoke of begging as highly unusual. Indeed the practice was frowned on all across the American frontier. Even the most economically hard-pressed settlers felt a need to avoid begging in order to preserve a positive image and maintain their self-respect as responsible breadwinners. Being seen as hardworking was of prime importance in times of hardship, when farmers had only one another for support. Every farmer had to pull his own weight. One historian of rural Minnesota cited the words of a southern Minnesota farm woman in the 1870s, who wrote to her unemployed husband during the hard times of that decade and beseeched him not to beg. The woman wrote: "I should be so ashamed to face people after begging my way to them."[11]

Minnesota government policy often reflected the need for self-reliance. In between the life of settled, responsible people and their families and that of itinerant hobos and tramps existed no middle ground. Respectable individuals down on their luck were quite simply not to ask for handouts, no matter what the cost to their own and their families' health and well-being. Swedes and Americans alike saw begging in the light of a family-oriented phenomenon, but public tolerance of it differed between the two countries. At the same time that begging was caused by real need, it brought down shame on those parents or children who had to resort to it, especially in America.

That shame stood in striking contrast to the extreme contempt showered — in both Sweden and Minnesota — on rootless tramps (Swedish *luffare*). Those were unattached males who wandered the countryside singly or in groups. They often looked for temporary work but at times were the cause (or object) of local disturbances. In Minnesota such men were under constant public scrutiny. Many were accused of crimes and given jail sentences. Public condemnation of their habits began as early as the 1860s in Watonwan County. The St. James Journal regularly reported on the arrival of tramps. According to the reports, they were not humble and starving family members whose situation people could lament but also feel sympathy for. Rather, they were seen as lice-infested, lazy, thieving, lying, and drunken individuals outside the pale of proper society.

The St. James paper described the comings and goings of several tramps who were crippled. The dismissive tone of the reports indicated that their physical handicaps made them even more suspect than their able-bodied brethren. At one point the paper also told of three tramps who were engaged in a fight in a boxcar. One was killed and another badly injured. The editor concluded (August 27, 1887):

"When tramps are not preying upon the public they turn and rend [injure] each other." On August 14, 1888, the newspaper reported on another death. One tramp pounded a fellow tramp to death in the business district of the town itself. The St. James Journal could write (September 17, 1887) about "three villainous tramps [who] loafed about St. James on Sunday — they did nothing but drink whisky and keep full [drunk] all the time." The paper even described the case of one luckless wanderer who unwittingly tried to burglarize the home of the Watonwan County attorney. For his bungled attempt the man received a thirty-day jail sentence, which the paper reported on with a barely disguised sense of glee.

Some wanderers were punished for their crimes, but others lived high on the hog, in the view of the St. James editor. He reasoned (May 26, 1888): "Few tramps really suffer for the necessities of life. If it is cold or damp and they need a fire, and dry kindling is scarce, they tap a [railway] car wheel, taking the waste packing from the box and thus securing material that insures a hot blaze." While many of those itinerant men committed crimes or drank to excess, the local populace victimized others. Many Minnesotans began to forget the important distinction between tramps and those settled but unemployed persons who were reduced to begging for their families. In the end, all those who asked for alms were lumped in the same general category of shame.

Lars carried with him to America a famine-era custom well known to the Swedish proletariat. Caroline's statement, supported by other members of the Kansas Lake settlement, that Lars intended to go off begging in November, 1872, concurs with accounts from Värmland that those accustomed to begging there had their most active period in the late autumn months and during the time closest to Christmas, when farm families were preparing sausages, meats, and bread for the holiday season.[12] Caroline described Lars's begging trips as frequent and of varying lengths. She said:

> *He had been away the winter before [1871] and many other times begging and at one time he remained away from four to five weeks. Other times he would be gone from two to three weeks. He generally brought back something to eat and sometimes clothing and money.*[13]

As a settled farmer, Lars had little reason for continuing such a practice in Minnesota. Yet possibly he himself viewed his begging as a form of enterprise fully appropriate for a man of his social class back home in Sweden. He never tired, for instance, of telling Swedes at Kansas Lake of all his upcoming trips. Wandering the country-side of southern Minnesota asking for handouts made him hard to distinguish, however, from the many tramps afoot in the region. In that context, people in Watonwan County looked down on him for his begging.

Even though Caroline failed to condemn Lars outright for begging, she stated she herself took care of the Kansas Lake household at all times. Implicit in her comments was the fact that she performed both male and female jobs on their farm. That imbalance in gender roles was guaranteed to direct scorn toward Lars among old-line tradition-alists in the Swedish settlement, who expected him to be a strong male presence and in full control of his family. Caroline said, however, that Lars's main aim was to gather enough money through begging to re-turn to Sweden, where he wanted to find his brother in Stockholm.

While Lars's begging puzzled American observers, it was his vio-lence that most angered the Swedes and aroused fear among them. Swedish settlers continued talking about the firearm Lars borrowed and what he might use it for. As the talk went on but nothing was done, Andrew, Charles, Hogan, and John Peter Johnson planned one evening in October, 1872, to take the gun away from him forcibly. Ho-gan described the foray:

> *Andrew and myself went one evening to take a gun*
> *away from Lars, or started to go, and went to within*
> *20 or 30 rods [110 to 165 yards] of Lars['s] house and*
> *then concluded not to do it — I then went home and I*
> *think Andrew went home also. I heard a noise soon*
> *after I left. I had parted from my brother only a moment*
> *or so before. I don't know who made the noise but I think*
> *it was Lars. Thought I recognized his voice.*[14]

It was Charles's father who stopped them by invoking an ancient Scandinavian dictum against attacking a man unawares after dark. Charles was the first to back out. Hogan then followed. As he neared home, Hogan again heard a noise, as of "Lars Johnson scream[ing]." After that Charles also heard screams.[15]

They were the sounds of a fight. Andrew took the long way home. Instead of going straight from Charles's house to his own, he followed the more beaten path leading by Lars and Caroline's house. As Andrew passed by, Lars yelled out in his direction and threw an ax at him. Andrew turned back and struck Lars over the head, leaving injuries that several persons still observed a week later. Caroline put a stop to the fracas:

> *It was seven in the evening. I recollect what was done there.*
> *My husband had been chopping wood. I was in the house*
> *and heard a noise outside as if two men were fighting and went*
> *outdoors and saw Andrew and my husband there fighting. I did*
> *not see Andrew when he came. [I] saw my husband throw*
> *an ax at Andrew. Lars was soon bloody.*[16]

Caroline added:

> *When I went out I saw the ax; it lay on the ground. Neither*
> *had it in his hands — They [Andrew and Lars] had hold of*
> *each other at this time — I told Andrew to leave my husband*
> *alone and the fuss stopped and Andrew started toward his house*
> *at once.*[17]

Caroline noted that the blood on Lars "came from his head, [and] ran down his hair on [the] back of his head." She also said Lars went several days without washing the blood from his head or clothes.[18] Strangely, Caroline neglected to say how she could have seen Lars throw the ax if she did not see Andrew approaching her house and if she stayed indoors until after the fight started. By seven on an October evening, it would have been completely dark outside.

Nevertheless her description of the fight and Lars's failure to wash the blood from his wounds spread quickly around the settlement and by late 1872 most people at Kansas Lake were fully convinced Lars was insane. As a result, Charles and Andrew abandoned their vigilante approach and decided to address the situation through legal channels. In October they went to Madelia to seek advice from probate judge H. S. Willson. Charles, who did most of the talking, asked:

> *What to do with a man who was insane and of whom*
> *the people in the neighborhood were afraid and Mr.*
> *Willson said he had better be sent to the Insane Asylum*
> *and he [Willson] made out papers for this purpose.*[19]

H. S. Willson ordered that Dr. Hiram Neill was to visit Lars and examine him for signs of mental illness. At the same meeting with Willson, Charles and Andrew took out papers "for Mrs. Lars Johnson to commence an action of divorce against Lars."[20]

Dr. Neill rode out to Kansas Lake only days after Lars and Andrew's fight. He examined Lars outside his house.[21] Dr. Neill saw the injuries on Lars's head but did not treat them. He went there, he said, specifically to interview Lars about his alleged insanity. Dr. Neill stated his findings: "I made examination as to his being insane and concluded he was insane or not of sound mind. I think his was melancholy insanity."[22]

After that, Caroline had to meet her dilemma head on. She could either attempt to send Lars to a mental hospital or try to divorce him. Both steps were more difficult to implement than informal talk made them sound. Was her wish to be free of Lars great enough to pursue the question all the way through the legal system? Did she have the money to pay for a divorce suit? In the summer and early fall of 1872, Caroline hesitated. Yet other community gestures toward sending Lars to the state mental hospital moved ahead. After Dr. Neill examined Lars, a warrant was issued to commit him. It fell on the shoulders of deputy sheriff Frederick Messer to take Lars into custody and deliver him to the mental health authorities. Messer started out with every intention of obeying those orders, but he eventually backed down. He stated bluntly why he failed to carry out the task: "I went to Larse's house to take him to St. Peter [insane asylum] by virtue of the warrant. I thought he was not crazy enough to take there."[23]

Likewise, Caroline explained that by November of 1872 she gave up on the idea of a divorce.[24] In a way it was a regrettable decision. Seen from a national perspective, her chances of winning against Lars were reasonably good. Divorce laws were restrictive in that era, but innocent spouses who had been victimized by abusive partners stood a good chance of obtaining a divorce. The period after 1850 witnessed extensive changes in divorce results across America. A sharp increase occurred in divorce cases heard and divorces granted. Nationwide the number of divorces rose from barely under 10,000 in 1867 to just over 25,000 in the early 1880s.[25] In those years, divorce ceased to be a middle-class or upper-class phenomenon. It spread among the working classes as well. It became possible to file for divorce not just for adultery or related causes but also on the broader grounds of abandonment, lack of financial support, or cruel and inhuman treatment.[26]

Caroline would have had little trouble gathering evidence that Lars's abuse of her was both mental and physical and also cruel. She would seem to have had one other advantage also. Divorce stopped functioning as a predominantly male prerogative. Across the country, large numbers of women began exercising the right of divorce. As the second half of the century wore on, women outnumbered men as plaintiffs in divorce cases. In some areas of the country, women made up as much as seventy-eight percent of the plaintiffs in divorce courts.[27]

In theory those changes indicated that Caroline had the odds in her favor against Lars. However, there was a local stumbling block. The strong national divorce trends were not as evident in Watonwan County. During the 1870s and 1880s around ten divorce cases were heard there. All but one were filed by husbands against their wives, and in each case the husband won his suit.[28] Those facts would suggest that the local culture discouraged women from filing for divorce. Even if some people in the Swedish settlement encouraged Caroline and helped to prepare preliminary divorce papers for her, she must have bowed to community pressures and decided her chances of winning in local courts were slim.

Complicating that situation was Caroline's position as a victim of Lars's violent tendencies. In all likelihood, she feared Lars would harm, or even kill, her and the children if she took steps to leave him. Indeed Lars showed definite signs of what a later age has defined as domestic abuse or intimate partner violence. Modern studies have identified two categories of batterers. The first is a grouping of men with dependency issues. Men in this category are generally insecure, have low self-esteem, and are psychologically dependent on the women they marry. Typically the men enter marriage thinking their wives are their reason for living. When the women prove unable to fulfill such unrealistic expectations, the men feel let down and physical abuse follows.[29]

Domestic abusers are generally terrified by the thought of abandonment and blame their spouses for their own dependence. Eventually they erupt in violence against their wives, thus expressing with blows their contempt for women, in spite of their dependence on them. A common tactic is stalking the wife. Men in this category have often been abused as children and bullied by their peers. As a result, they end up patterning onto others what has been done to them. Men with attachment disorders make up the other type of domestic abuser. For such men violence is less spontaneous and more of a calculated act. Their abusive behavior is impersonal and often preceded by acts of arson, theft, or cruelty to animals.[30] These men are frequently sociopaths, who use violence against many different targets, not just wives or partners.

A frequent motif in the lives of men in both classes of abusers is the problem of childhood attachment, or the lack thereof. Inconsistent, neglectful, or rejecting parenting of these men often results in attachment problems later in life. As adults they are commonly irrationally jealous and intolerant of rejection. They commonly suffer from depression as well.[31]

Lars showed a string of abusive traits. The Kansas Lake settlers noticed his feelings of insecurity and fear of abandonment, and Lars's encounter with American culture reinforced those emotions. He did not know English and was afraid of losing his home, being divorced, or sent to the mental hospital. In brief, he feared being cast adrift. In marrying Caroline, he surely expected to have his outcast state lessened. When that failed to happen, his jealousy of other men emerged. He tried to control Caroline's independence by dictating the terms of her employment and stopping her contact with other men. Lars's low self-esteem played a role as well. He spontaneously acted out his fears and anger by beating Caroline. He also performed aggressive posturing toward other members of the community. He obtained a gun and committed anti-social acts, such as throwing an ax at Andrew and exhibiting cruelty to animals. Caroline was, in brief, only one of his objects of hatred. She bore the brunt of his aggression because she was the closest person at hand.

Lars surely suffered from depression. Dr. Hiram Neill needed only one visit to diagnose him as a victim of "melancholy insanity," by which he can only have meant depression. In an environment in which other settlers labored constantly for survival and respect, Lars either begged or stayed at home. His imaginings fed his fears of bodily harm and his irrational jealousies. Those imaginings eventually became self-fulfilling prophecies when others at Kansas Lake lost patience with him or began to suspect his intentions. Underlying his depression were, beyond any doubt, serious attachment problems. He repeatedly left Caroline and the children for weeks on end. He showed disregard for his some of his neighbors' good intentions by returning tools in bad shape and threatened to shoot other neighbors. Caroline demonstrated a fine feel for understatement when she stated that Lars was not on good terms with any of his neighbors. Her fear of his unpredictable behavior was doubtless the decisive factor that convinced her to give up on the idea of a divorce.

So as people abandoned their thoughts of insanity declarations and divorce, the month of October, 1872, drew to a close on an inconclusive note. Early November gave little promise of improved conditions. Violence and threats of violence, both by Lars and against him, had increased since the summer. People close to the conflict made that clear. Hogan reported: "I heard Lars Johnson say he would shoot Andrew Johnson." Hogan added blandly: "Don't know as Andrew gave [him] any cause for his threat." On the other hand, Andrew was heard saying that Lars and Caroline ought to be separated and, if no one else appeared willing, he would do it himself.[32] Those attitudes pointed to one unmistakable problem. The bands between Lars, Caroline, and Andrew, which drew taught in early 1872, were stretched to their breaking point toward the end of the year.

In November, the biggest event was Election Day. It was a time for men to gather in town and celebrate. For many of the recently naturalized immigrants, it offered a glorious first chance to vote in a national election, a privilege denied them in Europe. Andrew, Hogan, and their father all went to town that day and cast their votes. For Lars, the festive holiday took on no special significance. He stayed at home the entire day.

For weeks Lars had continued talking about going away to beg. Finally the time drew near. He left his home before sunrise on November 8, just days after Election. Caroline described that fateful time. She said Lars arose on a Friday morning and put on a pair of pants, a shirt, and a vest. She continued:

> *I think Lars got up the morning he left before light. It was moon light and about 4 a. m. when he went away. I think he got up about 3 o'clock. The night before he said he wanted to get up early and go away. He told me where he wanted to go — he said he was going begging, he told me he was going to some place but I don't remember the place.*[33]

Caroline said she also got up, put on a petticoat, and started a fire. Lars had a breakfast of potatoes, bread, and milk. When her son began to cry, she went back to bed.

Caroline reported she lay in bed and watched as Lars left the house. After he closed the door, she never saw him again. According to Caroline, the couple had not argued. All she remembered Lars saying to her was "that he did not know when he would come back."[34] Caroline claimed she met no more adults that weekend. The next week she visited Charles's father and told him Lars had gone away begging again.[35]

On Andrew's farm things were as routine as they seemed at Lars and Caroline's. Andrew spent the whole day of November 7 repairing a stable. In the afternoon his mother came to him and announced they were out of flour. Since it was late, Andrew decided not to do anything about it that day. Instead he left home early on November 8 and went directly to Charles's house to borrow flour. Andrew said he waited until daylight to start off.[36] If that was the case, he was out long after the time Caroline said Lars set off in the early morning darkness.

Charles got up at four o'clock that morning. That was not particularly early since local residents, some of whom did not have lamps but saw only by the light of their fires, reported going to bed at eight or nine each night and rising before first light. Later in the morning Charles found Andrew waiting at his front door. Andrew sat and talked while Charles filled his sack with flour. After a few minutes Andrew shouldered his sack and walked back home. Andrew said he met no one else that morning, either coming or going.[37]

Under such conditions, seemingly so ordinary, Lars left home. No one admitted seeing him on the pathway leading away from home or out on the open prairies. In fact, if what people said was true, no one at all — either his family members or neighbors — set eyes on Lars that whole day, or in the days following. That account sounded straightforward enough. From such a simple chain of events, however, Andrew's and Caroline's lives, already a tangled skein of conflicting desires and stories, became increasingly — in truth, nearly hopelessly — complicated.

Chapter VII
Missing Lars

With Lars gone, Caroline carried on as usual. She worked and cared for the children. Andrew and Charles came over and cut wood for her. Seeing Caroline was alone, Andrew's mother went to her farm one evening and stayed overnight. Around the neighborhood some settlers began noticing that Lars was gone, but they remembered he had recently talked of leaving. So most thought little more of the matter. A few stated, however, that they heard Caroline say her husband "disappeared" rather than "went away."[1]   Still, there seemed little chance Lars would have trouble out on the road, since the weather was ideal for early November. The area had no snow and the lakes remained ice-free.

The sense of calm lasted barely a week. As it turned out, 1872-1873 had more than just an ordinary Minnesota winter in store, and Lars left home only days before the first dreadful blasts struck the prairies. The onslaught started in the form of an unforgettable blizzard in mid-November. Caroline and her children woke up one morning soon after Lars's departure and found their farm buried in snow. The storm hit without warning and left many people snowed in and cut off from the outside world. It was a threat to life and limb. One writer described the coming of that blizzard: "Following came the boreal winds sweeping the snow along in drifts and blockading every house. Several families were closed in their primitive residences for days and were finally helped out by neighbors."[2] Some settlers who were out-doors when the storm hit had barely enough time to find their door-ways before being blinded by the blowing snow.

After the snow stopped, temperatures dropped to twenty below zero. Under those conditions Caroline was left to fend for herself and her children. The four of them huddled together until the worst had passed. Then neighbors, including Charles Johnson, returned to help, but in the days following that Caroline was unable to clear snow and provide for the children and the animals by herself. As a result, she was forced to move.

Caroline first asked Charles's father if she and her children could spend the rest of the winter at that family's home. The elder Johnson said there was not room for all four of them. Only Caroline and the youngest child were invited to stay. The daughters Annie and Isabel would need other accommodations. Instead Caroline moved her household to Andrew's home. She described the move in this way:

> *I took my children and went to Andrew's to stay. I got very cold and the snow was deep and I went there to stay through the cold weather — I took our cattle there also about a week after we went. Andrew's mother and all her folks asked me to come there.*[3]

Charles later remembered his father's negative reply to Caroline. He commented matter-of-factly: "There was a large snowstorm in the fall of 1872. It came from 12 to 13 November. She [Caroline] went up to Andrew's after this storm. She first came down to stay at our house but father objected, he said he had no room for her." What Charles neglected to mention was that reporters who assessed the storm in its aftermath concluded that it was the worst ever experienced in Minnesota at that time of year.[4]

When Caroline moved, Andrew carried her belongings to his house. It was terribly crowded but they were all warm and safe. During that time Andrew and Caroline became physically intimate. Going from neighbors to lovers took place smoothly. They were living together in a one-room house with five other people. They worked, ate, and slept together. Annie gave the clearest indication that their affections were mutual. She saw Andrew kissing Caroline and Caroline kissing him back. She listened to them talking while they were still in bed in the mornings. Annie explained: "I heard Andrew tell mother he liked her and he put his arm around her. All of this was after father [Lars] left."[5]

Andrew himself said he had no sexual relations with Caroline until a month after the storm. Then the two slept together at her house and later at Andrew's place. Andrew said this happened after "she told me Lars had begged money and gone to Sweden." The understanding Andrew got out of Caroline's comment was that Lars either would not come back to America until he found his brother or not come back at all. That was a message Andrew apparently accepted without question.[6]

By Christmas of 1872, no one in Long Lake township could doubt Andrew and Caroline's feelings for each other. The severe weather gave settlers little time, however, to ponder Lars's continued absence or his wife's special living arrangement with Andrew. A second, and even more terrible, blizzard blew in at the beginning of January and came to be known as The Great Storm of 1873. (Figure 23) That blizzard swept down suddenly on a mild day and left several feet of snow in its wake. One survivor wrote of the general debilitating effect:

> *[The day of the storm] was a beautiful day, like spring.*
> *In the afternoon, like a thunder bolt out of a clear sky*
> *sprang the great blizzard of January 7, 1873, and lasted*
> *three days and nights. Three days and three nights that*
> *storm raged without slacking up once.*[7]

Another victim added in graphic terms:

> *A frightening roar was heard in the northwest and, looking,*
> *one could see a great white wall reaching from the clouds*
> *to the earth, coming at the rate of forty miles an hour. It was*
> *a blizzard, filling the air with frozen snow and driving it forward*
> *with the fierceness of a gigantic sandblast. No man or beast can*
> *face it. One turns instinctively from it, and once turned and*
> *started there is no such thing as stopping. One is driven onward,*
> *while unmercifully whipped by the frozen snow until, in sheer*
> *exhaustion, the ill-fated traveler sinks into the drift.*[8]

Across Minnesota, seventy people died in the storm, although early reports listed as many as 800 dead.[9] In the January blizzard many froze to death following pathways or wandering blindly in opposite directions from their destinations.[10]

The <u>Mankato Herald</u> (January 18, 1873) reported that it "was the most fearful [storm] ever experienced in Minnesota since its settlement and the list of casualties already received is frightful." The newspaper's reporters later surveyed the area along the Chicago & Northwestern railroad from Mankato southwest to the Iowa border and confirmed that eighteen people had frozen to death and countless others had lost limbs because of frostbite (January 25, 1873). The blizzard killed eight people in Watonwan County, along with livestock by the hundreds. The storm and its after-effects occupied people's minds and interrupted communications for weeks. If Lars Johnson was missing, he was only one of many in the same boat.

In Andrew's one-room house all seven persons — Andrew and his parents as well as Caroline and her three children — waited out the January blizzard for three days and nights. The difficulties they endured were enormous. One Watonwan County woman who lived through the storm told of a relative who left Minnesota after the winter of 1873 and refused ever to set foot in the state again because of her dreadful memories of the blizzard.[11] Later accounts gave a fair approximation of conditions following the 1873 storm. In mid-February of 1881, a similar blizzard struck the Minnesota prairie. On that occasion local newspapers devoted far more space to the difficulties in the countryside than newspapers had in 1873. <u>The St. James Journal</u> (February 19, 1881) reported that the first to be laid low by that storm were the rail lines. Trains were blocked by seven feet of hard-packed snow and then "almost buried from sight by drifting snow." Engines soon died for want of fuel. A crew of 200 men tried digging out one train stranded near St. James, but in two days they succeeded only in uncovering the engine and one car.

The newspaper followed that notice (February 19, 1881) with a report on the condition of the blizzard's second important casualty, the distant farming populace. The roads to town were completely blocked for weeks and farmers had to come on foot and carry their supplies home with hand-drawn sleds. The paper added: "Some have come at a distance of ten, twelve and fifteen miles. This is a greater hardship than any in the village would have to undergo had the railroad remained blockaded a week or two longer."[12] If communications could be disrupted so badly in the 1880s, they were surely affected far worse a decade earlier. With the even more primitive roadways of the early 1870s, privations then were greater and the long-lasting effects of the blizzards worse. The St. James Journal concluded as much in 1881 (February 19): "If the late storm [of 1881] had been accompanied by cold weather it would have been the equal of the great storm of '73 and much suffering would have followed."

Caroline stayed at Andrew's until the worst of the winter season of 1872-1873 was over. By March of 1873, she and the children were back at their own farm. That spring Caroline rented seven acres of her land to Andrew. Altogether he had nearly forty acres of his and her land ready to cultivate by the middle of April. However, being at their own farms was only partly a resumption of a normal pace of life. People's whisperings about the two turned to open and wild speculation, which soon showed its darker side. Once gossip got started, it continued unabated in the community, and words of suspicion were directed at Andrew and Caroline in equal measure.

Chapter VIII
New Problems

As the New Year of 1873 progressed, farmers in Long Lake township noticed that several months had passed but Lars was still missing. At first only the settlers at Kansas Lake talked about it among themselves. Then people began to voice their feelings more widely across the county. Some decided Lars had got lost or even died. For those who disliked him, such a thought surely came with a sigh of relief. Others were not so easily satisfied and spoke up. Disapproving of Andrew and Caroline's affair, they asked why nobody was looking for Lars. One newspaper carried a notice to that effect. An anonymous contributor to the <u>St. James Herald</u> (March 28, 1873) reported rumors were rife that Lars "has been foully dealt with." Yet suspiciously, the writer noted, neither Caroline nor the local residents bothered to find out what had become of him. While rumors about Lars's disappearance were widespread, search efforts were clearly not.

When Lars still had not returned by April of 1873, talk in the county swung back and forth. People started rumors. Some believed Lars finally went fully insane from the constant pressure on him and committed suicide during the winter. Others felt he fell in the lake and drowned as he was leaving home in November. Still others pointed to the love triangle between Lars, Caroline, and Andrew. They believed Andrew and Caroline plotted to murder Lars and then run away and live together. Another faction suspected that Andrew, in a fit of passion, killed Lars by himself sometime after Lars left home on the morning of November 8.

As the months went by, those stories spread ever farther and farther afield. People altered and embellished them with each retelling. Some told how Lars had wandered aimlessly across the countryside until the November blizzard overtook him and he froze to death in the fields. Others, who surely knew nothing of the way Lars and Caroline's family lived, said Lars was murdered on his farm by a conniving hired hand. The killer then took what he could of the dead man's possessions and ran off with Caroline.[1]

A few told an even more imaginative tale. According to them, Lars had gone off to northern Minnesota to work at logging. In November of 1872, he unexpectedly returned to Kansas Lake from his logging camp and discovered Andrew and Caroline were having a love affair. Caught in the act, the two killed Lars, bound his feet with a rope, and sank his body in the lake.[2] Surely the omission of begging and the substitution of the word logging, with its implications of strong masculine pursuits on Lars's part, made the story far more exciting for those willing to believe in such a wild tale.

As more and more stories spread, the county authorities at last gave in and investigated. On April 10, 1873, they arrested Andrew and Caroline on suspicion of murdering Lars. The arrest was based on little more than general assumptions and hearsay, since there was not a shred of evidence that Lars was even dead. Andrew was dragging his farmland at Kansas Lake when the sheriff arrived to take him to court and face questioning. They then drove to Caroline's and arrested her as well. Andrew and Caroline, who had Annie with her, were driven to town in separate buggies to prevent them from talking with each other. Since the two spoke in Swedish, which the sheriff did not understand, the unreasonable fear was that Andrew and Caroline might invent an alibi for themselves on the way to town. Oddly, having the local Swede Charles Westman in one of the sheriff's buggies did not alter that line of reasoning.[3]

Andrew and Caroline appeared before the justice court in Madelia on the 10th, 12th, and 13th of April, 1873. J. W. Seager, a young attorney from St. James, represented them. He later told how he listened patiently to the long, slow process of translating the Swedes' testimony to English and took careful notes on what was said. Andrew, Caroline, Annie, and other Kansas Lake residents were called as witnesses. Svenska Nybyggaren, which from that point on took a special interest in the case, had its local correspondents on the scene. They made it clear that the tone of those hearings was less than pleasant. An example was the growing hint of antagonism between Caroline and Annie. Reports showed that Andrew and Caroline told the court similar versions of what had happened in the fall of 1872. Annie later claimed that the two had also tried to construct a story that Annie herself could tell, which would agree with Andrew and Caroline's own testimony.[4]

Annie insisted that her mother and Andrew anxiously repeated to her that she must testify as they instructed her to, that is, that she was awake in the early morning of November 8 and saw her father leave home alone. Confusingly, Annie first made that very statement to authorities but later contradicted it, arguing that she had been asleep and did not see Lars depart.[5] In the midst of those contradictions, J. W. Seager had an easy time defending Andrew and Caroline, since Lars's body remained missing. Yet the talk in the community did not lessen. Pernicious gossip, rumors, and fickle public opinion continued to raise their ugly heads. The general public went on bringing up wild assumptions about Lars's disappearance, which it took as proof that Andrew and Caroline plotted to murder Lars. That sentiment influenced local officials to keep an eye on Andrew and Caroline, even if they could not detain them in custody.

After a while, the storytelling calmed down to the point that even some previously suspicious people began changing their minds and agreeing with the more realistic sounding argument that Lars had died in one of the snowstorms. Thus, they argued, Andrew must be innocent. Svenska Nybyggaren (April 17, 1873) attributed those changing feelings to the strong suggestive power of rumor. An excerpt of the newspaper's comments read:

> *Rumor at once pronounced the judgement that Andrew in*
> *consultation with Lars's wife murdered him. Thus many*
> *issues and guesses developed in which people convinced*

> *themselves that they saw proof of Andrew's guilt, a situation*
> *explained by the fact that they [issues and guesses] came about*
> *merely through the powerful misleading effects of rumor and*
> *wagging tongues. The insane Lars is now assumed, since*
> *rumor has turned, to have wandered about and begged and so*
> *perished on the prairies in the severe blizzard of January 7.*
> *What the facts are in reality only the Almighty knows. If a*
> *murder has been committed, it cannot be concealed in the long*
> *run. It is said Andrew can no longer be detained in jail; he is*
> *probably innocent and thus should be released.*[6]

Surely enough, Andrew and Caroline were freed. Andrew returned home and resumed his spring farming. Even so, he was clearly shaken. Though on his own again, he was not above suspicion. That thought and the general finger pointing aimed his way made him restless. Added to those worries came Caroline's discovery that she was pregnant. She must have broken the news to Andrew in March or April of 1873.

With his troubles doubling and trebling, Andrew left Kansas Lake. It happened suddenly. He first talked with his family and some neighbors about going to St. Paul to find work and then mentioned Wisconsin, where he wanted to recoup money he had lent out to a Swede there in the late 1860s. In the end, he headed west. The rail lines in and out of Watonwan County were closed by snow from January 7 to April 10, 1873. Andrew departed from Watonwan County just two weeks after the tracks reopened and in the middle of his work in the farm fields, which he left unplanted. Abandoned was Andrew's team of oxen. Hogan first took care of them, but he was later forced to return the team to their original owner, since Andrew had not yet paid for them. For a while, Hogan also tended to a cow and calf Andrew owned, but he then sold them.[7]

Across Minnesota and Iowa railroad jobs were still available, though no longer as plentiful. Andrew stopped first in Sioux City, but could not find any employment there; so he went on to Nebraska. In Omaha he got work in the Union Pacific Company's machine shop. He gave no address to his parents and failed even to explain to them which direction he was heading. Caroline said he intended all along to return to Kansas Lake. She discounted claims that he fled because he was responsible for Lars's disappearance and feared being arrested again.[8]

When Andrew left Watonwan County, he avoided St. James. He told Caroline of his destination but could not afford to take her along. He later said he knew she wanted to join him, and he expected her to do so. She did not go with him because she had no money. She soon found a way, however, by selling two of her cattle for coach fare. She caught up with Andrew in Iowa a week later and then lived with him in Omaha "as his wife."[9]

In leaving Kansas Lake, Caroline had to fib. Telling Hogan that she intended to visit friends in adjacent Brown County, she asked him to deliver her to the rail station and then care for her children while she was away. Hogan drove her the four miles by oxcart and left her at the Butterfield station. She waited on the platform until he departed and then bought a ticket to Sioux City, where she caught up with Andrew, arriving there a week after him.[10] Hogan also remembered Andrew's and Caroline's departures. He said Andrew left on April 18 or 19 and Caroline only four or five days later.[11] Hogan and his parents ended up caring for her children for over four months after that time.

Much later, Andrew explained that he left Long Lake township for points westward not only to find work but also to avoid meeting people who might recognize him. He called himself by his father's name of John Johnson to dissociate himself from anyone's recollection of Lars's disappearance. Andrew was asked if he could have found work in the spring of 1873 in St. James, which had a roundhouse and other railroad shops. Andrew did not seek work there, he replied, and did not know if any was available.[12] His clear aim in leaving was to put some distance between himself and Watonwan County. At that task, he succeeded.

Andrew and Caroline had just over two months together in the summer of 1873. They first stayed for a week with a Swedish family in Sioux City and then rented space in a residential area of Omaha. She stayed at home during the day while he was at work.[13] During the adventures of that spring and summer, Andrew and Caroline must surely have realized their lives were changed forever. She had begun with a line of small but deceptive prevarications and then left her children behind at Kansas Lake without saying when she would return to them. In that way the separate living arrangement between Caroline and her two daughters, which Charles Johnson's father suggested after the snowstorm of 1872, eventually came to pass. Andrew, in turn, suddenly left his farm. Moreover, after seven years in America, he abandoned for good his marriage to Johanna Persdotter, his wife in Sweden, and committed himself to a liaison with Caroline, the outcome of which hung in a precarious balance.

Besides wishing to remain unknown in Omaha and needing to deal with Caroline's pregnancy, Andrew faced another problem. He had never lived apart from his immediate family for any longer period and no doubt missed them. In early July of 1873, he asked a Swede in Omaha to write a letter to Hogan for him asking how things were back home at Kansas Lake. He signed the letter "John Johnson." No one in Watonwan County had yet discovered where Andrew and Caroline were, and the letter took Hogan by surprise. Unable to read, he asked another Swede to read it out loud to him, and looked for another man to pen a reply for him. Hogan explained:

> *The first I heard of Andrew after he left here [Kansas Lake] was from Omaha. I got a letter from him whilst he was at Omaha. The name signed to the letter was John Johnson. I did not know whether the letter was from him or not. I can't read or write. I got some one to read the letter, a man who was working with me on the road read it, but I don't recollect his name. I had a short letter written in reply. Andrew Lieberg wrote for me.*[14]

News of Andrew's letter spread quickly across Watonwan County, and it soon came to the attention of A. B. Stone, the county sheriff, who wired law officers in Omaha to inquire about Andrew's presence there.

As soon as the spring thaw of 1873 opened up communications again, events across the prairies followed one after another at a feverish pace. Unknown to Andrew and Caroline at Omaha in early July of that year, a happening had already taken place at Kansas Lake that would put Watonwan County journalists to work full-time and rapidly set the local legal community in action.

Chapter IX
Finding Lars

In early 1873 Andrew and Caroline's affection for each other was an open secret. Not surprisingly, the pressures mounted on them with time. After only a few months, they left their Kansas Lake home suddenly and with a degree of secrecy that was not altogether unlike Andrew's quick departure from Sweden seven years earlier. As a response to hard times, he left farm and family members on both occasions. By the spring of 1873, most in the local community saw Andrew and Caroline's action as a panic-induced flight. As a result, more and more people began blaming them, not Lars, for the troubles at Kansas Lake. Therein lay an important change of public attitude.

While people at home talked and wondered, Andrew and Caroline's life in Omaha began settling into a routine as spring turned into summer in 1873. Quite likely the couple even felt a certain sense of peace in their new environment. Omaha was a growing and lively city of around 30,000 with a strong base of Scandinavian immigrants. The ethnic community consisted of merchants, artisans, and laborers, which Andrew's work skills fit into nicely.[1] Andrew had steady work, while Caroline enjoyed a few weeks of leisure time. Surrounded by Scandinavians, they had no need to venture out into the English-speaking community. Instead they settled in and carried on as husband and wife.

Farther north, at Kansas Lake, the planting season ended in May, and the first real spring weather arrived. The last week in May was typical. The week before had been warm, offering hopes of a bounteous crop. The morning of May 25 dawned sunny and bright, reinforcing those hopes. In the evening light, Christine Johnson, Charles's mother, walked the 400 yards from her home down to the waterfront to carry out her wifely chore of fetching water for the household. There, among the vernal greenery, something caught her eye. She hesitated before venturing nearer. Then she could see it was a body. At that point she realized she had stumbled, fully unexpectedly, upon the remains of Lars Johnson. His body was floating quietly near the bank where the small creek at the northwest corner of Kansas Lake emptied into the lake.

At first Christine was shocked. Then she noticed there was something almost idyllic or calming in the scene before her. The sufferings of the most troubled man at Kansas Lake were now over, and his body had taken its time in finding a spot where it could rest securely against firm ground at the lakefront. Christine Johnson viewed the find for a moment and then alarmed her husband and son. The two men hurried to the scene, studied the body, and then pulled it partly up on dry ground. They sent word to others, and the news spread rapidly across the countryside. By the end of the next day, most of the men in the area had gathered at the lake and viewed the body.

Hogan Johnson was one of the first at the site. When he got there, Lars's head lay on the bank but the body was still in the water. Hogan described seeing three fractures in the skull. John Johnson, Charles's father, supported Hogan's comments. "The head was split in three directions," the elder Johnson said. John Johnson added that the body was clothed in "a pair of pants, a vest and a shirt" but it had no shoes on.[2]

The injuries that were immediately visible had been incurred with great force. In places the scalp was ripped off the skull. The body showed signs of having been in the water for a long while, since the exposed skin was weather-beaten. Hogan was one of a group of men who buried Lars, but they did not specify the exact spot. It might have been near the congregation's tiny meetinghouse on the east bank. Or they could have chosen ground at the new church building, if indeed it had been built by that time.[3]

If Lars was not laid to rest at the church, the men surely interred his body on the west side of the lake, near the spot where it was found. Charles Johnson came the closest to indicating that the men buried the body in the fields west of the lake. His comments were more detailed than Hogan's but failed to give the exact burial site:

> *I was present when he [Lars] was taken out of the water.*
> *When taken out he was carried about 15 rods [83 yards]*
> *and laid on the prairie. The body layed there from noon*
> *until about 4 o'clock P. M. Then it was buried. I saw him*
> *buried and helpt to burry [sic]. I was also there when the body*
> *was taken up from the same grave where I saw him buried. I*
> *saw Drs. Neill & Overholt take the skull out. That was in the*
> *fall of 1872 [actually1873?].*[4]

This statement by Charles Johnson was typical of the confusing comments concerning the finding and later exhuming of Lars's body. It was stated, perplexingly, that the body also was exhumed in 1874. If those statements were completely accurate, then the corpse was dug up and examined twice, that is, in 1873 (for a coroner's inquest) and again in 1874. Upon exhuming the body in 1873, doctors Hiram Neill and George Overholt, removed the head from the casket. The existence of a casket was a sign that Lars was buried with at least some care, though neither Hogan nor Charles mentioned any funeral service.[5]

The descriptions of the exact conditions under which Lars's body was found and the way it was examined grew as muddily unclear as the location of his grave. Hogan Johnson remembered May 25 and 26, 1873, as warm spring days, during which the heat had its way with Lars's body, but Hogan seemed to contradict himself about where Lars's body lay. After stating that he first saw it at the lakeside, he then said: "When I first saw Lars Johnson's body it was some 8 rods [40 yards] from the lake. It was then quite warm weather and the body was badly swollen."[6] Dr. Hiram Neill, who came to the site the very day Lars's body was pulled ashore, had another impression of that late-May weather. He recalled that the warm, sunny weather on the morning of the 25th had turned bad by the afternoon and the task of examining the corpse was disagreeable. Dr. Neill said: "I made the examination under difficulties, it was cold, and I was in a hurry and it was a bad [unpleasant] job. The body when I saw it was in pretty good condition. It had the appearance of having been in the water a long time."[7] Even the location of the major injury to Lars's head was called into doubt in his testimony. While others present at the site described the most lethal fracture as being on the right side, Dr. Neill remembered seeing it on the left side.[8] Yet he admitted he was cold at the time and his work hasty.

Authorities immediately assumed foul play was involved. They wished to know how the body could have ended up where it did in the lake. Since Andrew and Caroline were still the prime suspects, law enforcement men asked how or why the two would have put Lars's corpse in the north end of the lake, if they lived at the south end. Charles Johnson suggested the answer. He said it was possible the body entered the water in the fall season at the southwest end of the lake, and then emerged farther northward in the spring. (Figure 24) Charles told how the south wind pushed the ice to the north end of the lake and broke it up there each April or May. Charles estimated the depth of the water at only two or three feet near the shore. Since just two Kansas Lake farmers had boats, the implication was that whoever put Lars in the water had no boat and was unable to reach the middle of the lake, which could be up to eight feet deep.[9] Therefore, it was assumed, the supposed perpetrator(s) in haste, and also desperation perhaps, sank the body in the shallow water near the bank.

At last officials had Lars's body, but now they had no Andrew or Caroline. They waited for over a month. The arrival of Andrew's letter to Hogan later in the summer put the final piece of the puzzle in place, in the minds of Watonwan County officials at least. Andrew failed to explain what motivated him to send that letter, other than homesickness. Sending it may have expressed a naïve notion on his part that he was at a safe distance from the law, or it may have revealed a wish to face up to the realities of Lars's disappearance, regardless of his actual role in it. Intended or not, the latter eventuality came to pass.

Omaha police quickly located Andrew, and sheriff Stone left Watonwan County for Nebraska by train. Andrew was at work at the Union Pacific railroad shop in Omaha on July 9, 1873, when sheriff Stone appeared and arrested him. Andrew was given barely enough time to collect his pay before being taken away. Stone escorted Andrew and

Caroline back to Minnesota. The sheriff had them in Madelia by July 12. Andrew explained: "The sheriff brought me from Omaha to Sioux City then to Madelia and then took me to Mankato where I have ever since been in Jail."[10] Svenska Nybyggaren reported on July 17, 1873, that Lars Johnson's killer, Andrew Johnson, along with Caroline, was undergoing questioning. For Andrew and Caroline, the romance of that summer ended abruptly. Their return, under arrest, to the budding settlement areas of Watonwan County caused a sensation, as the news passed by word of mouth and was quickly picked up by the local press.

In Madelia, Sheriff Stone took them immediately to Justice of the Peace W. W. Murphy and their arrest warrant was read aloud. Thomas Rutledge, the Watonwan County attorney, filed a charge that Andrew Johnson "on or about November 8, 1872," and with "malice aforethought killed Lars F. Johnson by striking him on the head with an ax or other sharp instrument." Both Andrew and Caroline waived an examination. Since Watonwan County had no proper cell space, both were placed in the Blue Earth County jail at Mankato.[11] There the accused couple waited out the rest of the summer.

Andrew and Caroline remained in a state of limbo. The jailhouse was located next to the Blue Earth County courthouse. The jail and the courthouse stood on the slopes high above, and only blocks away from, downtown Mankato.[12] Andrew and Caroline had the freedom to walk the grounds of the jailhouse and talk with each other. From there they had a view out over the lush greenery of the river valley and the local community.

Their jailers treated them humanely. Both were given medical attention, Andrew for a respiratory condition and Caroline because she was pregnant. Andrew explained his complaint: "I have a disease of the lungs — I have pains and then my nose bleeds — I have been treated by physicians since I have been in jail — I have a cough. It tires me to walk. I have had this difficulty about seven years."[13] The ailment was possibly tuberculosis, and Andrew may have contracted it even before he left Sweden. His years laboring on the railroad, living in primitive housing, and struggling at farming surely worsened the malady.[14] By 1873 he faced a grim but not hopeless health situation. Caroline, in turn, was nearing the third trimester of her pregnancy, but she remained physically fit.

Conditions were tolerable. Still, jail was jail. Surely the two were troubled. Regardless of the difficulties, their devotion to each other during those months spoke of a total commitment. As the summer wore on, they decided to get married. They were wed in the Mankato jail. Charles Otto, a Mankato jeweler and justice of the peace, married them on August 20, 1873, at which time Caroline was seven months pregnant. The marriage certificate gave the newlyweds as Andrew Johnson and Caroline Anderson (the Swedish Andersdotter), an indication Caroline had taken her maiden name again. The Blue Earth County sheriff John Diamond and his wife were the signing witnesses.[15]

Few weddings have been stranger. Andrew was a legally married man from Sweden committing himself, in a jailhouse in Minnesota, to a bigamous relationship with the pregnant widow of the man he was accused of murdering. The few observers who possibly knew the details of Andrew and Caroline's past could only have wondered. Did Andrew think of Johanna as he wed Caroline? Or had he decided, or been forced by the course of events, to assign Johanna Persdotter to his past? And what future, if any, did the two envision together as they waited for their murder trial to begin?

Given the circumstances, they must have seen marriage as the only plausible way of stating the depth of their affection and the main hope of giving legitimate legal status to their as yet unborn child. Or perhaps Andrew decided nothing at all. He was so deeply embroiled in his problems that they alone dominated his thoughts, and his past in Sweden may suddenly have been put on hold, seeming, as it were, to be part of a different world, both geographically and mentally. It was during the tumultuous times in 1873 that Andrew broke off all contact with Johanna Persdotter.

Andrew found his plight growing even more difficult as fall turned to winter. At first, he had no attorney. Finally the state appointed an up-and-coming Mankato defense lawyer named M. J. Severance to his case, but neither Andrew nor Severance knew the other's language. Also Caroline was expecting their child soon. Then came the clinching blow. In February of 1874, Andrew was formally indicted in district court in Madelia and charged with murder. His trial was set for the spring.[16] Caroline, on the other hand, was in jail for just under eight weeks. The State of Minnesota later dropped charges against her, because of her pregnancy. Caroline was released into the custody of A. B. Stone and the Watonwan County sheriff's office in Madelia.

Even her exit from jail was dramatic. <u>Svenska Nybyggaren</u> reported (September 11, 1873) that the Watonwan County sheriff took Caroline from the Mankato jail in early September to save her from the miseries of prison life. While eight months pregnant and living in the sheriff's home in Madelia, Caroline crawled out through a window of his house one night and ran away, although it was not clear where she went. She may have acted in the hope of seeing her children, who by then had left Hogan and his parents' care and gone to other families. Or perhaps she wished to visit Andrew in Mankato, or just escape the public eye.

In any case, Caroline's trip was short. <u>Svenska Nybyggaren</u> predicted she could not get far, unless she had friends to whisk her away. The newspaper was right. Any such friends failed to materialize, and by mid-October, 1873, Caroline was back in Madelia. On October 17, 1873, she gave birth to her and Andrew's daughter, christened Nellie Christine and known thereafter as Christine. The girl was named after Andrew's mother Christine and his sister Petronella (Nellie).[17] After the birth, Caroline returned to Kansas Lake with her two youngest children, John Albert and Christine. She took up residence in the home of Andrew's parents. Her future there was uncertain, and money was in short supply. As the trial approached, Andrew's family could only wait in their crowded farmhouse and hope.

Chapter X
Early Trial Reports

Andrew's 1874 murder trial was held in Minnesota's sixth district court in Madelia, with Judge Franklin Waite presiding. After ten months of biding his time in the Mankato jail, Andrew was finally put on board the westbound train and taken back to Watonwan County. His trial began on May 5. The proceedings were held in the narrow confines of Madelia's old wooden courthouse. An early local historian called the State's case against Andrew "perhaps the most sensational murder trial in the history of Watonwan County."[1] Regional newspapers described the community as all abuzz with excitement over the trial. The St. James Journal commented that the proceedings aroused "considerable attention," and the editors of the Madelia Times and the St. James Herald announced their intention of printing transcripts of the witnesses' testimony to satisfy the public's hunger for immediate news from the courtroom.[2]

Despite all the hooplah, the essence of the case was simple. Seven years after he left Sweden in 1866, Andrew had twice been arrested in America on suspicion of homicide, and in 1874 he was at last being tried for murdering Lars. In preparation for the trial, the county made arrangements for the witnesses subpoenaed from Kansas Lake to stay at a boarding house in Madelia. That meant that nearly all the many Johnsons, as well as other residents, from the Swedish settlement were in attendance throughout the trial. An added complement of curious citizens made the Madelia courtroom woefully overcrowded and the atmosphere hot, muggy, and intense. Most of the early hours on the first day were devoted to preliminary procedures.

Deciding on a jury came first. Andrew and his defense attorney, M. J. Severance, successfully challenged several prospective jurors, including two Swedes who were excused from serving on the jury because they "could not read or write the English language and did not understand the [spoken] language." Another twenty were eliminated due to personal bias, an indication that feelings about the case were running especially high. Finally, an all-male jury, with no ethnic Scandinavians, was selected. A Swedish American from Madelia, Oscar F. Wennerstrand, a former Watonwan County sheriff (1864-1865), was then sworn in as the official translator. That was a job Wennerstrand was uniquely qualified for. At thirty-seven, he was approximately the same age as the principals in the case. He was also a native of Sweden and a farmer in Madelia township. In addition, his wife Elizabeth was born in England, a fact that helped Wennerstrand to become fully bilingual.[3]

Those called to testify by the prosecution included what, to an uninitiated observer, was a bewildering array of Johnsons. They were: Caroline Johnson; Hogan Johnson; John Johnson (Andrew's father); Annie Johnson; Christine Johnson (Andrew's mother); Charles Johnson; and a second John Johnson (Charles's father). Also called was Dr. George H. Overholt (a St. James physician). The defense called: J. W. Seager; H. S. Willson (the former Watonwan County probate judge, 1870-1873); Dr. Hiram Neill; John Johnson (Andrew's father); and Andrew himself.[4] An interested observer at the trial was George P. Johnston, a native of New York State, mentioned previously as the man who became a Republican Party political candidate from Watonwan County in the 1880s. Like the Swedish Johnsons, George P. Johnston had come to Watonwan County as a young man in the late 1860s. In time he became a leading citizen of the St. James community. Years later, he reappeared as a prime, if mysterious, player in Andrew's life.

Considering the alleged killing of Lars and deciding on the guilt or innocence of Andrew seemed a cut-and-dried matter. A violent death occurred and a likely suspect was on trial. What little information the legal people knew about the Swedes' past history was supplemented by other details that came to light, such as Lars's and Andrew's varying temperaments and physical energy levels. Those presented interesting personality profiles, whose differences made up a sure recipe for conflict. Each felt affection for Caroline, a fact that sowed discord between them. In turn, Caroline was tied to one of them by marriage and romantically linked with the other. She first had children with Lars but drifted steadily toward Andrew for employment and comfort, and later even for marriage.

There were complications, however. Other facts, which would seem salient, were not common knowledge. That Lars had long suffered from social exclusion before leaving Sweden and that Andrew already had a wife and children in Veinge presented potential complications that the American authorities and the general public in Watonwan County alike seem to have remained completely unaware of. Indeed trial officials made no visible effort to learn or record anything additional about Lars's, Caroline's, or Andrew's personal histories before their arrival in Minnesota.

Uncertain were the precise details of Lars's death, the horror of which could only be guessed at. Lacking in the court papers, furthermore, was an admission of guilt by Andrew. He steadfastly maintained his innocence before the trial, and his official plea to the court at the beginning of the proceedings was a firm "not guilty."[5] That fact raised the question: What alternative explanation of Lars's death could defense counsel Severance offer? Considering the many details missing in the preliminary legal papers caused the mystery of the case to deepen.

Negative public sentiment about Andrew and Caroline grew steadily throughout 1873 and 1874. That many forgot their previous disagreements with Lars and began voicing prejudice against Andrew was reflected in the pages of <u>Svenska Nybyggaren</u>. When the paper began following the case, it was willing to reserve judgement about the parties implicated in it. The paper consistently weighed wild rumor off against logical possibilities. Its major conclusion denounced hearsay and gossip and supported the idea of Andrew's innocence.

After Lars's body was found, the paper changed its tactics. In the summer of 1873, it began describing Andrew as the guilty party (June 5, 1873). Later on (July 17, 1873), it openly referred to him as the murderer (*mördaren*).

Caroline's reputation suffered as well. Her "immoral" connection with Andrew was held against her in the community, a fact that must have left her feeling condemned in the public eye, even though she was not legally held responsible for Lars's death. The presence of public moral censure against Caroline was alluded to in the pages of Svenska Nybyggaren. On July 24, 1873, it reported that "Andrew Johnson och hans frilla" (Andrew Johnson and his kept woman) had been committed to jail in Blue Earth County. In reporting on Caroline's leaving the sheriff's home in Madelia, the paper condemned her actions in moralizing tones (September 11, 1873): "The proverb 'the person who does ill can suffer ill' finds here a regrettable dramatization."[6] Significantly, Andrew was nowhere referred to in such loaded and denigrating personal terms. In fact, that was one of the gestures of respect accorded to him.

There the respect ended, however. Before Andrew's trial was even over, Svenska Nybyggaren jumped to the conclusion that Andrew deserved to be declared guilty and convicted of the charges against him. In comments published on May 12, 1874, but written before the trial began, the editor spoke of:

> [the details surrounding the] crime Andrew committed
> about a year ago. The murderer disappeared shortly
> thereafter in the company of the murdered man's wife,
> but both were apprehended in Omaha and brought back
> to Madelia, where punishment for the criminals is not
> likely to be neglected.[7]

There was no way to mistake whom the word "criminals" referred to. That mood of pre-judgement persisted and grew ever stronger among newspaper editors and private citizens alike long before Andrew's murder trial began. When the court finally began questioning witnesses, people were at last allowed to speak their minds for the record. None of the individuals who were called forward appeared reluctant to tell what they remembered about Lars and his disappearance or Andrew and Caroline's various actions during the previous three years.

Chapter XI
On Trial

The drama of the 1870s leading up to Andrew's trial was played out in an almost totally Swedish social setting located on American soil. The testimony of the trial was prolonged and detailed, giving a graphic description of the numerous events and some of the personal motivating factors involving the Swedish settlers. In some instances different witnesses described the same events and personalities in diametrically opposite ways. Those inconsistencies suggested that a lack of clarity existed in some witnesses' minds. If contradictions appeared, they were at times due to the fact that witnesses were speaking of events and personalities that went back anywhere from one to six years. Nevertheless, in their comments as a whole the subpoenaed witnesses portrayed in depth the thoughts, living conditions, and actions of the Nordic settlers around Kansas Lake. The case went beyond the purely ethnic aspects, however, and revealed universal motifs, such as divided affections, forbidden love, unbridled jealousy, and violent death.

Judge Franklin Waite was in the last of his five years on the district court bench (1870-1874). He was a long-time veteran of southern

Minnesota courtrooms, having traveled the district under the most primitive of conditions during the years before the coming of the railroads. First as a Mankato lawyer and then as an elected judge, he had dealt with a novel array of civil and criminal cases since he arrived in Mankato in 1860, from his native New York state. A lifelong Democrat, Waite fought for community rights against the greed of private parties and large companies and the encroachment of railroad interests on public lands. Those actions earned him the reputation among conservatives of having decided biases and marked opinions.[1] In the final result, however, Waite was known for his uncompromising honesty and strict impartiality in court. Those qualities stood him in good stead during Andrew's emotionally charged trial. The judge ran the proceedings with a firm hand.

Since Judge Waite assumed all those participating were acquainted with the basic details of the case, the proceedings offered nothing in the way of preliminary background information. After the jury was chosen, the trial moved ahead straightway with an account of the happenings at Kansas Lake in the early 1870s. As the clerk of court recorded them, questions and answers from the prosecution and the defense came in a staccato fashion and careful transitions from topic to topic were rare.[2] However, the attorneys were constantly probing witnesses for inconsistencies in their individual testimonies. All the witnesses (except for Charles Johnson, the two American physicians, J. W. Seager, H. S. Willson, and Frederick Messer, the Watonwan County deputy sheriff) testified in Swedish, while interpreter Wennerstrand translated for the court.[3] Wennerstrand worked patiently, but not without glitches, at explaining what the Americans and the Swedes were saying to each other.

To some degree the steady questioning partly masked the fact that the attorneys for both sides were working at definite themes, which they pursued with energy. They began by probing Caroline, the first person on the witness stand. She was the key to both the prosecution's and the defense counsel's arguments. Because of that, the accuracy and clarity of her testimony were of prime importance. In the months after she escaped from the sheriff's house, she had kept up regular contact with both her daughters, Annie and Isabel, as well as with Andrew. She had ample time to think and rethink what she would tell the court. Hers became a ticklish and nervous testimony.

The first theme the State broached was her relationship with Andrew and the talk of a divorce from Lars. In response, Caroline in fact said little about her devotion to Andrew but emphasized her dislike of Lars. In 1872 she heard about the divorce papers Charles and Andrew took out on her behalf. She said she welcomed news of them but never actually saw the papers and had no idea which attorney issued them. Caroline explained that the decisive incident in her decision to seek a divorce was the fight between Lars and Andrew that she had broken up in front of her farmhouse. Caroline denied that she had any romantic connection with Andrew before Lars's disappearance.[4]

Caroline's mentioning of divorce papers aroused interest in that topic. When Charles Johnson took the stand, attorneys also asked him what he knew of the issue. Charles replied that a divorce summons was issued. However, his statements about the fate of the summons created a degree of confusion, which here requires some explanation. A gifted youth of only twenty-two who spoke several languages, Charles, along with his father, had a history of giving legal advice. Charles's father especially was known as an amateur student of legal affairs. He was a man "who not only learned English quickly but studied American law so that, though he had no legal education or documents, he was able to give legal advice to the farmers in his neighborhood."[5] He was known familiarly on both sides of the Atlantic as "the lawyer" and was something of a self-appointed expert on local affairs in general.

Following Lars and Caroline's move to Kansas Lake, John's son Charles exhibited the same type of interest in their Swedish neighbors' problems. Charles's family place at Ör parish in Dalsland was barely forty miles from Caroline's home in Värmland, a fact that drew Caroline to Charles and his parents for advice and socializing at Kansas Lake. Since he came to America as a child, Charles was, in addition, the only adult in the Swedish circles at Kansas Lake who spoke Swedish and English in a fully bilingual manner. In 1874 Charles was active as an intermediary among those subpoenaed by the district court. At the boarding house in Madelia where the trial witnesses were staying, Charles informally surveyed the prospective witnesses, including Caroline, to ascertain what they were able to testify on Andrew's behalf. They answered him in some detail, even if this action had little, if any, effect on the eventual outcome of the trial.

Along with Charles, H. S. Willson was asked in court about his part in writing out the divorce writ that Andrew and Charles had mentioned. Willson said he issued a summons to begin an action of divorce, but he could not say whom he delivered it to. Willson concluded: "I don't think I put any authority on this summons for anyone to serve it. None is necessary in the District Court." When queried for the second time under oath, Charles was as much in the dark about the summons as Willson. All he recalled was that he did not know what became of the divorce papers. "I did not give them to Andrew," Charles stated. Andrew, in turn, knew little more about the matter. He thought the papers were given to the sheriff. "We left all the papers we had with the Sheriff," he said. Here Andrew showed his own confusion, for he misidentified the deputy sheriff Messer as the county sheriff. Deputy sheriff Frederick Messer then told the court he received the divorce summons, but since it was either Charles or Andrew who was authorized to serve it, according to Messer, the deputy gave it back to them.[6]

Making no progress with that theme, the court dropped it and moved on. In short, Charles Johnson's confident actions and statements about some aspects of the case were mixed with his uncertainty about the fate of the divorce summons. In connection with Andrew's trial, Charles's relative youth and inexperience surfaced at critical moments and created as much confusion as clarity, with the further result that his well-meaning efforts often failed to help resolve pertinent issues.

A second important theme that the attorneys focused on concerned the events of November 8, 1872. Caroline could only repeat to the court what she had earlier told others about that fateful morning. She claimed that Lars went off begging that day. He told her the name of the town he was going to, she repeated, but she could not remember it. When he left home that morning, she expected him to return. He departed before daybreak but never came back. She did not look out to see which way Lars went, and she did not see Andrew anywhere in the vicinity of their house that day. Nor had Caroline viewed Lars's body after it was found and buried or when it was exhumed. She maintained she was innocent of Lars's death and denied the prosecutor's insistent claims that she knew more than she was telling the court about Lars's disappearance. She described as untrue, for example, the allegation that in November of 1872 she informed Charles's father that something terrible had happened at her farm, which she needed to talk about.[7] Despite further probing, she stuck to her story.

What Caroline did, in fact, after 1872 was to conduct herself as though Lars was part of her past. She did so in some of the things she said in court as well as in her actions in private life. The most obvious sign of the latter tendency was that she began living openly with Andrew and his parents and had a child with him. Those were facts she made no efforts to conceal in court. Her wish by the early 1870s was to begin a new life for both herself and her children — and she wanted that life to be without Lars. Obviously, Andrew seemed the better partner. Those thoughts were implicit in her testimony and visible in the things she had done in 1872 and 1873.

The court, in its right, wanted more information about November 8. It asked Charles Johnson to expand on what he remembered. Charles said he noticed nothing unusual at first when Andrew came to his house with his empty flour sack that morning. While Charles made up a fire, Andrew came in, said good morning, and took a seat. He "was quiet in his actions" and talked a bit before asking to borrow flour. At the same time, Charles added: "I noticed an unusual appearance about him then. I noticed a trembling in his voice and he looked excited." Andrew said goodbye when he left.[8] Charles's father later testified simply: "His [Andrew's] face looked pale." However, John Johnson admitted that this thought had not occurred to him while Andrew was there to borrow flour but only at the time of the trial, two years later.[9] The power of suggestion was clearly at work in this bit of testimony.

Andrew was the next to explain his actions on that fateful morning. He stated in exact terms what he did on November 8:

> *I took a sack to carry the flour in. I did not stop on my
> way there (to Charles's house). I did not stop at Lars
> Johnson's house that morning. I don't remember of
> seeing any of his family that morning. At John Johnson's
> I saw Charles and his father and mother. They were all up.
> I went to borrow flour and got about a half of a two bushel
> sack full. After getting the flour I went home and I did not
> stop at any place before arriving home.[10]*

Andrew stated he knew nothing about Lars's whereabouts that morning. He said his neighbors, not Caroline, first informed him Lars was gone. In fact, he maintained, strangely enough, that he first learned of Lars's absence two weeks after Election Day, that is, a little more than a week following the November blizzard of 1872.

The only other person with any first-hand knowledge of what went on at Lars and Caroline's on November 8 was eleven-year-old Annie. She was one of the most vital witnesses called to testify. As a child, she was under enormous pressure, given the gravity of the moment and the tumult she had already gone through. In addition to appearing at the Madelia hearings in 1873 and a coroner's inquest that same year, she had also been taken, when she was only ten years old, to the site where Lars's body was found on May 25, 1873, and exposed to the gruesome process of identifying it as her father's. Then in 1874 she had been present and watched as his body was exhumed and the head examined separately. Now Annie took the witness stand in district court for yet another grueling session. Still, she retained her focus and supplied valuable, if not unquestioned, insights on Andrew and Caroline and November 8.

Of all who testified, Annie had the kindest words for her father. She stated: "Father was good to me[.] He whip[p]ed me sometimes but not very hard. I did not know father was crazy, they said he was crazy but he was not crazy. Father was mad because Andrew wanted to see Mother." When asked if Andrew and Caroline's interest in each other was something she told Lars about, Annie said she had no need to. "He knew it," she replied directly.[11]

Following the move to Andrew and his parents' home, Annie heard Andrew talking affectionately to Caroline. Furthermore, Annie stated that at different times Caroline instructed her what to tell authorities about her father, first at the hearings in 1873 but especially before the district court in 1874. However, attorney J. W. Seager, who represented Andrew in 1873, testified before the district court that, despite his careful note-taking, he had seen no signs of such coaching in justice court.[12]

By implication Seager questioned whether all of Annie's statements could be taken at face value. Here a gray area arose in determining the relative truth of Caroline's and Annie's testimonies. On one hand was the possibility that Caroline made up her account of Lars's movements on the morning of November 8 and insisted that Annie support her mother's version of what took place. Out of a basic moral sense and a love for her father, Annie may have defiantly gone against her mother and given an actual description of events, as she recalled them. On the other hand, the defense argued that Annie was too traumatized by her father's disappearance and the later sight of his dead body to remember details accurately. Therefore it insisted that her comments could not be given the same weight as those of the adult witnesses.

Annie's relationship with Caroline after Lars's death was troubled. At an impressionable age the daughter lost her father and also whatever sense of family cohesion they had known. Her anger over that loss was implicit in the girl's testimony. Since Andrew and Caroline's return from Omaha, Annie had not lived with her mother. She stated in district court: "I now live at Mr. Barge's. Mother was there 2 or 3 days ago. Mother told me then not to say that Andrew whip[p]ed father."[13]

Here an indication emerged about Annie's living arrangement. By late 1873 she was in the home of Daniel and Elisabeth Barge. A couple in their mid-fifties, the Barges lived in nearby South Branch township.[14] They were Mennonites and took Annie in, from Hogan and his parents, as an act of humanitarianism. Caroline visited Annie more than once at the Barge residence around the time of the trial. On those occasions she had the chance to try to influence her daughter's thinking, but the court got no truly objective feedback on the efforts she actually made in that direction. Annie's repeated statements that her mother coached her could neither be credited nor discounted.

There was no doubt that accompanying Hogan to view Lars's body in 1873 and also viewing the exhumation later on left an indelible imprint on Annie's mind. Those sights coupled with her father's sudden disappearance haunted the girl long afterward. In court she described a vision she had:

> After father went away I saw something come to our
> house and stand up like a person that had no head on.
> This was a long time after father went away. Plomstead
> [a neighbor's child] saw the same thing in the daytime. I
> heard noise about the house this night.[15]

Annie's report of ghostly sights bears a stamp of authentic believed experience. Tales of ghost sightings, including those of headless bodies visiting death scenes in the late autumntime, were widely known in the folklore of Sweden. Clearly Annie and the Plomstead child were influenced, through the power of suggestion, by such tales as told by older Swedish residents around Kansas Lake.[16] The children were frightened by the stories and by the memory of viewing Lars's dead body and then seeing its detached head being removed from the grave.

Particularly important was Annie's impression of the night and morning of her father's disappearance, as she retold it in 1874. She had no memory, for example, that he had any breakfast, as Caroline claimed. In fact, Annie testified that Caroline and Andrew instructed her what to say in that respect: "They [Caroline and Andrew] were both talking and wanted me to say he ate bre[a]d and butter and went to beg and that he had a cap and pants and vest on."[17] She also stated: "I said at Madelia [in April, 1873] I was awake when father went away, but I was not awake. When at Kansas Lake on examination before the coroner [in the fall of 1873] I said the same thing and Mother and Andrew told me to say so."[18]

Annie had spent time observing Andrew and Caroline after the snowstorms of 1872 and 1873. She often listened to them talking. She said, for example, that she once overheard Andrew telling Caroline he intended to leave soon for Sioux City.[19] Though appearing to be a set of impromptu comments, other parts of Annie's description were a series of responses to the prosecutor's questions, which were not recorded along with her testimony. Annie's account had direct bearing on (and at some points contradicted) Caroline's earlier testimony. Annie told the court:

> I was at Madelia before the Grand Jury last winter. I don't think I told what I knew there — I told them[,] the grand jury[,] then anything they wanted me to tell — I heard Andrew tell mother once after father went away that he would like to have her — When father and mother were scolding [about Andrew] the night father went away, I guess mother got up and went out doors. I heard a noise as if some one was walking on the ground and it woke me up, when I woke up mother was in the house. I don't know whether father was in the house or not. I then went to sleep again — I wanted to get up to see what the noise was and mother was in the room and told me to lay down there was nothing wrong — father was gone then. I heard a groaning noise out doors and was going to get up and go out

and see what it was and mother told me to lay down.[20]

Later Annie said she woke up again while it was still dark and found that Lars was at home but not Caroline. Lars told Annie her mother had left the house.[21] Annie's comment that Lars was chiding Caroline about Andrew as the family went to bed the night of November 7 was an indication of an unpleasant atmosphere in the house. It was also a clear contradiction of Annie's own words in April, 1873, and Caroline's testimony in district court in 1874 that she and Lars had not argued the night before Lars left.

Annie's only fully inexplicable statement came when she told the court: "When we went to St. James on the examination mother told me not to say that father said he was going St. James to take up Andrew."[22] It was uncertain what she meant by the words "take up." Possibly the idea was that Lars intended to go to town to charge Andrew with assault for the beating he inflicted on Lars in October, 1872. If so, it was clear why Caroline would not wish her daughter to make that information public, since it would have cast Andrew in an even more suspicious light in the eyes of the authorities. In sum, Annie's words must have riveted the listeners, who could speculate on what she meant with the above statement and also imagine the dying Lars's last moments as well as the mysterious footsteps outside Annie's window.

The attorneys kept coming back to the theme of Andrew and Caroline's relationship. How long had they known each other? And when did Caroline first move to Andrew's? Caroline admitted to knowing Andrew since 1871, that is, since she and Lars arrived at Kansas Lake. Andrew said they first met in 1868. Several people were polled about the second question. Charles Johnson stated that Caroline moved to Andrew's farm in late November or early December, 1872. Hogan believed it was in the middle of November sometime. Hogan was with his parents at Christmas in 1872 and saw Caroline there then. Andrew, once again, gave his reply:

> *Lars Johnson's wife and children came up to our house*
> *to live. They came a short time before Christmas. Mother*
> *asked her to come there. I did not ask them to come there.*
> *They staid at our house most all winter. They were there*
> *about 3 months.*[23]

Caroline herself stated, oddly, that she went to Andrew's three months after Lars left; that is, she moved in February of 1873. She was quoted twice as saying she moved to Andrew's three months after Lars disappeared.[24] However, in all fairness, it is possible to imagine she actually said "three weeks." Although the Swedish words *månader* (months) and *veckor* (weeks) are not similar, Caroline's comments went from her Swedish through the Swedish-American interpreter's English to the English of the English-language court reporter, thus leaving room for misinterpretations. If Caroline's words were recorded correctly, they presented one of the most noticeable inconsistencies in her testimony, ones that were difficult to explain away.

Not long after she moved to Andrew's farm, Caroline became pregnant. She stated in court in May, 1874, that she then had another child, who was "about 6-months old" and fathered by Andrew. Caroline's reckoning indicates that the child was conceived around January or February of 1873, approximately three months after Lars "went away." Whereas the court identified the child as her daughter Christine, Caroline, in an unusual twist, described this six-month-old child as a boy. She stated at another point: "My boy is about six months old. The Defendant [Andrew] is his father."[25]

Caroline's statement was surely recorded incorrectly in court. Beyond all doubt the child born to Caroline in 1873 was a girl. She must have referred to the child in Swedish as "mitt barn" (my child). An unconsciousness process of alliterative association with the "m" and the "b" in those words may have prompted interpreter Wennerstrand to translate them incorrectly as "my boy." If such was not the case, Caroline made a slip of the tongue and inadvertently identified her son John Albert as Andrew's child when in truth she was being queried about the daughter Christine.

Only one fact was clear in the question of paternity. Andrew and Caroline were inextricably linked through the nativity of their daughter. If Andrew was also John Albert's biological father, he and Caroline must have carried on a long-distance romance somewhere between St. James and Waseca over a considerable period, perhaps while Lars was off on various of his begging trips. The main relevance that the question of John Albert's birth father had to Andrew's trial lay in the prosecutor's need to establish further reasons why Andrew and Caroline wanted to get Lars out of the way, that is, to live together with their two children, John Albert and Christine. The State's efforts to establish that motive proved inconclusive.

Soon two days of questioning had passed and the State had still other themes to pursue. It wanted to learn exactly how Lars died. When the prosecution asked if Andrew's path to Charles's house would have taken him past Lars's farm on November 8, Charles Johnson replied: "In going from his [Andrew's] house to ours if he took a straight line [he] would not go very near Lars Johnson's house — yet there was a path way running near Lars Johnson's house."[26] Andrew admitted he always went from his place to Charles's along the pathway past Lars and Caroline's farm.[27] (Figure 10) Clearly some people imagined Andrew passing by the supposed place of death at a critical moment on the alleged fatal morning. Such thinking involved large assumptions, however, since the court failed to specify either the place or the time of Lars's death. Nor had anybody explained why Lars's body was found in stocking feet but with no shoes on and wearing no coat, if he had been leaving on a long trip in early November when cold weather was setting in. The prosecutor suggested that Lars actually had a coat with him as he left home, but that he flung it aside as he fled in fear from his attacker. The defense quickly rebutted that suggestion by illustrating that Lars owned three winter coats, none of which anybody had ever seen or found in the fields after November 8.

Still, evidence was swiftly mounting against Andrew in the minds of the court — and perhaps against Caroline as well, though she was not on trial, at least not formally. Caroline guarded herself cleverly on one level. She stolidly maintained her innocence and gathered support to the effect that she was the victim of Lars, not the victimizer. At the same time there was little in her testimony to exonerate Andrew. In fact, neither she nor Charles, the defendant's best friends, said anything of substance to support Andrew's plea of not guilty.

The sensational nature of the case increased when the examining physicians were called to testify. Authorities exhumed Lars's body to allow the coroner and Drs. Overholt and Neill to study its injuries once again and explain the cause of death. The detached head was examined in minute detail. Several of the approximately twenty persons (including Hogan and Charles) who helped bury the body attended. Also present, as mentioned above, was Annie, whose attendance was one of the more grotesque aspects of the whole proceeding. It was highly unusual that the eleven-year-old girl was taken to view the exhumation but not her mother Caroline.

The medical examiners testified to the district court that the main wound, if delivered by a human hand wielding a sharp instrument, would have caused instant death.

Andrew's defense argued that Lars either jumped or fell into the lake and drowned and the head wounds were incurred after his death. The two doctors were queried about this possibility. The effect of ice, which could be as much as six inches thick, dashing the dead man's body against the large rocks lining parts of Kansas Lake could have produced such injuries, the medical men stated. However, they were divided in their comments. Dr. Overholt said simply: "There is nothing unreasonable in supposing that these wounds might have been made by floating ice." Dr. Neill agreed only in part. He stated: "I don't think all the wounds could have been made with ice, but they might be so made." To another question he replied: "I don't think the wound to the temporal bone could have been made with ice."[28]

The physicians' statements did not help Andrew's defense. As Charles's father testified, Andrew had been heard to "say at one time that Lars ought to be killed. This was in the summer of 1872."[29] The prosecution created a scenario: Andrew and Lars met on the pathway between Lars's and Charles's farms as Lars went off to beg and Andrew to borrow flour. Andrew overpowered his smaller adversary, beat him to death, and disposed of the body. The absence of an eyewitness or even the lack of proof of when and where Lars died would seem sufficient to give the jury pause. However, the missing details seem not to have damaged the State's case. Neither was there any indication that the defense questioned this matter. Assumptions of Andrew's guilt did not take into account the fact that Caroline was also up at the supposed time of Lars's disappearance or that Annie later testified to hearing groaning and strange footsteps just outside her house, not on the pathway between the farms.

Andrew's main support came from his parents, who swore he was at home every night during the week Lars disappeared. Yet part of John and Christine's time on the witness stand was spent denying allegations that in 1873 they told the justice court that Andrew was away on two different nights in early November of 1872, once to borrow tobacco from his brother to treat a toothache. In addition, Andrew's father, who was now over sixty, admitted to having extremely poor eye sight. He stated in court: "I can see [only] a little."[30] He could positively identify Andrew only by the sound of his voice.

Charles's father tried to support the defense's argument of suicide. John Johnson told the court: "I have on various occasions heard Lars threaten to kill himself — I don't recol[l]lect the first time but it was prob[ab]ly in Oct. 1872."[31] Dr. Hiram Neill concluded his testimony by reiterating his description of Lars as a n'er-do-well. Though clearly damning of Lars, much of this testimony had the cumulative effect of showing the reasons various persons would have had for harming Lars. Not the least among them was Andrew himself.

By the time Andrew took the stand, the court had been in session for four days. Under oath Andrew acquitted himself well, knowing that the future and his freedom were at stake. His own testimony had a truthful ring, which caused some in the audience to rethink their prejudice against him. He made few of the seemingly contradictory statements that characterized Caroline's comments.

The questioning went quickly to the matter of the fight Andrew had with Lars and what caused it. Was it ill will or alcohol? Andrew replied that he sometimes bought liquor and took it home, but not often. However, he admitted to drinking beer and whiskey in a St. James tavern with Hogan and Charles the day he beat Lars in October of 1872. He had two or three glasses of beer and two glasses of whiskey. Andrew explained that in anger he struck Lars about the head that evening with a walking stick he often carried.[32] Yet Andrew claimed he would have passed on by and not talked with or harmed Lars had Lars not thrown the ax at him. Despite that comment, Charles testified that Andrew told him, as the two rode to St. James together the next week, that he would have beaten Lars to "eternity" if Caroline had not interrupted them and sent Andrew on home.[33]

Andrew said he did not worry much about the risk of Lars shooting him. In fact, he had never actually seen Lars fire off the gun he carried. Still, there was enough fear in the air for Andrew to stay away from Lars's farm. Though Andrew was in the vicinity of Lars and Caroline's house on the morning of November 8, he insisted repeatedly that he knew nothing of Lars's departure from his and Caroline's house. Specifically, he argued that he knew nothing of any events on Lars and Caroline's farm that day. Andrew stated emphatically:

> *I did not have anything to do with the disappearance of*

> *Lars Johnson — I had nothing to do with the killing of*
> *Lars Johnson either directly or indirectly — I never*
> *inflicted any injury on him or used any violence except*
> *at the time I whip[p]ed him as I have before testified —*
> *I don't know what became of him. I never saw him dead —*
> *I never had anything to do with concealing his body.*[34]

M. J. Severance continued to argue that Lars died either by accidentally falling into the lake or by taking his own life by drowning.

By the time Andrew finished testifying, both sides had plumbed their major themes. The testimony came to an end on Friday, May 9. Both the prosecution and the defense gave their final remarks that afternoon. Surely the concluding session and the words of the State instilled a sense of foreboding in Andrew's family and friends. In the late afternoon Judge Waite handed the case over to the jury. The general public listened intently and then filed out and spread the news around town.

Chapter XII
The Verdict

The details of Andrew and Caroline's living conditions or their feelings for each other elicited little sympathy from the jury. The general public may have hung on every word of the testimony and would doubtless have listened even more intently if they had known all the facts of Lars's and Andrew's lives. The authorities, on the other hand, took a practical, no-nonsense approach and zeroed in on what they saw as the core of the problem. The testimony made it clear that Lars, already suspicious of Andrew, became especially incensed when Andrew and Caroline were seen together in St. James in the fall of 1872. Soon thereafter occurred the fight between the two men at Lars's house. As Lars told Dr. Neill, he obtained the gun because he was afraid of Andrew. [1] Lars's troubled mind and the competition with Andrew for Caroline's favor gave rise to the turmoil on the two farms.

As a result, the jury faced three choices. One was M. J. Severance's argument that Lars died by drowning. Another was that Andrew and Caroline killed Lars together. According to that view, Andrew passed by Lars and Caroline's house on the morning of November 8 and chanced upon them in the midst of an argument (a continuation of the "scolding" Annie referred to), whereupon the two clubbed Lars and sank his body in the water. The third possibility was that Andrew encountered Lars alone, murdered him, and put the body in Kansas Lake by himself.

Though the official charge stated that Andrew acted with malice aforethought, no evidence emerged to prove a careful, premeditated, or orchestrated killing. The idea that an unknown fourth party might have been out on that early morning and killed Lars was not considered, although the footsteps reported by Annie theoretically could have been those of such an individual coming to their house, leaving it, or passing close by. Certainly Lars had enemies other than just Andrew.

Some reasonable doubts about Andrew's guilt must have existed, not least of all because of the discrepancies in the testimony by Caroline and Annie. Still, the jury opted for the third choice. The jury foreman announced a guilty verdict at an early morning session on May 12, which was incidentally Andrew's father's sixtieth birthday. In the words of the <u>St. James Herald</u> (May 23, 1874), the jury found sufficient grounds to believe that a "willful and deliberate murder" had taken place. The verdict held up despite defense counsel Severance's request that the jurors be polled separately, "which was accordingly done and to which the Jurors all answered yes [that is, guilty]."[2] A brief glimpse of the drama of that moment shone through in the words of the clerk of court:

> *The court ordered Andrew Johnson to stand up and asked him*
> *if he had anything to say why the court should not pronounce*
> *sentence against him. And the prisoner said he was not guilty.*
> *The court then proceeded to sentence the said Andrew Johnson*
> *as follows: That you Andrew Johnson are sentenced to the state*
> *prison at Stillwater in the State of Minnesota to hard labor during*
> *your natural life[.]*[3]

Therein lay Judge Waite's pronouncement on Andrew's fate. M. J. Severance asked for a new trial. Severance based his argument on the assertion that the jury foreman had signed his name to the court papers on the wrong page. The Minnesota Supreme Court later refused the request.[4]

Immediately following the announcement of the verdict, George P.

Johnston filed a charge against the county attorney and several other citizen friends of the prosecution, but the nature of the charge was not revealed and the court dismissed it.[5] That was the first of several actions on Johnston's part pertaining to Andrew's case.

Judge Waite had valid reasons to argue that he conducted Andrew's trial in a fair and honest manner. Primitive living conditions and uncertain agricultural techniques at the time marked the Watonwan prairie as a frontier area, but the social infrastructure spoke of a settled, civil society. The law enforcement bodies and the legal and judicial system met with the demands of state government. The lawyers on both sides of the case were competent members of the bar and the judge a respected and qualified official. Even if the trial was held in a ramshackle courthouse, the proceedings followed the letter of the law. Bearing the burden of proof, the prosecution followed approved protocol and presented circumstantial evidence that led to Andrew's conviction.

Throughout the proceedings, the State endeavored to establish a motive for Andrew to murder Lars. Reasons were near at hand, that is, the general disagreements between the two men, Andrew's anger over Lars's abuse of Caroline, and the conflicting love interest. The existence of a motive on Andrew's part was reinforced by the sworn testimony that Andrew had been heard to say that Lars and Caroline should be separated and that he might do so himself. He also reportedly said that Lars ought to be killed. Those bits of testimony were judged as admissible in court. They must have carried considerable weight with the jurors, even if other allegations — such as suggestions that Andrew and Caroline were making love in the harvest fields and that Caroline asked Andrew to kill Lars — were called into question or might be viewed as hearsay.

The testimony by the medical men strongly suggested a violent death. In that respect, certain aspects of Andrew's personality seem to have spoken against him. That Andrew had the propensity to carry out such a violent act could be seen as clear and demonstrable. Andrew was physically stronger than Lars and had not only threatened him with bodily harm but, by his own admission, had once injured him. In addition, he was alleged in court to have beaten his own father once with a stick when John Johnson failed to comply with his son's wishes.[6]

Andrew and his father denied that allegation, but Andrew's various actions presented a series of personality traits that combined nurturing and caretaking with volatile tendencies.[7] Indeed volatility was a trait often attributed to natives of Halland by its own local authors, who saw natives of the province as humble in the realm of material attainments but highly accomplished in verbal skills. Those writers described Hallanders as quick-witted, fast-talking, and eager to leap into the fray when verbal battles commenced. They were noted for their rapid retorts and striking witticisms. Cunning and clever were the words one Halland writer, a native of Breared, associated with the populace of his home district.[8]

In short, Andrew very possibly fit the description of a certain impetuous Halland personality type. The district court jury members in Watonwan County may well have intuited that possibility, even though they knew nothing, naturally, of the stories in Sweden about Hallanders' personality traits, real or imagined. The jury likely reckoned that Andrew imposed himself on Lars and Caroline's marriage, much as Annie's testimony had indicated, but his impulsivity kept him from fully thinking through the probable long-term consequences of his actions. To the jury's way of thinking, those consequences opened the door to a possible act of violence.

With a motive for the alleged crime and a propensity to commit it established, the prosecution next approached the question of whether the defendant Andrew had the opportunity to carry out a killing. The ready answer was that both Lars and Andrew were out on the pathways in the dark on the morning of November 8, where they were assumed to have met and an argument ensued, which led to Lars's death.

With such details the prosecution built a strong case. Andrew and Lars had a past history that suggested murder as a logical outcome. There were voices against Andrew, a motive on his part, Lars's body as evidence, and a set of circumstances that was assumed to offer Andrew the opportunity to kill his adversary. Judge Waite abided by the jury's decision and pronounced sentence in accordance with it.

Looking back on Andrew's trial more than a century later, one is tempted to consider it in a different context. From a present-day perspective, certain aspects of the case raise questions. The strongest impression left by the written documents that survive from that time (here meaning the wording in both the legal papers and the popular press) is that the prosecution was highly motivated to obtain a conviction in the case and in the most expedient manner possible. It can only be assumed that public pressure influenced the county attorney's conduct of the case. Lost in the prosecution's haste was a deep-seated interest in searching for the truth. It was obvious that concerns for the societal and moral issues that might result from a thorough examination of Lars's death were missing.

In the defendant, Andrew, the jury had before it an illiterate immigrant awash in a foreign culture and with limited or no ability to understand the legal language of American judicial proceedings. The difficulty was not just a straightforward linguistic one. Knowing right from wrong if a murder had been committed was a universal given, and with the help of the interpreter, it was possible, of course, for the Swedes and Norwegians to grasp the utterances of the court. A deeper problem existed. Andrew, his family, and the Long Lake township immigrants, like newcomers in any world setting, suffered from split loyalties and a divided heart syndrome. On one hand, they had committed themselves to a new life in America, and they devoted their energies to that experience and the future of their adopted country.

In that respect, scholars have described a three-step process of ethnic assimilation into mainstream American culture. The first step entails participating in the activities of society at large. That includes entering the job market, speaking English, moving away from the ethnic neighborhood, and voting in elections. The second step involves economic advancement toward middle-class standing. The final stage allows for ease of movement for individuals within the wide array of identities and attachments that are features of a diverse society.[9] In the early 1870s the Scandinavians in Long Lake township had only begun working their way into the initial stage of assimilation. They had entered the agricultural economy and started voting in general elections. Otherwise they were novices in American culture.

On the other hand, the Watonwan County Scandinavians' emotional and civic life was rooted in the soil of Sweden and Norway. The culture of those lands, though oppressive in many ways, was their birthright. In America the first-generation immigrants understood the law of the new land, but in their heart of hearts it was not their land. In contrast to the remembered cushioning effects of settled, centuries-old communities in Scandinavia with shared concerns and sympathies, they found little balm for their specific ethnic troubles and concerns in the broad cultural spectrum of America. As a result, they were caught up in a quandary, that is, how to deal with the legal and social realities and the language of a country in which they were not yet at home but in which they desired to be loyal participants.

Such feelings complicated the stress they experienced during Andrew's trial and its aftermath. While observing and participating in the courtroom proceedings, the immigrants must have struggled to understand the forces that had placed them at such a crossroads in their community life. They now had a foot both inside and outside two different cultural systems at once, the Scandinavian and the American.

The Minnesota judiciary appears to have had little sympathy for, or even understanding of, this immigrant plight. Neither did the authorities at Andrew's trial show any interest in looking behind the scenes at Lars's, Caroline's, and Andrew's behavior. One can hardly help suspecting that a rush to judgement took place, expedited by public sentiment and facilitated by ethnic stereotyping. In that context, commonly held perceptions of ethnic groups or societal subgroups could easily be marked by pre-judging, or what one writer described as impressionistic views.[10] Identifying individuals as belonging to a particular non-mainstream group made it easy to label them as "other." The most flagrant example of that tendency appeared in The St. James Journal's repeated denunciations of the societal subgroup of tramps. The paper viewed those itinerant men who passed through Watonwan County as a collective danger to the community. In all certainty the men represented a wide diversity when it came to personal motivating factors and societal encounters, but the newspaper criticized them in a blanket fashion without making any attempt to inquire into their individual backgrounds or the varying causes behind their way of living.

Scandinavians could also be lumped into a generic grouping, identified according to ethnic markers. Scandinavians were said in the local press to be excessive drinkers and to have difficulty learning English. They also spoke an incomprehensible Nordic tongue and were said all to look alike. Those stereotypes were reinforced by the fact that the incoming Scandinavians, like people in ethnic in-migrations in any world setting, began arriving on the prairie in large numbers and formed their own particular settlements, which could cause the majority culture to view them as being outside the pale of conventional manners.

In Watonwan County those who spoke English and were born in America made up a numerical minority, but they conformed to a broader national power group in terms of social, cultural, linguistic, and economic influence. They could label newcomers by the extent to which they differed from American conventions. Naturally, a number of Americans were accepting and understanding of immigrant habits. In other people's minds the criteria of appearance, speech, dress, customs, and living space could contribute to the formation of an ethnic stereotype. Since the Scandinavians did not, in most cases, master English, they were vulnerable to suspicion because they could not be understood, or were understood imperfectly. Since the immigrants' responses to cultural situations were not identical to those of native-born citizens, the word of American law enforcement agents in court cases could be viewed as more credible than the testimony of the foreign-born. In addition, when Scandinavian Americans voted for Norwegian-American or Swedish-American political candidates, they could be charged with voting only along ethnic lines. Surely the stereotypes often contained some grains of truth, but those truths were offset by the broad and injurious inaccuracies present in them. The negative valance outweighed the positive.[11]

Testing the above claim on the trial of Andrew Johnson would seem to indicate that, before the district court jury in 1874, he faced a stacked deck, in cultural terms. Since Scandinavian-speaking prospective jurors for various reasons were all rejected for jury duty, the seated jurors were all native-born Americans and might have found it easier to understand and believe the English-language prosecutor than the ethnic defendant. In this respect, an important question arises concerning whether the jurors were all culturally competent to decide on the case. First were they wise enough not to pre-judge Andrew because of his romantic involvement with Caroline, which came after Lars's disappearance? And were they sophisticated enough to understand the differences in mores between Swedes and Yankees? Second, were they prone to judge Andrew as guilty because he fled to Omaha? The answers were likely no and yes. In the first case, Andrew's romantic liaison with Caroline and the birth of their child were signs of a deeply felt emotion, but they were not sufficient to prove he killed Lars. In reference to the second point, the jury seems not to have been concerned about two basic concepts: that is, that avoiding the law does not show guilt or that flight is not the same as evasion.

On the stand in 1874, various witnesses were led by the State to demonstrate a tendency known as retroactive construction of events.[12] Charles and his father both recalled, for example, that Andrew looked nervous on the morning of November 8, though they were being asked to think back nearly twenty-four months into the past. Likewise, the prosecution repeatedly asked witnesses to recall scenes that would seem to indicate Andrew and Caroline were romantically involved or that Caroline was urging Andrew to murder Lars. The attempts were to construct a probable cause and scenario for Andrew to commit murder, but they were all built on memory and insinuation. In present-day law probable cause cannot be taken as evidence of a crime. Nor does it equate with proof beyond a reasonable doubt.[13] In the end result, the State produced no tangible evidence that Andrew killed Lars. Andrew was poor, foreign-born, loved the dead man's wife, and was in the wrong place at an unfortunate time on the morning of November 8. The last two aspects made him a viable suspect, but they did not prove he killed Lars.

The transcript of the trial against Andrew gave no direct cause to believe that anyone in court — either witnesses, attorneys, judge, or jury — truly knew what happened to Lars, or that any witnesses were trying to hide anything of major importance, with the possible exception of Caroline. The documents now at hand suggest that convicting Andrew of murdering Lars on the testimony present in court was tantamount to clutching at straws, or tailoring and re-tailoring the testimony to fit a pre-conception that one poor immigrant murdered another, just as minority individuals have always been "known" to kill others in the same social class. That tailoring process was aided by sentiments planted in the public's minds by stereotyping comments on minorities in the popular press of the day.

The popular response to one crime case near Watonwan County exemplified that stereotyping tendency. It was the case of Nels Hast, a Swedish immigrant carpenter from Faribault County. Hast was charged with murder in 1870. He was convicted in 1871 and sentenced to life at Stillwater. His trial and conviction took place in the same district court as Andrew's. Hast's encounter with the law resulted from disagreements in the village of Wells, Minnesota, between Norwegian and Swedish immigrants concerning pride in their respective nations and arguments over the celebration of November 6, Sweden's former unofficial national holiday. Hast was convicted of stabbing a Norwegian immigrant to death when he mistook him for a native-born American. Hast's complicated motives reinforced the belief among many persons, as the idea was expressed in the local press, that non-mainstream individuals were likely to attack and injure their fellows, when they were not posing a serious threat to settled, respectable members of the dominant English-speaking culture.

According to The Wells Atlas, a group of "gentlemen" or "citizens" of the town of Wells, that is, resident English-speakers, was enjoying a sedate dinner of oysters at a local hotel dining room on the evening of November 6, 1870, when they became aware of an ethnic riot among Norwegian and Swedish workers down the street. They learned that the fight had then spilled over from a local tavern into the town square. The citizens interrupted their meal to quell the tumult. After stopping the street fighting, they made a raid on the boardinghouse of the immigrant "ruffians." The local citizens restored order and learned that a Norwegian had been killed in the fighting. They soon arrested Hast, who earlier had told his Swedish friends that he had actually intended to kill one of the town's Yankees, not another immigrant, since he considered the native-born residents a greater threat to his safety than the Norwegian immigrants.

The Wells Atlas facilely dismissed the killing of the Norwegian as "unprovoked, not committed for any purpose," when in truth there was historical and documented friction between Norwegians and Swedes on both sides of the Atlantic in that period, which could result in aggressive actions. At the same time, there were even more sensitive issues of culture, language, and economic standing between all immigrant groups as a whole, on one hand, and the settled English-language population of Minnesota, on the other. Hard feelings about those differences could easily rise to the surface at inconvenient times. In Hast's case, he openly admitted to the killing, but the clear anti-immigrant approach to his case among the general populace did little to lessen ethnic tensions. Classifying people either as citizens and gentlemen or as immigrants and ruffians, as the Wells editor did, was the easy path to describing the friction that existed, but it was hardly a useful means of reaching a deeper understanding of the social differences that caused disturbances such as that in Wells.[14]

The St. James Journal gave voice to that same type of bias when it wrote, as noted above, that when tramps were not victimizing settled society they turned on and beat one another. Svenska Nybyggaren uttered similar pre-conceptions by passing judgement on Andrew as Lars's murderer even before he was indicted or his trial began.[15]

The basic tenet of the American judicial system is equality under the law.[16] Being a member of an ethnic minority, like Andrew, in an English-language courtroom in rural Minnesota in the 1870s was, it may be assumed, a potentially precarious situation. While circumstantial evidence was presented at Andrew's trial, forensic evidence indicating a time and place of death, a murder weapon, and eyewitnesses to the death were all missing. If Andrew was the guilty party, the prosecution seems to a modern sensibility to have failed to prove it. Andrew was viewable as an expendable entity, easily dispatched, and the jury acted swiftly on the prosecution's case.

Examining the practices of the past by the standards of our own day is, of course, to be done with care. We run the risk of overlooking the validity of the State of Minnesota's case against Andrew, as the judicial system judged it in the nineteenth century. Even in our own day, he would doubtless have been the prime suspect. If nothing else is gained by looking back on his trial through different lenses, we see illustrated how the burden of proof has changed during the past century-and-a-quarter. It is noteworthy that the guilty verdict satisfied most people of Andrew's time, but not all. The St. James Herald (May 16, 1874) reported that Andrew's conviction came as a disappointment to some observers: "It is said by his conduct during the trial, [that] Andrew succeed[ed] in gaining the sympathies of many who were in attendance at court, and that he still protests his innocence of committing the murder."

That attitude buoyed Andrew and his family's spirits temporarily. Still, he and the concerned immigrants in Long Lake township had had ample time to prepare for the worst, and the verdict can hardly have come as a surprise, given Andrew's many months of jail time since 1873 and the strong feelings the case elicited among the general public.

Surely Andrew was depressed and fearful of the future. Being scared of prison would be a natural reaction. In the end, however, there was nothing to be done. His family had no choice but to say their goodbyes and retreat to Kansas Lake. Even if they resolved to visit him as often as possible and send letters to the prison, weeks or months must have passed before they heard from or saw him again. When they next had contact with Andrew, he was only one among hundreds of convicts at the Minnesota state penitentiary. In the eyes of the law, he had entered prison as a duly convicted felon and was there to stay.

Chapter XII: The Verdict

Chapter XIII
The Response

On May 14, 1874, Andrew was taken away to prison. The new Watonwan County sheriff James Glispin delivered him to the Stillwater state penitentiary that same day, and his name was entered in the Convict Register. The prison's admissions book noted merely how tall he was. It added that he had a scar on his left hip, was ruptured, and did not smoke. It added inaccurately that he could "read English but not write it." For two years thereafter he served his time.

Just as Andrew left Sweden in 1866 without viewing his third son by Johanna Persdotter, so he went to prison at Stillwater in 1874 without seeing his daughter by Caroline again. Christine was seven months old when he left for the penitentiary. In their turn, Andrew's parents lived on at Kansas Lake after 1874 with the site of Lars and Caroline's nearby farm as a constant source of mixed memories. In all, the family took the experience as a devastating blow, which functioned as a source of unabated daily sorrow. As far as the records show, the elder Johnsons bore that sorrow in silence.

During the first period following the trial, Andrew's cause did not seem completely lost. In Mankato defense counsel M. J. Severance continued to pursue the case energetically. Severance (1826-1907) was a born leader. He eventually became one of Minnesota's leading criminal defense lawyers and later a district court judge in Mankato from 1881 to 1900. In the mid-1870s, Severance kept working in the firm belief that his client was innocent of killing Lars. He filed a further appeal with the Minnesota Supreme Court in June of 1875, but the court turned it down.

Then in April of 1876, Severance applied for a pardon for Andrew. Severance sent the pardon application to Governor John S. Pillsbury (in office 1876-1882).

Pillsbury was known for his firm stance against crime and his encouragement of stiff sentences for offenders, as well as for an extreme, individualist approach to societal questions. In light of those attitudes, Severance's application for a pardon seemed unremarkable to the authorities in Pillsbury's administration, and it was obviously unconvincing to the Governor himself, who delayed acting on it.

Given those delays, Andrew and Caroline's prospects were, naturally, bleak indeed in the mid-1870s. Andrew's only hope was for an act of executive clemency. Caroline had little choice but to remain in Watonwan County. She lived at Kansas Lake with Andrew's parents, Hogan, and her two youngest children. Her actual comings and goings during that time were limited and her feelings under wraps. From time to time she could visit the daughters Annie and Isabel in neighboring South Branch township, where they lived as servants and wards in two different families. Otherwise she stayed close to her in-laws' farm.

During that time M. J. Severance's formal proposal for Andrew's pardon still lingered on for week after endless week at the Capitol. Eventually the Governor considered it, but he quickly refused the pardon. In the end, Pillsbury's assistants lost Severance's letter. Only the transcript of Andrew's trial, submitted as a part of the pardon application, remained. With a note of finality, one of the assistants at the state capitol building scrawled a note across the front of it: "Application for Pardon of Andrew Johnson, convicted of Murder. Filed April 1876. Refused. File away."[1]

There the matter rested until Caroline dropped the biggest bombshell of all. In an affidavit of June 30, 1876, handwritten and notarized by M. J. Severance and sent to the Governor's office in St. Paul,

Caroline confessed to killing Lars herself. The affidavit was a follow-up step by Andrew's counsel to counter Governor Pillsbury's pardon denial.

Caroline told attorney Severance that Andrew took no part in the killing of Lars. He had no knowledge of what happened to Lars until she told him in June of 1876, a few days before she submitted the affidavit. Here appeared the only concrete reference to her seeing Andrew at the prison. Yet even there Caroline was imprecise in revealing what she told Andrew. Her confession said only that she informed Andrew "of some of the facts connected therewith." Though the wording was Severance's, the thoughts were her own.

Caroline briefly explained her new version of the events of November 8, 1872. After announcing the day before (November 7) that he intended to go off begging, Lars readied himself that day to leave early on the morning of the eighth. During the night, however, he and Caroline argued. Lars then turned violent. In fright, Caroline left the house and started off on foot to Charles Johnson's for help. The killing happened, she stated, in the following way:

> *That is to say, in the night time — my husband said Lars Johnson and myself were quarreling in bed, when he became violent and threatened me so that I got up and went outside toward the house of Charles Johnson a neighbor — Lars Johnson followed me in his stocking feet and had a club in his hands and struck me in the back — I turned around [and] got the club away from him and struck him on the head and knocked him down. I then went into the house[;] — soon after I went out — found that he was dead and I carried him half a mile and put him in the Lake where his body was found in the following spring, and further saith the deponent not, except that she is willing to be examined before any public authority touching the matter referred to in this affidavit.*[2]

The paper was signed "Caroline Johanson." The handwriting was shaky, showing an uncertain hand.[3]

The pent-up fury Caroline felt toward Lars was palpable in her words. Angered by Lars's striking her, she turned to face him, as she told the story. Those who were willing to believe her could see the scenario unfold in the way she then described it: At the critical moment Caroline gained the upper hand and struck back at him. Her first blow easily led to the second and third. The readers of the affidavit could remember that Annie reported waking up at one point that morning and noticing her mother was gone but Lars was still at home. Perhaps Lars left soon after Annie went back to sleep, and the fatal confrontation between Caroline and Lars ensued on the path to Charles Johnson's. In his anger, Lars surely intended to do Caroline grievous bodily harm.

Pulling a dead body from the vicinity of their farm to the lakeside would be no easy task. Yet the ground there was level and with the help of adrenaline Caroline could have managed if she dragged Lars by the shirt and vest that on May 25, 1873, were found still hoisted up over his head. Nobody would have seen Caroline in the dark, and Annie had already fallen asleep again, according to the daughter's testimony. If Caroline dragged Lars's body half a mile to the bank, she must have walked at least a quarter mile from their farm before Lars caught up with her.

Most all sources stated that the major injury to Lars's head was on the right side. If Caroline dealt him a right-handed blow, it must have originated from behind and come across from his blind side. If Caroline delivered the fatal strike, she acted with a large degree of physical strength and exceptional fury. The injuries were not limited to a single blow but consisted of several. If readers of the confession assumed that Caroline was right-handed, they could imagine that Lars relinquished the club and turned his back to her, after which Caroline struck at him from behind and across the right side of his head.

The Governor's office left no documentation telling whether they responded to Caroline or M. J. Severance personally after the two filed the affidavit. Regrettably, her confession had little effect, except to increase gossip around Watonwan County. The Minnesota authorities made no effort to test the truth of her confession and took no legal action. In the absence of a follow-up investigation, it was impossible to determine the truth of her statement. Neither was Andrew released from Stillwater. As The St. James Journal wrote of the matter nearly twenty years later (January 6, 1893): "The woman in the case [Caroline] afterwards stated that she, and not Andrew Johnson, committed the murder but no credence was placed in her story [by the authorities]." Clearly the county attorney and the State ignored the background of domestic abuse Caroline experienced as a possible and sufficient motivating factor for her to commit an act of aggression. In their eyes, the legal system had followed due course in convicting Andrew. There they allowed the matter to rest.

After 1876 nothing was left for Andrew but to wait out the rest of his days behind the walls of the Minnesota state prison. Caroline was also left in limbo. The affidavit of 1876 was her last public statement concerning the death of Lars. Whatever her true role was on November 8, that day was to prove only the beginning of her inner struggles and her sense of divided loyalties, not their culmination. What she told Andrew and his family after those times remained their private affair. She lived thereafter without uttering a single additional word about the dire happenings at Kansas Lake. She had the rest of her life, however, to sort out the events of the early 1870s in her own mind.

Chapter XIV
At Stillwater Prison

On a hot, muggy day in 1887, a lone nineteen-year-old Swedish woman arrived at the entrance to Stillwater state prison. She paused and gazed up at the imposing structure before her. Beckoning outside were fresh air, verdant countryside, and freedom. Inside were musty hallways, regimentation, and despair. It was a scene that filled many strong men with trepidation. Fortunately for Amanda Elizabeth Gustavsson, there was nothing to fear. She was a missionary, who came to Stillwater in the spirit of love and forgiveness, not as a female convict.

Amanda Gustavsson traveled to Stillwater on that summer day so many years ago for a study tour of the prison. Despite her youth, she had a serious bent. She left Sweden with her family when she was only twelve. While living on her parents' farm in Wisconsin, Amanda began her Christian work. Later she moved to Minneapolis and St. Paul. There Amanda became an evangelical missionary who carried on her church work across Minnesota and western Wisconsin.[1] An extrovert, she met the challenges of her calling with resolve and clear-cut goals. At Stillwater prison she showed those very qualities, facing the dark corridors and hardened visages without flinching.

Amanda's tour of the Stillwater facility showed her its standard features. She visited the deputy warden's office, the cellblocks and workshops, the prison yards, and the penitentiary chapel. She saw the institution as it was — a foreboding place offering none of the cheer and little of the hope of her evangelical world. Nevertheless her visit turned out to be of special significance, because of an eye-opening observation she made there. Among the multitude of convicts in their drab prison garb, Amanda spied out several fellow Swedes. Amanda herself stated: "I became deeply impressed with the thought that there must be some of my own countrymen among the many forms which met my sight, and God put the thought into my heart to seek permission to speak to them in their native tongue."[2]

Meeting Swedish convicts was a situation Amanda's background and the growing mythology of Swedish America had not prepared her for. Were not Swedes in America hardy pioneers who tamed the frontier or strong workers who built railroads and kept industry prosperous? Had they not inherited qualities of honesty and democracy in their homeland and practiced them in America? How did the existence of Swedish-American convicts fit into the equation?

Not one to let such questions stand in her way, Amanda took action. She asked the Stillwater warden, H. G. Stordock, for permission to stay until the next day, a Sunday, and preach a sermon in Swedish. She returned on July 24, 1887, and spoke for over an hour in the prison chapel. Stillwater's inmate newspaper, The Prison Mirror, featured her in its inaugural issue from August 10, 1887.[3] Astonishingly, the paper stated that fifty Swedish prisoners attended her sermon. In the words of a convict reporter, she assured "her hearers that they possessed her deepest sympathies in their hour of sorrow and trouble, and lifted her voice to God in plaintive and earnest appeal for their salvation."[4]

Amanda spoke to the inmates "upon the birth, life, and death of our Savior" and appealed "with all the power and earnestness of her Christian heart and nature, to those in her presence to give their hearts to God." The Prison Mirror concluded that "in tender and impressive language" she "melted many stubborn hearts to tears" and "left within their breasts a new-born hope of a nobler and better life to come."[5]

At Stillwater penitentiary Amanda saw and sympathized with individuals paying dearly for their offenses against society. Among that group was Andrew Johnson. Regardless of his true role in the death of Lars, Andrew was not differentiated from the gray mass of other convicts Amanda encountered at the prison. He surely was one of those who heard her preach that Sunday.

In 1887 Andrew had been in the state penitentiary for thirteen years and now called it home. At that time the prison was in its fledgling period, much like the state of Minnesota. Population figures reflected the steady influx of settlers to the state. From a total of only 172,000 inhabitants in 1860, Minnesota's population increased to 1,300,000 in 1890 and surpassed the 1,750,000 mark in 1900. The arrival of Scandinavians contributed significantly to that total.[6]

Stillwater prison grew with the state itself. Opened in 1853 while Minnesota was still a United States territory, the prison stood on marshy land at the north end of the city of Stillwater. It consisted of a three-story building, which contained six cells, two dungeons, a workshop, and an office.[7] Living conditions were primitive and escapes frequent.[8] By 1886 the facility had expanded to a state prison with 582 cells and 387 inmates. The prison was renovated and expanded after Andrew arrived, but it remained cold and dank, with poor hygienic conditions and few recreational facilities. As the century neared its end, the penitentiary population continued to grow. By the first day of the fiscal year 1889, the number of inmates reached 437. Until 1890 the average age of the convicts was relatively low. In 1888, for example, sixty-four percent of the prisoners were under thirty.[9]

The first professional penologists to serve as wardens were Albert Garvin, who held the position in 1891-1892, and Henry Wolfer, who was Stillwater's warden from 1892 to 1899, then again from 1901 to 1914. A former administrator at the progressive Joliet state prison in Illinois, Wolfer took important steps to modernize the penal system in Minnesota. He worked for inmate rehabilitation, often counseling convicts on a one-to-one basis. By means of such hands-on work, he first came into contact with Andrew and began studying his conduct.[10]

Wolfer worked to disseminate information and increase awareness of prison conditions. He also enforced a well-ordered routine. The names of all incoming inmates, the so-called "fresh fish" such as Andrew in 1874, were entered in the Convict Register as the inmates were admitted to the prison.[11] Along with the convict's name, the following information was recorded: inmate number; county and court where convicted; nature of crime; sentencing date; length of sentence;

and place of birth and/or parentage. Personal features of the inmate, such as height, weight, and distinguishing physical characteristics were also kept.[12] In Andrew's case, prison officials recorded only the barest details in that regard.

Including Andrew, 335 Swedish Americans served time at Stillwater in the years before World War I.[13] Who were they? The answer lay in the nature of the Swedish-American community itself. The overwhelming majority of Swedish immigrants were humble working folk seeking a better life in the United States. They were successful en masse. Their hard work and loyalty enabled them to aid in building a new nation. They carried on their social lives in an informal way and associated almost exclusively with people of their own working class background. Like Andrew, they were mainly workers from obscure settlements and had virtually no personal visibility in the "high culture" of American or Scandinavian-American social, business, and intellectual circles.

The majority of those sent to Stillwater prison fit that same pattern. Though their crimes were diverse, the Swedish-American inmates tended to fit a general mold. They served their time and eventually left the penitentiary. The average length of time they served was 3.5 years. With the help of institutions, family, friends, and their own will power, most of Stillwater's Swedish-American convicts were peacefully re-assimilated into the civilian community. The majority resumed their former places in everyday routines and made their own — albeit small — contributions to ethnic and social life.

In 1874 Andrew Johnson became the tenth of the Swedish Americans admitted to Stillwater and the third convicted of murder. The average age of Swedish Americans at sentencing was thirty-four. Andrew fit that statistic nearly perfectly, since he entered Stillwater at age thirty-three. Of the Swedes he shared his prison time with, the most common transgression was theft, whether in the form of larceny, burglary, embezzlement, robbery, or swindling. Most acted alone in committing crimes, and the majority performed their misdeeds without long-range planning. Nearly all ran afoul of the law despite having clear ideas of right and wrong. Several were mentally ill, and they were eventually transferred to mental care facilities.

A total of 298 Swedish-American inmates were listed at Stillwater by occupation. Of the 298, 123 were unskilled manual laborers.

Thirty-six farmers and three farmhands made up the second largest group, followed by twenty-three carpenters. Others practiced several different trades before their incarceration. There were painters, blacksmiths, masons, teamsters, tailors, and shoemakers. Once again, Andrew fit the mold. He was a practical man and a life-long farmer, laborer, and carpenter.[14]

Other categories gave insights into the pre-prison lives of the Swedish-American inmates Andrew would have known at Stillwater. In terms of education, 242 were able, or said they were able, to read and write English and had at least an elementary school education. Twenty-five were illiterate or had "no education" at all. In terms of religion, the affiliations of the Swedish-American convicts reflected a strong Protestant orientation. A total of 172 inmates were Lutheran, while another sixty-seven said they were Protestants. Alcohol use was the greatest personal vice of the Swedish Americans. Prison officials considered as many as 144 of the 335 inmates as "intemperate." Only eight were abstinent. Another 147 were either temperate or moderate drinkers.[15] Here again Andrew placed in the middle of the field. He had little schooling, was of a Lutheran background, and, as far as is known, drank only moderately, even if alcohol played a significant role in his fateful 1872 fight with Lars.

Andrew was unusual in one important respect. Most inmates were in the prison for only short stays. Andrew's life sentence promised him no other future than Stillwater prison. He lived the same regimented life as all other convicts, but with less hope than most. Andrew, and all the others as well, wore the "penitentiary stripes," consisting of a hip jacket, woolen pants, and a skullcap.[16] His cell was like those of all other inmates, too. It measured 5' by 7' and had an iron door. In addition to towels and bedding, he had a Bible, a water jar, and a shelf for books. In the corner of his cell, sat a cast iron night bucket, which was emptied only once a day. When he marched to the dining hall for breakfast each day, Andrew performed the same ritual as all his fellow inmates. He carried his night bucket along and emptied it on the way.

Discipline was strict. With his fellow convicts, Andrew marched in lock step to and from his cell and lived under the rule of enforced silence. These were the rules Andrew was introduced to from the very beginning of his time at Stillwater:

> *The prompt rising of each prisoner in the morning at the sound of the gong, followed by his personal hygiene, dressing, washing cuspidors, making his bed, standing for the count; no lounging on the bed during the noon hour; standing with his right hand on the cell; retiring at nine o'clock at night; sitting erect, arms folded, eyes to the front in the dining room until the signal was given to eat; gesturing to communicate with those dispensing food; no gazing into cells when marching back and forth from the cells; and similar rules governing their behavior in the chapel.*[17]

Being silent was intended to give inmates time for personal reflection and reformation, while working in the prison industries was meant to instill self-discipline.[18] Andrew saw those rules relaxed only toward the end of the century, as the prison began observing national holidays and allowing freer conversation for convicts on special occasions.

Andrew's respiratory illness disappeared in prison, but that was with little help from Stillwater's health facilities. Physicians visited the prison only periodically, and the infirmary remained primitive until the late 1800s. Andrew's process of recovery was never explained, in fact, since the official prison reports on its hospital system and the physical condition of inmates failed to mention a single visit by Andrew to the prison medical staff through the years. As was true of other inmates, Andrew could bathe each day with a bucketful of water in his cell, until showers were installed in the early 1890s. Before the late 1880s cells were lighted with gasoline lamps or candles. After electricity was introduced in 1888, each cell had a ten-watt light fixture. A modern heating system was added in 1886.[19] Andrew worked a nine to eleven-hour day at a job in the prison carpenter shop. His place of work allowed him to escape much of the repetitious drudgery of prison convict labor. As a carpenter, he had the chance to move from job to job around the grounds. In his earliest months in the shop, he made and decorated a wooden sewing box, which he had sent to Caroline as a token of his affection.[20] (Figure 14)

Few convicts were able, or had the inclination, to record their feelings about prison life. In 1910, however, a former Stillwater convict, writing under the pseudonym of John Carter, published an article on inmate life. John Carter described an era that came three decades after Andrew's admittance to the prison, but Stillwater's was, in many ways, a static environment, where the daily routine varied little through the years. Certainly the grueling psychological effects remained the same. According to John Carter, prisoners were "oppressed by a multitude of rules, many of them seemingly unnecessary, overweighted by silence, [and] overwhelmed by solitude."[21]

They had only one brief exercise period per week, which was on Sunday mornings, and even then only if the weather permitted. Otherwise they breathed fresh air just during the short moment each day when they passed the few yards from their cell buildings to the workshops. The prison environment was, in John Carter's view, "unnecessarily dark and inconceivably foul." In illustrating a typical day in prison life, as a convict such as Andrew would see it, the author wrote:

> To attempt to bring conditions of life in Stillwater clearly before the readers' eye, it will be advisable to detail a day's routine. At 5:45 the gong rings. This sounds like a very ordinary and necessary procedure, but the morning gong is the insistent fact that disturbs one's dream-fancies, the everlasting reminder of one's status in life. At the sound of it, seven hundred men get out of bed, wash, dress, and tidy their cells. At 6:15 they march to breakfast in the dining-halls. Breakfast over, they return to their cells for a moment, but shortly march out to the shops, beginning work promptly at seven o'clock. Work continues until noon, at which time a recess is taken for dinner. At one, work begins again, and it continues until six, when comes once more the silent march, and by 6:15 every man is locked in his cell.[22]

Prison food left much to be desired. John Carter remembered the same regular offerings: three good breakfasts and dinners each week to which were added four bad ones. The good meals came on consecutive days, a situation that left inmates hungry much of the rest of the week. When not working, eating, or sleeping, inmates were left to their own devices in the cells. Unless they were able to sleep twelve hours every night, the only way to pass the time was by reading. John Carter wrote: "A man shut in a cell is virtually forced to read, if he wishes to keep sane."[23]

Despite ongoing reforms, the type of discipline Andrew lived under remained rigid. One historian wrote of prison life at Stillwater: "The whole atmosphere in which the inmate lived was negative, frustrating, and repressive."[24] Andrew was introduced to this feeling on his first day of incarceration, when his head was shaved and he spent the first night alone in his cell. In the months and years that followed, he adjusted to the routine but still felt the threat of punishment for as many as fifty different in-house offenses.[25]

The punishment most commonly referred to was solitary confinement. The rooms for solitary (known as "the hole") were lined with iron and had double doors. They were entirely dark and until 1887 remained poorly ventilated. In each one was an iron ring placed four feet from the door, to which a prisoner might be handcuffed. Andrew was never subjected to such treatment, but numerous Swedish Americans in his day spent countless hours in solitary. One example came near the turn of the century. Then Dan Peterson, a thirty-eight-year-old immigrant cook from St. Louis County who was convicted of robbery, spent a total of 148 hours in solitary for "skirting his work" and "for not doing a [full] day's work."[26]

Those inmates, like Andrew, who served long terms could see a veritable Scandinavian subculture develop through the years. Despite the rule of enforced silence, the Scandinavian convicts could carry on clandestine conversations in the secrecy of their Nordic tongues. They would have had much to talk about, as a cavalcade of bizarre and violent happenings passed before their eyes. A few examples, some of a truly abominable nature, gave a small taste of what Andrew witnessed or heard about. In 1876 the notorious Younger brothers, of the Jesse James/Younger gang, were captured in Watonwan County and brought to Stillwater, where responses flooding in from the civilian public turned them into celebrities of a perverse sort, whom all the convicts knew about.

Years after the Youngers arrived, Charles A. Burling, a twenty-five-old Swedish-American baker from Minneapolis convicted of burglary, entered the prison and created tumult. He surpassed Dan Peterson's record and served 438 hours in solitary confinement for making violent physical assaults and using foul and abusive language toward prisoners and non-prisoners alike. Burling was later scalded to death at his prison work place, a violent end that bore the earmarks of retaliation by a fellow prisoner for some unnamed assault.[27] Another year John Dutzinski, a Galician immigrant convict, attacked a Swedish-American inmate named Junior Danielson. Danielson was a bricklayer convicted of grand larceny. After an obscure dispute, Dutzinski bashed Danielson across the head with his iron night bucket and crushed his skull while the men were on their routine march to break-fast one morning. Danielson died on the cell house floor as guards looked on helplessly.[28]

In that venomous and depressing environment, Andrew watched the years go by. For a man accustomed his whole life to open spaces, prison confinement must have been a horrifying experience in the beginning. He likely lay awake many nights in his cell wondering about his situation and replaying the course of his trial in his mind. He surely had other events of the past in his thoughts as well, includ-ing his immigration, his marriages, and his children, who grew up without seeing or knowing him. In the long run, however, there was no choice in Stillwater but to adjust to the realities there, harsh and unforgiving as they were.

Andrew's name came up from time to time at the prison. As early as 1874 Stillwater officials reimbursed him for a parcel of vegetables he had grown in the prison gardens. In 1878 he contributed $1.00 to the prison's Organist Fund, to increase the salary of the organist who played in the prison chapel. During the fall and early winter of 1883, he was released from work and confined to his cell for several days because of sickness. Those days included November 8 (the mel-ancholy eleventh anniversary of Lars's disappearance) and all of the Christmas season (December 24-26).[29]

In addition, throughout the years 1875 and 1876 Andrew regularly sent money from his prison earnings home to Caroline at Kansas Lake. In January and June of 1875, officials forwarded $8.10 and $16.20 from Andrew "to his wife." Not knowing he had two wives, prison managers understood, of course, none of the irony or ambiguity in that phrase. Slightly larger amounts went from Andrew to Caroline in April and May of 1876. In 1877 and 1878 the disbursements paid in Andrew's name started going "to [Andrew] himself" with noth-ing paid out to Caroline. The only exception came in February, 1878, when once again a cash payment of $20.00 went from Andrew "to [his] wife." After 1878 the prison disbursement ledger ceased to indi-cate which persons the convicts' funds were paid out to.

Andrew was not without a certain earning power through the years. In the mid-1880s his personal account was regularly granted sums of $60.00 and $70.00.[30] So he could have sent significant sums of money home, if so inclined. Those are the only concrete details available on Andrew's prison life. They revealed little of his mindset but showed that he was a steady and reliable worker and that for a while at least he kept up some measure of contact with Caroline. For the prison officials he remained a known and productive entity among the convict population. As the years slipped by, he worked, stayed out of trouble, and avoided punishment. Those qualities did not escape the personal attention of warden Henry Wolfer.

Andrew lived among the hodge-podge of varied and conflicting customs represented by the inmates and in the midst of the disease and violence that were rife at Stillwater. The prisoners were a polyglot population of ethnic and racial groups from all across Canada, Mexico, and the United States. An additional segment consisted of immigrants from every corner of Europe and a few from Asia. They brought with them a checkerboard of cultural diversity and adjustment difficulties. In fact, the number of inmates sent from Stillwater to mental institutions grew steadily as more and more of them proved incapable of adhering to the penitentiary routine, began inflicting injuries on themselves and others, or repeatedly feigned bodily injuries to shirk their assigned work.

The prison's physical plant did little to lessen those problems. One other convict lent support to John Carter's description of conditions. He wrote in the 1890s: "Bedbugs are so numerous they drive the average prisoner wild with pain and annoyance. The air is foul. The stench is almost intolerable."[31] Before 1873 Andrew had spent his entire life in the close company of his family. Isolation and separation were not accustomed parts of his existence. Even if he accepted his incarceration with a certain resignation, his hours there surely felt empty.

Relief from the monotony occurred seldom and unexpectedly. In 1884 the prison buildings burned twice. On both occasions Andrew was among convicts removed to temporary housing, which gave them a brief respite and a taste of the outside world, though that taste was surely bittersweet. Contemporary accounts told of prisoners being gawked at by citizens who lined the way and observed their movement.[32]

Religious services were also held occasionally in Nordic languages, as when Amanda Gustavsson came there to preach, but all regularly scheduled Sunday worship was, in the words of John Carter, perfunctory and uninteresting, as if the visiting pastors held out little

hope the convicts might mend their ways.[33] The prison library offered loans of over 5,000 religious and secular books, which included
eighty-six Norwegian and Swedish titles. Swedish-American maga-
zines and newspapers, which the prisoners themselves subscribed to,
also made the rounds in the cellblocks.[34] Reading was not Andrew's
strong point, however, and knowing little English he must have spent
long hours in his cell just thinking.

Yet there were a few people to sympathize and commiserate with.
One other Swedish inmate worked alongside Andrew at the prison
carpenter shop. That was the convicted murderer Nels Hast. He
entered Stillwater three years before Andrew. Hast served his time
with good behavior until the Governor of Minnesota pardoned him
in 1883. Andrew and Nels Hast had more than their Swedishness,
carpentry skills, and rural backgrounds in common. The same judge,
Franklin Waite, sentenced both of them to life at Stillwater. The courtroom proceedings and their lengthy sentences were experiences the
two men could discuss in secret together while they shared working
space at the prison.[35]

As Nels Hast left Stillwater, Andrew stayed. Uncertain are the
methods he devised to avoid further serious physical illness and
maintain his mental health. Through the years his thoughts must repeatedly have drifted back to Sweden and the Minnesota prairie, even
if memories grew dimmer with each passing year. At times the series of happenings that brought him to prison could seem the work of
blind fate, at others the inevitable product of his own desires. During
his early period at Stillwater, Caroline may have visited him regularly
and given him some hope. M. J. Severance was also preparing the
pardon application for him. But those hopes faded fast.

In time the reality of Andrew's situation surely became indelibly
imprinted on him. The unfailing ring of the prison gong would have
sent the strongest signal. Task-oriented as it was, that routine served
as the impetus that kept him alive. Work — barely the "hard labor'
he was formally sentenced to — was surely his salvation. At the same
time, the prison gong, which woke prisoners in the early morning and
sent them to bed at night, was what John Carter described as the everlasting disturber of a convict's dreams. Another writer summarized
the situation more prosaically:

> His [the convict's] environments force him to dwell

continually upon the depths of degradation to which he
has fallen, and he suffers the keenest possible mental torture;
but after passing this period he begins to readjust his viewpoint
and adapt himself to his surroundings.[36]

No doubt this description captured the development of Andrew's thoughts during his long incarceration. The memories of his encounters with Lars and the feelings he had for Johanna Persdotter and Caroline surely stayed with him for a lifetime. In prison perhaps he experienced guilt over his actions or felt he had been betrayed or used as a scapegoat by the legal system and those he knew at Kansas Lake. If he grieved over such matters, he had long, lonely years behind bars to canvass his feelings. Working alone through his many emotions — being his own therapist, in other words — could not have been easy. A full recovery would have required years of introspection and personal evaluation.

In brief, the psychological effects of Andrew's penitentiary experience cannot have been other than traumatic, longlasting, and sobering. In prison, he lived, as it were, in a vacuum, as part of a stable and never-changing routine. Outside the walls of Stillwater prison, change was in the air. After the 1880s agriculture gradually started thriving on the Minnesota prairie. After the nationwide economic problems of the early 1890s, the Gilded Age began and with it an era of unprecedented economic prosperity. That upswing affected life in Watonwan County as well. It was from that life Andrew was fully separated. To fall back on for moral support outside the prison, he had only his family. Yet contact with their world was hard to maintain. Visitors and letters were all he had to remind him that the places he knew and the people he loved still existed anywhere except in his reveries.

Even for those who cared most about him, everyday life took precedence. They carried on with work, could not think about him everyday, and did not send letters more than occasionally. Still, a few caring souls kept trying. On her 1887 Stillwater visit Amanda Gustavsson sent out prayers for a better life to come. Some people in Watonwan County took such sentiment to heart. Through the years they raised several petitions for Andrew's release. Despite their best efforts, not enough people signed the papers. Memories of Lars's violent demise influenced the responses of Kansas Lake residents for years after his death, and the suspicions many oldtimers harbored toward Andrew and Caroline did not die easily. Their attitudes remained negative. As the 1890s began, Andrew entered his third decade behind the walls of Stillwater prison. The parties concerned for his welfare were filled with mixed emotions. They kept on hoping for the best but had no grounds for optimism.

Chapter XV
Caroline: A Riddle

While Andrew languished in prison, Caroline went free. Sometime between 1876 and 1880 she left Kansas Lake and returned to Madison, Wisconsin. With her on the trip back eastward she took her youngest children John Albert and Christine, but left Annie and Isabel behind. Several separate factors in combination prompted her move back to Wisconsin. Foremost was Caroline's relationship with Andrew's family and the other Swedes in Watonwan County.

After 1874 Andrew's parents continued to welcome Caroline to their home. They offered her and her children a helping hand out of a sincere sympathy and understanding for her difficult position in the community. Andrew's mother was the person who had invited her and the children to their house after the first blizzard of 1872. During the years 1874 and 1876 those bonds strengthened. The Johnsons lived on at Kansas Lake feeling torn and devastated but with hopes alive nonetheless. The ensuing period between the refusal of the pardon request and Caroline's 1876 affidavit was a time of stress and crucial decision-making in the crowded household.

Despite their goodwill, the dynamics of the Johnson family's relations grew problematic. In the first place, they all felt confusion in the aftermath of losing a son, a brother, and a husband upon Andrew's incarceration. If Caroline loved Andrew, as her behavior indicated, her conscience may finally have motivated her to make the public declaration of guilt, in June of 1876. Another possibility is that Andrew's parents, his brother, and M. J. Severance pressured Caroline to file the 1876 affidavit, either out of a continued sympathy for her or a newfound disappointment. That disappointment could have come about if, in the spring of 1876, Caroline revealed information concerning Lars's death that the others had not known before.

Perhaps she told them she killed Lars and the news left Hogan and his parents dumbfounded. They must often have wondered about Caroline's true role in Lars's disappearance but failed to believe the worst. If Andrew and his family from the beginning accepted unquestioningly Caroline's story that she knew nothing at all about Lars's fate, they surely were unusually trusting people or very naïve. At any rate, hearing from Caroline's own mouth that she was the responsible party would have been a sobering note that could tip the balance of the family's faith in her. By way of contrast, Caroline, Andrew, and his family may all along have shared a secret knowledge of how Lars died and then did their best to maintain a united front in planning their lives and facing the court system as well as the community at large. Sadly, the family did not reveal publicly how much they all knew or when they knew it.

Another uncertain part of the equation was John and Christine Johnson's feelings about Andrew's two wives, Johanna in Sweden and Caroline in Minnesota. Certainly the general attitudes of Swedes and Americans of that era toward various sexual practices and housekeeping arrangements differed. What might appear in America to be unusual forms of cohabitation or irregular sexual unions were far from uncommon among ordinary folk in Sweden, a country that was untouched by many of the puritanical strictures of the Victorian Age. To most rural Swedes in the past, marriage was a four-step process, which involved both secular and ecclesiastical definitions. To the commonfolk marriage officially began with an engagement. Following that the couple moved in together, thus completing the second step of married life. Having children was the third step. Many Swedes considered those three actions sufficient for a complete and binding married relationship, and in the secular and legal world they functioned in exactly that way. The formal church ceremony, if and when it occurred, supplied the final ecclesiastical touch and was recorded by the bishopric in which each couple resided.[1]

In other words, settled and committed Swedish couples customarily celebrated a church wedding only after pregnancy occurred or following the birth of a child. In many cases cohabitation or an engagement was seen as a trial period to find if a union between two young people could result in compatibility and children. In brief, rural commoners usually married in church after having children, not in order to have them. As a result, the number of children born to unmarried but cohabiting parents in Sweden (*oäkta barn*) was high, at least according to the Church of Sweden's strict official definition of what constituted a marriage. To the general public, living together and having children spoke of a binding and honored commitment. This pattern was the one followed by Hogan and Andrew and their wives in Veinge in the early 1860s. Both couples married in church only after Hanna and Johanna became pregnant, but they were surely considered permanent committed couples long before the wedding ceremony took place.

In less happy scenarios, younger Swedish workingwomen were often taken advantage of by their employers or by men of higher social standing. For the victims, such practices were, naturally, unwelcome and unfair, but most were powerless to stop the men's advances. The compromised women and their families were forced to live with the consequences, which included, of course, shame and unplanned pregnancies. The victims managed as well as they could and usually suffered in silence.[2] Furthermore, married men or established wage earners were known to have female lovers or mistresses (*frillor*), to the extent they could afford or accommodate such liaisons. That was the very sort of illicit relationship <u>Svenska Nybyggaren</u> accused Andrew of having with Caroline when the two were in Omaha in 1873. In brief, Swedish commoners tolerated pre-marital and extra-marital affairs, though not always by choice. Certainly the Church of Sweden discouraged such practices, though it was never successful in stopping them.[3]

As products of that culture, John and Christine Johnson must have felt that Andrew and his wife in Sweden were separated, in 1873, by several years and many thousands of miles and were unlikely ever to meet again. Thus Andrew's relationship with Caroline did not come as a total surprise to his parents. Yet whatever the general level of tolerance, bigamy was not accepted in Sweden. In America at the time, bigamy was defined as a crime, but not an important one.[4] Despite that fact, it would have been openly condemned in churches across America if and when it occurred. Therefore, Andrew's parents clearly chose to keep information about Johanna Persdotter to themselves in Minnesota. Given the close communal life of the Swedes at Kansas Lake, it is difficult to imagine that the Johnsons succeeded in keeping the secret, that no one there, in other words, knew of Andrew's married life back home. Nonetheless Kansas Lake Swedes seem not to have been aware of it. Andrew's neighbors treated him as a single man, and Svenska Nybyggaren, which got its information from local sources in Watonwan County, reported (April 17, 1873) that Andrew was unmarried and lived with his parents.

As faithful Lutherans, John and Christine Johnson doubtless had cause to wonder at the behavior of their children's generation, but they resigned themselves to the fact that the American authorities were sure to remain indifferent to, or ignorant of, Andrew's situation as long as his two families stayed on opposite sides of the Atlantic. Still, Andrew's parents' acceptance of Caroline in Minnesota to some degree entailed forgetting Johanna in Sweden or at least pushing her further back in their consciousness. Whatever Andrew's parents' feelings were, many doubts of differing magnitudes and increasing intensity, on a broad spectrum of issues, existed on the farm at Kansas Lake in the mid-1870s. Important and unresolved questions about the past and the future surely weighed heavily on them all.

An added pressure was the hardships of the grasshopper (or Rocky Mountain locust) invasions, which stripped farm fields all across the prairies between 1873 and 1878. The insects arrived in Minnesota from the West, sometimes in clouds that darkened the sky. The swarms devoured all foliage in their path, and at times they were so heavy as to derail passenger trains. A resident of the nearby Nordic settlement at Odin, barely five miles from Kansas Lake, wrote of the destruction:

> *During the years of 1873 and 1876 the entire countryside*
> *was devastated by swarms of millions of grasshoppers*
> *resulting in partial or complete loss of all crops. White*

> *clothes or bedding, after washing, could not be hung to*
> *dry outdoors, as they would be devoured by the 'hoppers'.*
> *Farmers who were fortunate in not losing their entire crop*
> *helped those who suffered the most.*

The farmer remembered how he watched as swarms of grasshoppers, descending like a snowstorm, ruined his entire corn crop within minutes.[5] The Johnsons at Kansas Lake were among those who were hardest hit, since their farm also lay in the direct path of the invasion. Only nine days after Andrew was taken off to prison in 1874, the <u>St. James Herald</u> (May 23) reported on the first wave of grasshoppers in the area for that year.

The living conditions became especially cramped and tense at John and Christine's farm in those times, especially when the fierce winter of 1875, which rivaled that of 1872-1873, gave way to a new wave of grasshopper attacks after fair weather returned in April. Families in general were forced to tighten their belts even more than usual. At the turn of the century, a St. James resident looked back on the extent of the loss:

> *Everything was ruined and destroyed. Day by day the people*
> *of the county and Village were to be seen leaving the country.*
> *Many could not even raise sufficient funds to enable them to*
> *enter upon a journey to other points, and many hesitated and*
> *delayed in the hope that the little pests would make their*
> *departure. Thus did people live, 'twixt doubt and hope, for*
> *four long years. What were the prospects for the future, the*
> *outlook for the days to come? The people were destitute and*
> *actually suffering. They found themselves without money, credit*
> *or provisions — everything gone; swept away.*[6]

A single tangible comment on conditions in the Johnsons' Kansas Lake household showed the hardships involved. In 1872, Hogan had purchased his reaper and mower on two promissory notes, both co-signed by Andrew.[7] In 1875 the two notes were still unpaid. One local Swedish American commented on the financial difficulties farmers such as Hogan faced: "Some [farmers] had bought machinery and had to borrow money to pay for it paying 24 to 36 percent interest to the loan sharks[,] and machinery companies became owners of many farms."[8] The resulting losses were said to strip families of their "last defense against impending starvation," as the grasshopper invasion grew worse.[9]

In 1875 the St. James farm implement company took Hogan to claims court. He was charged with unpaid debts plus court costs. With the help of J. W. Seager, Hogan filed a statement of forfeiture admitting the delinquency and his creditors' right to collect the money (or re-claim the machinery). He requested, however, that such action be delayed so that he might gather money to pay the debts.[10] A tone of resignation emerged from Hogan's writ, which implied not only that he had been unable to meet the financial demands but also that other affairs occupied his mind. Grasshoppers and a family in crisis were at the top of the list. The Johnsons surely felt the hardships of their life in the Old World being revisited on them in the New World as well. Andrew's trial and conviction as well as the grasshopper plague put a strain on the family members' state of mind as well as their finances.

During the mid-1870s when Caroline pondered her and her family's difficult situation at Kansas Lake, the county lost eleven percent of its population, mainly due to the movement of destitute people out of the area. At the worst of the grasshopper scourge, Watonwan County officials reported they had only $350.00 in relief funds to distribute among seventy families, which resulted in a payment of just $4.00 per household.[11] Caroline and her two children surely left the county partly because of such financial hardships, or, alternatively, those financial troubles functioned as the push factor, the final straw, added to the severe social and psychological pressure Caroline felt, which eventually forced her to seek another life elsewhere.

Caroline seemed to leave Kansas Lake without looking back. In fact, moving on and leaving part of one's life behind may have been commonplace in some circles on the frontier. One writer has argued the following about pioneer life and the westward expansion in America:

> *Life in the nineteenth century did not involve for most people a commitment to permanence, tradition, and stability, at least geographically. More often than not, the roots planted in one place were left to wither while new ones were put down in another. Searching, hoping for a better way of life, thousands of Americans tried one spot for a time, abandoned it, and moved on again.*[12]

Some have seen that generation as one that moved on when difficulties arose and refused (or saw no need) to consider the possible consequences of their actions. According to this theory, people came and then went, taking their secrets with them, without perceiving the need to explain their innermost desires and regrets to other people, or to inquire of others about theirs.

Indications point to just such a situation in the Kansas Lake settlement. By the time of the Kansas Lake Swedish Lutheran Church congregation's twenty-fifth anniversary celebration in 1897, only sixteen of the thirty-seven charter members were still in the community. In romanticized but telling terms, the congregation's official anniversary handbook later summarized the relative state of permanency (or impermanency) among the original congregation members:

> *In 1896, 21 [charter members] had died or moved away, and only 16 remained as members, indicating that the Swedes of that day had itching feet — that they were a restless lot, and found it difficult to settle down. The Viking spirit was still strong in their blood, leading them on to new and ever newer adventures.*[13]

Regardless of what Caroline was seeking as she left Kansas Lake, she was not alone in pulling up stakes and moving on. When she emerged from the ravaged farmlands of southern Minnesota in June of 1876 to speak with Andrew at Stillwater prison, she was surely already on her way out of Watonwan County, psychologically speaking. Approaching the penitentiary walls and experiencing the grime and foreboding aspect of the penal institution could cast a pall over the strongest of individuals, with the exception of teenaged missionary Amanda Gustavsson. Even in the best of conditions, Caroline would have experienced some apprehension on that early summer day. Her visit must have come after a long period of soul-searching and a desperate search for answers. The tenor of her conversation with Andrew was surely affected by that feeling. It must have been tense, if not overwrought.

On that day Andrew possibly took the initiative and told Caroline to forget him, to go on her way, and start a new life. By 1876 the brutal truth had made itself felt. He had no prospects of leaving prison or rejoining her. Andrew was doomed to die in Stillwater, wearing prison stripes. Or Caroline may have told him her story of killing Lars and asked Andrew to forgive her for not being forthright about it from the beginning, only to find herself rejected in anger by Andrew. Or she may have belatedly discovered his marital status in Sweden and responded with shock and rejection and announced her plans to leave the area for good.

An outside possibility was that the two had a secret agreement from the start, dating all the way back to 1872, which they agreed to finalize upon her prison visit. Certainly they had had ample time in Omaha and the Mankato jail to discuss the most intimate topics central to their lives. That fact made it difficult to believe they lived together for so many weeks without ever discussing at length the details of Lars's disappearance or Andrew's former life in Halland. Yet it is possible they did not. Whatever they said at Stillwater in 1876, Andrew and Caroline's relationship and marriage came to a definitive end after her visit. In all likelihood, the aftermath also caused Andrew slowly to start cutting back on financial payments to Caroline from prison after 1876.

For Caroline there was no future at Kansas Lake. As she departed Watonwan County for the second time, Hogan surely took her to the station once more. She must have passed reasonably close by the foster homes of Annie and Isabel, barely two miles away. In 1877 Annie reached confirmation age, the church's so-called age of reason. Knowing how to act toward her older daughter, therefore, must have been hard, even agonizing for Caroline. Simply walking away from the girl or trying to explain why she was leaving but not taking the two daughters along can only have presented special difficulties, as it would for any but the most unusual of personality types.

What Caroline told the girls as she left, if anything, was never revealed. Neither did she tell them her whereabouts once she reached Wisconsin. Nor did she ever correspond with Andrew and his parents, Charles Johnson, or any other member of the Kansas Lake community once she was gone. In addition to Annie and Isabel, the individuals hardest hit by the chain of events were Andrew's parents. In less than ten years, they lost a son, three daughters-in-law, and seven grandchildren to prison, emigration, or death, not to mention the four small daughters of their own who died in Sweden during the 1840s. Those many losses reinforced the notion that John and Christine's was an embattled high-risk family. However, they bore the disappointment of those losses stolidly and bravely.

Considering the circumstances she encountered at Kansas Lake and others she created for herself, Caroline was forced in the 1870s to make personal decisions of great, even heart-breaking proportions. Regardless of which step she took, someone's emotional life, and not least of all her own, was certain to be placed in jeopardy. Not even the most callous frontier settlers or those who considered her behavior with Andrew as immoral could have remained unmoved by a plight such as hers. In that regard, attempting to shed light on the question of how Caroline responded mentally to her dilemma leads one to examine the social background she lived in.

The southwestern Minnesota farming frontier of that era was a rough-hewn social environment. Even in good years, most farmers had difficulties making ends meet, which necessitated conformity to a conservative collectivist mode. During economic recessions conditions could turn truly desperate. Many stricken farmers looked for work away from home, but those who were homesteaders often feared they would lose their rights to the land while they were gone if claim jumpers moved in or the government charged them with failing to fulfill their residency requirements.[14] The agricultural blight in Watonwan County between 1873 and 1878 caused just such an uneasy job market there. Still, many men shrugged off their apprehensions and sought work away from home.

With jobs scarce for men, the opportunities for women like Caroline were even fewer. Though growing numbers of rural women sought paid employment outside the home after 1870, jobs open to them were typically as "domestics, nursemaids, and in the needle trades," although "some women entered the professions as teachers, nurses, doctors, and at least one as a minister."[15] Caroline would have found no demand for such employees in Long Lake township, nor would she have qualified for them if they had existed. As a lone, uneducated woman with children, she could in fact have found no work to support her family around Kansas Lake at all, other than menial farm labor. A bustling rail center like St. James conceivably had more stable employment for women. Being unable to read and write or speak English would have nullified her chances in that environment, however, except possibly as a domestic. In many quarters the social stigma associated with Caroline, Lars, and Andrew would also have spoken against her as she applied for any openings on the local job market.

At the height of the grasshopper plague, the Minnesota legislature and the federal government gave relief packages to struggling households, which Caroline theoretically could have qualified for. Yet those were typically for as little as $1.00 to $10.00 per family. In 1849 the Minnesota territorial legislature, in addition, had passed The Act for the Relief of the Poor. The complete wording of that document placed the emphasis on all individuals being able to help themselves or, if that failed, to rely on relatives, which Caroline obviously was capable of, at least through 1876. Despite those aids, Minnesota leaders focused on ideas of self-help for ordinary citizens. Among the most stalwart proponents of that philosophy was Governor John S. Pillsbury, whose office refused Andrew's pardon application in 1876.[16] Pillsbury saw deprivation as a normal hardship (and one of the strengths of life) on the frontier and argued that the independence of the people would be damaged by state aid.

Like others in her social group, Caroline was left to live independently in an embattled situation. She had Andrew's family and her own mental resources to aid her. The loss of financial support from Andrew or of psychological and material help by his family could spell disaster for her and her children. Thus she was faced with acquiescing in that vulnerable position or taking steps to leave it.

Caroline and other women faced formidable barriers on the local as well as the state level. While the enduring popular image of pioneer life was one of brave and diligent farmers challenging and taming the wilderness, the frontier exerted a strong pull on people from the white-collar professions as well. As rail and trading towns grew up, the need for a local infrastructure in government, medicine, law, law enforcement, and commerce also arose. To fill that need came lawyers, doctors, former military men, and merchants from the East into the new towns west of the Mississippi. The influx of New Englanders was considerable.[17] The majority of those leaders were new graduates of medical schools, law students recently admitted to the bar, or discharged Union Army officers. In a spirit of adventure but also with an eye to financial gain, they opened medical practices, started law firms, or became county sheriffs and justices of the peace. Others founded businesses and banks.

The Minnesota prairie typified that line of development. Professional men left the East Coast, followed the expanding railroads, and staked out their territory in Mankato, Madelia, and St. James. Judge Franklin Waite was born in Vermont and grew up in New York State.[18] M. J. Severance, the most prominent of the group, was a native of Massachusetts. Admitted to the bar in that state in 1854, he settled first in Le Sueur County in 1856. After serving in the Union Army, he returned to Minnesota and followed the railroad to Mankato in 1870. By the 1880s his legal expertise and military record led him to the district court judgeship.[19] Following a similar path was J. W. Seager. Born in New York State, he was a graduate of the University of Michigan law school. In 1869 he came by train to Mankato. From there Seager continued by stage coach and mail wagon to Jackson, Minnesota, near the Iowa border, where he worked for two years before settling in St. James in 1871.[20] Those professional leaders had enlightened views. Severance was a life-long member of the Democratic Party, a supporter of the temperance movement, and a defender of the underprivileged. Seager, in turn, practiced philanthropy and lent his support to liberal religious causes.

Still, the professional men in the frontier towns were exclusively English-speaking and products of East Coast cultural and educational institutions. Their understanding of the languages and ethnic customs of immigrant groups in the farming areas was severely limited. In addition, the society in which they worked contained more men than women. Women were excluded from a voice in elections and from holding positions in public office and on trial juries.

Generally, there existed a conventional understanding of gender roles, but behavior could vary from community to community. In some cases Euro Americans moving onto the prairies removed old gender restrictions and social controls from back East, thus paving the way for more egalitarian relations between men and women. In other settlements men were seen as rightfully receiving preferential treatment over women in terms of legal rights, family roles, and social advancement. The result in such communities was that women became increasingly vulnerable to male dominance, or what one writer referred to as "men's brutality" to women.[21]

Caroline's years with Lars put her in line with that second category of experience. She suffered physical and mental abuse. Given the numerical superiority of males and the male-dominated governmental structures in Watonwan County, there must to an extent have existed an unwritten patriarchal law, which expressed clear gender expectations. Within limits, Lars was seen as the head of his marital relationship with Caroline, while her role as wife, mother, and farmhand could be viewed as passive, obedient, and proper. In those conventional terms, her later association with Andrew in Omaha as his "mistress" — though also seen as passive in nature — was a serious breach of the moral expectations placed on women, whether married or unmarried.

After Lars's death, the tide of public sentiment turned against Caroline, and she faced the problem of finding a way to stand on her own in the local community as a single mother and a target of blame. When she later assumed a "masculine" role (that is, claiming the responsibility for a violent killing and risking imprisonment), the law and the people of Watonwan County summarily rejected her affidavit as lacking in believability. Caroline's claim to guilt failed, simply, to correlate with ideas of female passivity common among ordinary citizens and leaders alike in her environment.

In taking such a facile stance, the authorities overlooked the enormous complexity of her situation. In time, however, it could not have escaped the attention of most involved in the case that at some point Caroline had concealed the truth about how Lars died, either in what she told the district court under oath in 1874 or in filing her affidavit two years later. Whether or not she lied to Andrew in private about Lars's disappearance must also have been a question in people's minds. Yet, sadly, the authorities made no attempt to delve below the surface of her statements and sort out the truth. By refusing to investigate her statements, they failed to take advantage of their chance to establish the relative degree of truthfulness and accuracy of her sworn testimony before the district court in 1874, which, of course, played a large role in Andrew's conviction. If she perjured herself in court, the charges would have been serious.

After the rejection of her affidavit, Caroline surely slipped into anonymity in Long Lake township. What she lost was the right to participate as a part of the symbol of the nearly sacrosanct pioneer American family structure. She faced the idealized image that on the frontier "father, mother, and children formed a cooperative, contented working team. The farmer moved westward [in the public's mind] with his 'Madonna of the Plains' to create civilization out of chaos." This Madonna of the prairie is the frontier woman one writer has described as the " 'wilderness Martha,' a dependable contributor to the economy as well as the social amenities of the pioneer world."[22] In contrast to that idyllic vision of farming life, Lars and Andrew, with Caroline in the middle, could be seen as coming to Watonwan County in the early 1870s and creating chaos rather than order. Lars and Andrew were now gone. So as long as Caroline remained at Kansas Lake after 1873, she was likely to reap the bitter fallout of blame for that disruption of life and its perceived cohesive social fabric, which took on almost mythical qualities.

Caroline might conceivably have revolted against the social restrictions, however, and taken a more daring path during the late 1870s. After the refusal of her affidavit, she conceivably made the conscious choice to walk away from all that was dear to her, making a clean break from her friends, some of her family, and Andrew. A decision to exorcise the past may have seemed her only avenue toward freedom from narrow moral codes and gender restraints. The fact that she broke all of her ties with people in Watonwan County may indicate the completeness of her breach with that life. Regardless of which path Caroline took (that is, submission to or defiance of the unwritten patriarchal law), the authorities' refusal to consider her affidavit stood as a watershed experience, which could offer her valuable insights into moral problem solving and her own tenuous position as a working-class immigrant woman.

Caroline faced significant moments of truth at Kansas Lake. They contributed to the complexity of her situation, and as Andrew went off to prison and settled into the routine there she had ample time to ponder her plight. She may have been forced out of Watonwan County by the censure of those closest to her, or she might somehow have found the inner strength to strike out on her own and leave Watonwan County behind her. In either case, she was forced to sacrifice much of her family life in departing from Minnesota.[23] In Wisconsin she faced the task of gaining psychological closure to the series of tragic events and rebuilding her own life. The move from Sweden to Minnesota failed. Now in Wisconsin her future was at stake.

Chapter XVI
Veinge Revisited

In the heat of a late summer day in 1882, two teenaged boys stepped off a southbound train in St. James. Traveling bags in hand, they must have stood on the platform and gazed out at the hot, dusty town before them. They were thin and wiry and wore the weary look of those who had traveled vast distances and were not yet certain what kind of place they had arrived at. Their natural reaction was to stop and rest a while. Then the boys could walk the main street, stopping people, and asking questions in broken English. The townspeople must have paused and listened distractedly. They had places to get to and excused themselves and rushed on. After a while, however, someone recognized their accent and answered in Swedish, whereupon the youngsters could explain in detail who they were and what they wanted.

They were eighteen and sixteen years old. They had crossed the Atlantic in June and then traveled cross country from New York City searching for their father. They hardly knew him but had heard much about him as children. Those who understood Swedish listened attentively. Some nodded in recognition and then offered them a ride.

Before day's end, the youngsters Nils Peter and Per August Andersson — Andrew's sons from Veinge — were standing on John and Christine Johnson's doorstep at Kansas Lake.

The boys' sudden appearance was certain to shock their grandparents but also cheer them. There on the vast, open prairie stood two boys who were at once strangers and still John and Christine's own family. In the expectant faces they could see the image of their son who sat behind prison bars. The welcome mat went out immediately, but getting acquainted must have gone slowly, since the one boy had been only a toddler when John and Christine last saw him and the second youth was just born when his grandparents left Sweden.

Of course, the boys asked about their father and life at Kansas Lake. Some bits of news were joyful, others extremely painful. In time John and Christine would have needed to set the boys down and tell them the whole story of the past sixteen years. The discussions must always have drifted back to Andrew. For his sons, the tale was a bitter pill to swallow. Nils Peter and Per August can only have listened incredulously and then asked their grandparents question after endless question until the truth sank in.

The talk did not end with Andrew. John and Christine were surely full of questions of their own. What was the news from Halland? What had happened in Veinge since they left there all those years ago? Who was still alive? And who was dead? What kind of talk made the rounds? Then Nils Peter and Per August had their own tale to tell. The news from those years in Veinge was both good and bad.

Not surprisingly, daily life back home had gone on without the emigrants. The ages-old pattern of rural poverty changed hardly at all. The poor gained little chance of upward mobility, and most of the old injustices remained. In the urban areas of Sweden, full democracy was on its way. The changes came painfully slowly in the countryside, and in the early 1880s they had barely touched the lives of farm workers in the inner districts of Halland. That sobering fact was illustrated by the fate of the families Hogan and Andrew left behind at Veinge in the 1860s. All were still alive, but not all was well with them. Nils Peter and Per August could tell their story, at least up until 1882. After that, news would have to trickle in to Kansas Lake year by year.

At Göstorp, Hogan's wife Hanna Andersdotter eventually left the tenant farm where she and Hogan lived between 1864 and 1866. Hanna and her two daughters moved back to Hanna's parents' home. In 1879 they left the tenant farm itself and took a step even further down to a small crowded *undantag* cottage on the outskirts of the farm, where they were still living when Nils Peter and Per August left Sweden. Through the 1870s and 1880s Hanna was destitute. She managed to survive on menial farm labor and the good graces and donations of neighbors. In 1880 the Veinge Poor Relief Board granted her some grain and six Swedish crowns in cash. That amounted to half support (*halv försörjning*) for her and her family for the whole calendar year. She apparently received no support from Hogan in America. In fact, by 1880 he seems to have broken all ties with Hanna. He commonly referred to himself at Kansas Lake as being divorced. [1]

After her father died in 1866, Hanna lived in an all-female household. With her were her mother, her older sister Svenborg, and her and Hogan's two daughters, Bothilda and Anna Johanna. In 1888 Bothilda married and moved away from home. [2] When Hanna's mother passed away, her household was reduced to four persons. [3] Still, their cottage was terribly cramped. It consisted of only a kitchen, a living room, and one bedroom. Hanna and her family were forced to gather moss, peat, and heather to heat the dwelling, much as the Swedes on the Minnesota prairie used corn stalks and hay to fuel their home fires. The site offered only marginal living at best, but the women persevered.

By the late 1880s the oldest of them was the mentally retarded Svenborg, whom Hanna cared for until Svenborg died of pneumonia in 1892, at the age sixty-six. Then came the next oldest, Hanna herself. Following was Anna Johanna. Though unmarried, she had a daughter of her own, Hulda Josephina, born in 1893. The child's baptismal record identified no father, and the Veinge church pastor at the time labeled her as illegitimate (*oäkta*). [4]

Against the odds, Hanna Andersdotter kept her home intact for over a quarter of a century after Hogan left her. During the years, her daughter Anna Johanna had two other children, for whom no fathers were officially noted. In 1899, she gave birth to a boy, named Bernhard Julius Håkansson, and in 1902 came a second son, Johan Gottfrid Johansson. Bernhard was originally given the last name Benjaminsson, and the accepted wisdom in Veinge was that his father was Benjamin Larsson, the brother of a prominent tradesman in Veinge parish.

Benjamin Larsson was said to have paid Anna Johanna a sum of money in order that he might avoid officially acknowledging his paternity of the child. [5] Anna Johanna was left as a single mother, scraping by on the very barest of incomes.

In contrast to the quiet nurturing and long-suffering bravery of Hanna Andersdotter, Johanna Persdotter chose a less passive course. Johanna was of a nervous disposition. When news from Andrew in America quit arriving in 1873, she began to wonder. By the end of the 1870s, her patience had run out. She took decisive steps to come to terms with the separation from her husband, but that process was drawn out over many more years than she might have expected. Her actions were grounded in an active feeling of dissatisfaction and the need for closure, but in other ways her story bore striking similarities to Hanna Andersdotter's life of patient poverty.

After Andrew left for America, Johanna Persdotter stayed on at Göstorp #6, in one of the small *undantag* cottages. The terms for the sale of Andrew's and his father's Skaftaberget farm in 1867 stipulated that Johanna be awarded the cottage and allowed to remain its owner for life, or until she might be reunited with Andrew. In that cottage she scraped out a living and struggled to raise the couple's two small sons. Like Hanna, she was described in the local church records as destitute. On several occasions after 1873, the Veinge Poor Relief board gave food and clothing to her and the children. In time, changes took place, however. In 1879 Nils Peter, then fifteen, left home to take a job as a farmhand in Skåne. In 1881 Per August, fifteen, moved to Göstorp #4, the same farm where his aunt Hanna lived, and also became a farmhand. [6] The closeness of those two farms allowed Hanna and Johanna to stay in regular contact with each other, but through the years they seem to have known little about Hogan and Andrew in Minnesota.

In the late 1870s Johanna Persdotter began moving back and forth between Göstorp and a neighboring farm named Bölarp. Bölarp was the home of her paternal uncle, Pål Esbjörnsson, who was the signing witness at Johanna's 1862 wedding to Andrew. At that farm, she met Johannes Swensson. He was a tenant farmer whose wife died in 1876, leaving him with four young children. [7] Johanna's increasingly strong relationship with Johannes Swensson led her in 1880 to file a suit against Andrew, fourteen years after he left her and went to America.

The legal proceedings Johanna initiated against Andrew lasted three long years. She first appeared before the civil court in Tjärby, Halland, in February, 1880. There she sat before the Swedish district court magistrates one day and asked for a divorce from Anders Johannesson, whom she could hardly have known by his Americanized name of Andrew Johnson. A simple unlettered farming woman, Johanna surely had a bad case of nerves as she addressed the gathered officials, but by her side sat Pål, her uncle, and Johannes, her prospective new husband. Johanna explained that Andrew gave up on his and his father's farm in 1866. In the spring of that year, he left for America, thereby deserting her, Johanna charged. Her divorce suit failed to add that Andrew left her in the seventh month of Johanna's third pregnancy.

Reluctant to act on the information Johanna filed, since it was considered hastily gathered and incomplete, the Swedish civil court postponed a decision on the divorce suit until the summer of 1880. By that time a committee of Veinge officials, including the local pastor and the chairman of the county council, was to gather complete information and then deliver a more thorough account of events surrounding Andrew's departure from Sweden. Their report came in June of 1880. The committee included five specific points, which stated:

a. that nothing negative could be said about Andrew and Johanna's life together at Veinge between 1862 and 1866;

b. that Andrew bought his father's farm at Skaftaberget but later ran into debt; he then had trouble keeping his affairs in order, and so he went to America to find a better life there;

c. that before he left Sweden he promised to send for his wife and children once he arrived in America, and he later made the same promise in his letters to her from America;

d. that during his first seven years in America, 1866 to 1873, he sent his wife money twice a year for the support of their children;

e. that no information from or about Andrew had reached Veinge during the seven years from 1873 to 1880. [8]

Those details led the Swedish court to decide, first, that Andrew deserted his wife out of "malice and aversion" to her. It declared, second, that Andrew's silence since 1873 indicated he had permanently abandoned Veinge and disappeared for good in America. [9]

As was common under Swedish law in the case of one spouse deserting another, the judge of a higher court in Hök allowed one year (beginning in October, 1881) for Andrew to come back to Halland and resume his marriage with Johanna. At the end of that twelve-month period (during which Andrew, naturally, did not appear), the civil court granted the divorce to Johanna and forwarded the case to the Church of Sweden's bishopric in Göteborg, which gave its approval in 1883.[10]   That action by the ecclesiastical officials made it possible for Johanna, then fifty-two, to marry Johannes Swensson, forty-seven, in September of 1883. [11]   With that marriage Johanna inherited four step-children and became legally free from Andrew after twenty-one years of marriage. He had been in Sweden for only four of those years.

The divorce showed that Andrew dealt in good faith with Johanna during the first years of his absence. Whether he neglected (or could not afford) to assure the passage to America for her and the children or whether Johanna refused to leave Sweden and join him in Minnesota was left unsaid. It is not certain if the Swedish court's phrasing "malice and aversion" reflected an underlying dissatisfaction on the part of Andrew toward his wife in Veinge. If so, the cause of those feelings was not specified. Very likely, the words malice and aversion were only formalized legal terms used to facilitate the divorce proceedings.

At Kansas Lake, of course, Andrew had shown clear signs of aversion toward Lars, but in his dealings with other people impulsive acts, rather than malicious ones, were more characteristic of him. Johanna's divorce suit implied that in 1866 Andrew, only in his mid-twenties, had grown restless in his farm routine at Göstorp. Then came the financial collapse. Suddenly he made the decision to leave for America. That move could be seen as one of great personal initiative, even intelligent foresight. Or it may have illustrated Andrew's rash tendency to run from problems once they grew especially severe, just as he did in 1873 when he moved from Kansas Lake to Omaha. Difficulties in "keeping his affairs in order," as the Veinge committee described his situation in 1866, plagued Andrew on both sides of the Atlantic. Either way, he left Johanna, in the divorce papers' words, "against her will." [12]   That Johanna chose to remain at Göstorp in her destitute situation later on in the 1870s, and not join Andrew in America, was a less easily explained decision on her part. As in so many other cases, the Atlantic Ocean once more had done its work as the great divider of families.

The Johnsons at Kansas Lake ceased upholding contact with their families and friends in Veinge after 1873, in all likelihood because of their shame at Andrew's conviction and their preoccupation with the grasshopper plagues. In the early 1880s no one in Halland knew that Andrew was in prison for murder or that he had married Caroline and committed bigamy. If known to the civil and church officials in Sweden, either piece of information would have made Johanna's divorce suit a much shorter affair than it turned out to be, since nineteenth-century Swedish law stipulated that long-term prison sentences and adultery were grounds for granting uncontested and immediate divorce.[13]   The letters and money from Andrew to Johanna simply stopped coming after 1873, for reasons that would have seemed more fiction than fact to the parishioners back home in Veinge. If the full story had been known, the news would have spread like wildfire in the home districts of Halland.

That news was not forthcoming, however, and so Johanna asked the Swedish authorities for permission to remarry, explaining that she and Johannes Swensson together would be better able to support her and Andrew's two sons.[14] That support turned out to be unnecessary. Fifteen months before their mother remarried, Nils Peter and Per August took matters into their own hands. By 1882 the boys had already left Göstorp to work on their own. Now they were ready to try a new move. They decided to try their luck in the New World. As children, the boys had surely asked about their father hundreds of times, but they were eager to know more. Only in America could they find out about him. Johanna sold her *undantag* rights at Göstorp when she moved to Bölarp and doubtless used part of the money from the sale to pay for her sons' passage to America.

And so the adolescent wanderers set off on a quest to find their father. All they had to guide them was a few old letters with an address showing the names of strange places: Watonwan County, St. James, and Minnesota. Both boys left for New York from the port of Göteborg in June of 1882.[15]   From New York they journeyed far into the heart of America until they arrived in St. James and found their grandparents.

Thus it was Nils Peter and Per August who first relayed information on the family in Minnesota back to the folks in Halland, after nearly ten years of silence on the Kansas Lake front. The concrete evidence to prove that was slim, but irrefutable. In July of 1892, nine years after his wife in Sweden re-married, Andrew received two letters from Johanna and Johannes Swensson.[16] The couple surely corresponded with Andrew throughout the ten-year period leading up to 1892, sending words of encouragement and good cheer, trying to make Andrew's life at Stillwater as tolerable as possible.

Chapter XVII
In a New World

The arrival of his sons in Minnesota was the first ray of hope in Andrew's life since 1876. After 1882 the branches of the family, which the ocean had sundered, began reuniting. When their initial shock wore off, the boys visited Andrew at Stillwater. There Per August set eyes on his father for the first time. Nils Peter, who had not seen Andrew since the age of two, also saw him with fresh eyes, of course. Before them sat a middle-aged man dressed in prison garb and marked by the years. The three talked and then the sons returned to southern Minnesota.

Nils Peter stayed for a while in Watonwan County and showed the same energy as Andrew had in his youth. In 1883 he moved to Stillwater and went to work. In that city he met a Swedish girl named Augusta Johnson. In May of 1884, Nils Peter and Augusta returned to Watonwan County. Reverend P. J. Eckman married them at the Kansas Lake church in what can only have been a festive occasion for John and Christine Johnson. Neighbors attended the ceremony and a Scandinavian couple, who lived just down the road from Nils Peter's grandparents were signing witnesses at the wedding.

Augusta was seven months pregnant at the wedding. In that sense, the young couple followed the Old Country custom of marrying as a result of a pregnancy, just as Andrew and Hogan had done in Sweden in the early 1860s. There were complications, however. Augusta gave birth to a son on July 21, 1884, even though there were doubts that Nils Peter was the child's father. Under Swedish law (and by Swedish custom) a man who discovered his fiancée was pregnant by another man had full legal grounds to break off an engagement or to be freed from promises of marriage. Nils Peter chose to overlook that situation and went ahead with the decision to marry, temporarily overcoming his doubts and reasoning perhaps that he was now in America with a new set of values. Nonetheless doubts remained in his mind.[1]

By the time they were twenty-one in 1885, Nils Peter and Augusta were settled as farmers in Sveadahl, just twelve miles north of Kansas Lake and only four doors away from Pastor P. J. Eckman's parsonage.[2] In that way Nils Peter, the lowly farmhand from southern Sweden, was transformed into a married and independent farmer in Minnesota, at least as far as outward appearances were concerned. Things went differently for Per August. He remained single and moved to Mankato in the mid-1880s, where he went to work as a manual laborer.

As a married man, Nils Peter found his obligations increasing rapidly. He continued farming in Sveadahl through 1885, but making a living at it proved difficult. In truth, the chance to move to Sveadahl was an emergency measure, which came in the nick of time to save him and his wife from sliding into poverty. With no financial resources and an infant son, Nils Peter and Augusta were badly in need of a start. The East Sveadahl congregation had a tenant farm near the church, and Nils Peter and his wife got settled there. Through the years the plot had been operated by a variety of newly arrived immigrants as a place to get their feet on the ground. The farm consisted of a tiny house and a few buildings. The soil was sandy and only marginally productive, giving small harvests of wheat and flax. It was, in fact, a Swedish-American replica of the type of tenant farm (*torp*) Hogan had worked in Halland in the 1860s.[3]

Nils Peter farmed while his wife kept house. P. J. Eckman baptized their son in the church at Kansas Lake, even though Nils Peter still had trouble coping with the possibility that he was not the birth father. In time, Nils Peter's financial prospects at Sveadahl began to seem little better than those of an ordinary embattled tenant farmer in the Sweden he had just fled from. Here he had food for thought. How independent was he in reality?

By late 1885 the young couple had itching feet. Looking to improve their lot, they eventually relocated to east-central Minnesota. In 1890 they came to Pine County, settling in the emerging village of Sandstone.[4] Augusta's sister was married to a stonecutter in Sandstone, and he helped Nils Peter get a job.[5] There the youngster found the great occupational passion of his life, stonecutting. Backed by large-scale investors in Minneapolis and St. Paul, developers in Pine County were beginning to exploit extensive deposits of St. Croix sandstone on the banks of the Kettle River. As a quarry center, Sandstone was incorporated in the late 1880s and became a thriving community by 1894. Hundreds of stone workers, attracted by abundant jobs and good wages, swelled the population.[6] In his mid-twenties Nils Peter joined a Sandstone labor union. Aside from a stint in St. Paul in 1900-1903, he and Augusta stayed in Pine County for eighteen years.[7]

In that politically conscious setting, they took part in and observed some of the historic events of Minnesota history. First was the labor movement. Working in the quarries offered advantages. In contrast to the conservative farming settlements of the prairies, Pine County had an organized industrial work force that pressed for on-the-job benefits and argued for egalitarianism. The hometown newspaper, the Sandstone Courier, regularly featured articles on the rewards of socialism, a sentiment that the local clergy often supported, both in the columns of the daily press and from their pulpits.

Nils Peter came to see stonecutting as an art. Through the years, however, his dedication to this work was countered by the questionable working conditions he was exposed to. The Sandstone quarries were hardly safe artists' studios. The labor was intense and hazardous. Men cut the stone with chisels and wooden mallets and transported the heavy stone blocks to the nearest railway line by the clumsy means of slow-moving ox teams. Accidents were common. Though young and strong, the men wilted quickly under the press of heavy labor. An added danger was the risk of respiratory diseases from inhaling the stone cuttings and dust from the drilling process.[8] The cloth face-masks the workers wore did nothing to stop the fine particles from entering their lungs. Nils Peter was not immune to those dangers.

His and Augusta's first years in Sandstone must have passed quickly, but there was trauma to come in the form of another of the many historic natural blights the Johnson family experienced. On September 1, 1894, they lived through the disastrous Hinckley firestorm. The largest conflagration in nineteenth-century Minnesota, the fire resulted from unusual heat and dry conditions across the state, which had built up during the summer and then led to the sudden fire. High winds, a temperature inversion, and low humidity spread the flames. The storm spread over 480 square miles, killing more than 400 people and burning six towns to the ground.[9] Many of the survivors in Sandstone escaped by train. One train packed with those fleeing the fire crossed the high railroad bridge out of Sandstone as the supporting girders collapsed behind the last of the cars. Others escaped on a Duluth-bound train that returned to Sandstone and picked up fleeing townspeople. Most of those who stayed behind in Sandstone perished, but some were lucky enough to find refuge in the Kettle River.[10]

Nils Peter's family was among those who took to the water. As the flames hit the town, Augusta gathered up her children and ran down to the riverfront. She led the children into the water and held them under for hours on end, allowing them to come up only for short gasps of air. The worst of the blaze passed in four hours. Still frightened, Augusta and the children waited in the water for a whole day and night until the danger was fully over. After that, they returned to the destroyed townsite to rebuild their home and start life over again. In addition to their house, they lost personal possessions and family momentos.[11]

Despite the hazards, Nils Peter and Augusta found their place in the sun in Pine County in the 1890s. (Figure 21) Life in Sandstone offered a workingman's environment that provided a sense of social comfort and solidarity. Ethnic diversity was alive and well in the quarry work crews. In addition to the other European groups in the area, the Johnsons lived among numerous Norwegian and Swedish workers' families. In nearby Askov a large concentration of Danish Americans added further spice to the ethnic mixing.[12]

At the same general time as Andrew's sons came to Kansas Lake and then left the area for Mankato and Sandstone, his sister Petronella rejoined the family picture in Watonwan County. She took the roundabout way. Petronella moved to Minneapolis sometime in the early 1880s. In the city she first found work as a domestic and later as a housekeeper at the Augustana Home, a residence for Swedish immigrant women and children. In 1883 Petronella married a Swedish-born man named John Olson. In the spring of 1890 the couple moved to Watonwan County and settled at Petronella's parents' farm so that she could care for them, as they retired from active farm life.[13]

Living with Petronella and John Olson in 1895 was an eleven-year-old boy called Aaron Olson. He made his home with them until the end of the 1890s.[14] Many in the neighborhood must have believed he was John and Petronella's son, but he was in fact the child born to Nils Peter and Augusta in 1884. They named him Aaron Reuben. Not having a child of their own and seeing Nils Peter's discomfort with the son he suspected was not his, Petronella and John Olson fostered her nephew's first-born as a gesture of family solidarity.

As the Kansas Lake Johnsons drew closer together again through the 1880s, Andrew was not forgotten. Yet he still had no prospects of release. As the 1890s got underway, he started nearing the end of his second decade at Stillwater. Behind prison walls in 1891, he marked his fiftieth birthday. Andrew occasionally got letters from his family. In 1892 two letters arrived from his sister. He also received two letters from John Olson.[15] Surely Petronella and her husband wrote to tell Andrew about his parents' state of health.

Visits to Andrew were apparently few and far between. Caroline saw him at Stillwater in 1876 and his sons in the 1880s. Otherwise only a single visit to the prison by a Watonwan County acquaintance of Andrew, other than his family, is known. In 1887 George P. Johnston of St. James visited the prison as one of a party of Minnesota legislators. The ubiquitous Johnston accompanied the group since he served at the time as a committee clerk in the Minnesota state legislature.

At the prison Johnston spoke briefly with and received a gift from Cole Younger. There the outspoken court clerk explained that he had a place in Minnesota history. Following their notorious and ill-fated raid in Northfield, Minnesota, in 1876, the Younger brothers were apprehended near Madelia by a posse of seven men under the leadership of W. W. Murphy, who presided over Andrew and Caroline's Madelia hearing in 1873, and James Glispin, the Watonwan sheriff, who delivered Andrew to Stillwater in 1874. Though George P. Johnston boasted to Cole Younger and prison officials in 1887 that he was one of Younger's captors, he served in reality only in a peripheral role. Johnston was a temporary deputy, who stood timidly in the background with other deputies and held the horses of the seven law officers who made the capture. Johnston's need for attention was clearly so great that it prevented him from telling the whole truth. Unfortunately, Johnston left no record whether he saw Andrew at the prison during that visit.[16]   The most likely assumption is that he did not see him there and that Andrew spent his time on that occasion, as he did year after year in Stillwater, locked away from the outside world in his cell block or busy at his post in the prison carpentry shop.

Chapter XVIII
Facing Freedom

Life at Stillwater dragged on at its dreary pace. The numbing routine had changed little since Andrew arrived there in 1874, and hope was scarce. His family stood by him in spirit, but there was little else they could do. His life sentence seemed as irreversible as ever. Then in 1892, just when everything seemed lost, hope appeared miraculously on the horizon. By the end of that year, dealings for Andrew's release were in the works. The developments were three-pronged and by the standards of Stillwater prison they happened with lightning speed. First, during the course of 1892, George P. Johnston circulated a petition for Andrew's release. All the previous attempts at petitioning had failed, but this time — defying all the odds — a large number of people signed it. Then a change took place in the Stillwater prison administration that spoke of more humane practices. Finally, a radical shift occurred in the prison population.

Those three points came together fortuitously. The petition led the way. Later on The St. James Journal (January 3, 1893) reported on it in the most detail:

> *Several unsuccessful attempts have been made heretofore*
> *to secure a pardon [for Andrew], and petitions have been*
> *circulated at various times to that end, and the last effort*

> *proved successful. A resident of St. James who lived near*
> *Johnson's at the time of the murder, on being questioned in*
> *regard to the crime and pardon, said: 'The crime was a brutal*
> *one, and no one thoroughly acquainted with its details would*
> *sign a petition for his pardon. New people have come in [to the*
> *county] however, and many of them have done so.' George P.*
> *Johnston was, we believe, mainly instrumental in securing his*
> *pardon.*[1]

The St. James Plaindealer also reported on the matter. It stated (January 5, 1893) that Andrew was a "life-termer; but his record in the prison being up to the highest mark, and other extenuating circumstances being considered" Governor Merriam commuted his sentence.

George P. Johnston's role in the petition was interesting. The son of a Madelia carpenter and agriculturist and himself a highly visible member of the St. James community in the 1880s, Johnston served for nearly twenty years (1875-1895) as the clerk of district court in Watonwan County, under the judgeship of M. J. Severance. Through the years Johnston worked assiduously for Andrew's cause. In addition to sponsoring the pardon petition, he had contacts with judges and penal authorities across Minnesota. The guiding hand of M. J. Severance was discernible behind Johnston's work. Though Severance had come to be one of the most influential men in southern Minnesota, he kept his interest in ordinary people alive.[2] As a judge, Severance officially needed to stay impartial in Andrew's case, but he could urge or instruct Johnston to manage Andrew's case from his base in St. James.

The shift in Stillwater's central administration took place when Henry Wolfer took the reins at the beginning of the 1890s. In large part Andrew owed his eventual freedom to Wolfer and the warden's faith in deserving individuals. Wolfer had well-thought-out views on penology, which were of an individualist but understanding sort. In Wolfer's mind, all inmates were on an equal footing in the prison setting and had the responsibility of answering for their own progress. Each convict was "a free, moral agent" who was to be given helpful encouragement to work out his own salvation along the lines of least resistance. If he chose to make war on society, the convict was also destroying himself.[3]

While penitentiary life in Wolfer's time remained anchored in the slower daily pace of earlier nineteenth-century society, the prison also operated in an era of rapid social change and ethnic mixing. Wolfer succeeded in introducing a humanistic spirit into that challenging environment. Among other reforms, he campaigned at the Governor's office for the commutation of long-term sentences to improve human rights for inmates. The result was that Governor William A. Merriam (served 1889-1893) agreed to grant conditional pardons to deserving men. Through the years, Wolfer had continued observing Andrew's positive habits and good behavior, and in 1892 the warden included Andrew among those prisoners he recommended for release.

Neither the petition nor the warden's efforts would have guaranteed success had prison overcrowding not entered the picture. It was the final and decisive factor. The State of Minnesota reported in 1894 that the Stillwater inmate population grew from 329 to 502 between 1892 and 1894, largely because Federal courts outside of Minnesota sent 108 prisoners to Stillwater during that time. In 1892 and 1893 Governor Merriam considered Henry Wolfer's recommendations and pardoned thirteen long-term inmates, clearly in an effort to relieve crowded cellhouse conditions. Those thirteen included Andrew.[4] In the end, the Governor officially commuted Andrew's sentence to twenty-one years.

By January of 1893, Andrew was a free man again. No one in authority expressed any opinion on either the right or wrong of his conviction in 1874. He had served his time with admirable conduct. Now practical concerns dictated changes and Andrew was released to make way for them. He was discharged on December 31, 1892, after serving eighteen years, seven months, and seventeen days.[5] The prison books explained that he was "discharged January 1, 1893, upon expiration of sentence, 21 years." They added that he was "released from custody Dec. 31, 1892, Jan. 1 being a legal holiday."[6] Andrew received over two years' credit for good conduct. In January of 1893, he was fifty-one years old. He had spent fully one-third of his life behind prison bars.

During those last days at Stillwater, Andrew's excitement must have been mixed with apprehension. Prison life was now a safe routine, but freedom beckoned irresistibly. George P. Johnston had long been busy on his behalf. Johnston's efforts included a December, 1892, visit to the capital in St. Paul, where he worked to help facilitate

Andrew's release. Still, Johnston's name appeared only twice in the Stillwater books. The first time was in the prison Correspondence Register for 1892, which showed he wrote to Andrew seven times during that calendar year, the last time only eight days before the prisoner's release. Officials noted only that the letters dealt with "business." Likewise, Johnston wrote letters to Andrew on his parents' behalf. Also received at the prison during 1892 were two "business" letters to Andrew from "Emil [M. J.] Severance" of Mankato.[7] It was not clear if Andrew learned to read during his time in prison or had others read the letters to him. The prison had a literacy school, which he may have attended.[8] Regardless of who read the letters, there was much in them to prepare Andrew for the outside world. He had ample time to look ahead to a new beginning.

Stillwater officials gave all prisoners being released $25.00 in cash and had them measured and fitted for a new suit of civilian clothes in the prison tailor shop. That included underwear and an overcoat for winter use.[9] Andrew would have stood in just such a suit of clothing as the gates of Stillwater prison swung open for him. On the last day of 1892, he walked out of Stillwater and breathed in the fresh air, his prison days behind him forever. He had reasons for joy, but the elements did not treat him kindly. Local newspapers reported temperatures well below zero in those early January days, as he began re-accustoming himself to liberty.[10]

The only hint about Andrew's journey away from Stillwater came in the second reference to George P. Johnston in the prison records. On January 6, 1893, Henry Wolfer wrote to Johnston in St. James. Wolfer thanked him for a letter, now lost but dated two days earlier, informing the warden that Andrew had arrived home. Wolfer added:

> *Glad to hear that Andrew Johnson arrived home safely.*
> *I sent his [carpenter's] tools next day after he left, and*
> *they are doubtless there by this time. I am glad that*
> *Andrew is out. I considered him one of the most deserving*
> *that has left this institution since I have been connected with*
> *it, and I feel that executive clemency in his behalf has been*
> *very wisely given.*[11]

By "home" Wolfer meant the St. James area. A cheerful group surely met Andrew. They would have presented an interesting sight. There were George P. Johnston, the self-important clerk of court; Andrew's two aging parents, one sick and nearly blind; Petronella and

John Olson; Andrew's increasingly Americanized sons Nels Peter and August Johnson, as they now called themselves; with Andrew himself, squirming in his unaccustomed and perhaps ill-fitting prison-made clothes. Their first stop was at his parents' farm, where Andrew began re-acquainting himself with John and Christine Johnson, seeing the world anew, and revisiting the old farmsteads at Kansas Lake. The family had reason for tears after two decades of separation.

Andrew's return had its ironic and sad side, however. Barely two weeks after he came home, his and Caroline's nineteen-year-old daughter Christine, who was only an infant when he went to prison in 1874, was married in a quiet ceremony in Wisconsin. Her husband was a Norwegian-American youth.[12] (Figure 16) Both before and after she married, Christine went on living, as she had done since childhood, with the mistaken idea that her father Andrew had been dead since 1873. He remained equally as unaware of his daughter's status in life. Andrew apparently learned nothing whatever about where she resided, how she lived, or when she got married.

Chapter XIX
Caroline in Wisconsin: Reinventing Her History

The sad fact that Andrew and his daughter Christine failed to learn about each other's life history, and that he did not attend her wedding, was traceable back to Caroline's actions in the 1870s and 1880s. Caroline returned to Wisconsin from Kansas Lake less than ten years after she left Madison in 1868, but those short years in Minnesota had caused her enormous trauma. As the 1870s drew to a close, there were troublesome inroads on her psyche that she needed desperately to come to terms with, or even try to erase. When she left Watonwan County, she knew exactly where she was going — and what she wanted to forget. Her sister Anna Maria and husband Adam Peter Jonasson were still living in Madison, where Adam Peter worked as a farm manager. In contrast to the diminutive Lars Johnson, Adam Peter was known in America as "Big Swede" and had the reputation of being hardworking, decisive, and responsible. Caroline steered her course back to them.

With Anna Maria and Adam Peter in Madison, Caroline found a safe haven from Kansas Lake and moved in at their home on the southwest shore of Lake Monona. It is not certain just when she came to Wisconsin, but she possibly arrived there in the first months of 1877. There were reports that Adam Peter and Anna Maria moved their family from Madison to Pulaski County, Missouri, in the fall of 1877, as the urging of his brothers, who had gone to Missouri the year before and settled near the village of Swedeborg.[1] If that was true, Caroline and her sister lived together in Wisconsin just a short time before the Jonasson family moved on.

Only one consideration complicates the notion that Caroline was in Madison by 1877. The existence of Stillwater prison records showing that Andrew had money forwarded to Caroline in 1878 may mean that she was still in Minnesota at that time or that Andrew and Caroline maintained contact with each other, even if indirectly, for a while after she arrived in Wisconsin. Whatever the sequence of events, Caroline and her two children at last became ensconced in Madison. Once again she honed in on an environment featuring a combination of freshwater lake and farmland similar to the Djupviken of her youth. At the end of the 1870s, she found work as a domestic servant in the home of Nathaniel Dean, a prominent Madison dairy farmer, merchant, and legislator.

Sometime before 1881 she formed a liaison with Gilbert Tingom, a Norwegian American. Caroline and Gilbert Tingom met in Madison, and they soon began living together, after which she took his last name. Soon the couple turned to small-scale farming. From the beginning, Caroline shared some information with Tingom about Annie and Isabel and where they were in Minnesota. That fact indicated that she also surely gave him at least a few details about Lars and Andrew, the fathers of her four children.

Gilbert Tingom was of common qualities. Born in Norway in 1845, he arrived in America in 1862. He was three years younger than Caroline and was handicapped by hemiplegia. The malady first occurred when he was only sixteen. Afterwards Tingom was lame in his right side and walked with a crutch. Because of those physical problems, he was no more energetic than Lars had been, despite his relative youth. Like Lars before him, he demanded that Caroline do the physical labor on their farm. The couple seemed to have little in common, except for their rural backgrounds and their dialects. His Norwegian matched up well with her western Swedish accent. Even if theirs was seemingly not a match made in heaven, Caroline and Gilbert both had needs the other could fulfill. If she wished a man to allay her single status and give her an aura of respectability in her new home, he in turn needed an able-bodied helpmate. Thus they struck a bargain that aided them both.[2]

In the early years they were together, Caroline and Tingom lived on her four acres in Madison, where they ran a truck farm and grew some tobacco. Around 1890 they moved to Token Creek, in Burke township, outside of Madison, and then purchased other parcels of land in Dane County.[3] In the years when John Albert and Christine were growing to adolescence, Caroline had three sons with Tingom. The first and third boys were born in 1881 and 1888. In between came their second son, born in 1884 and named Andrew after Caroline's father Anders Nilsson and Andrew Johnson. With the coming of children, Caroline and Tingom completed the customary secular marriage arrangement of their homelands, but they never went through with a church ceremony.

The new life Caroline made for herself in Wisconsin extended beyond her physical circumstances. She also recreated (or thoroughly revised) her Minnesota past. Her new acquaintances and family in Dane County learned from Caroline a version of her life from 1868 to 1876 that the people of Watonwan County would have recognized in only the dimmest of outlines, if at all. Lars Johnson, she reported to various people at different times, had died in an accident in Minnesota or passed away during the Atlantic crossing of 1868.[4] Caroline recounted that she next met Andrew Johnson, who either was killed or died of a heart attack in 1873 when John Albert was two and before Christine was born. Another version she gave of Andrew's fate held that he left Caroline in 1873 and was never heard from again. She explained that the family first lived with Andrew on a farm outside of Mankato, before they were forced to move in to Mankato itself after they lost crops to grasshoppers several years in a row. She said it was in Mankato that Andrew first went to work on the railroad.[5]

To people in Wisconsin, Caroline explained that Andrew had fathered two of her children in Minnesota, John Albert and Christine. About Annie and Isabel she said only that she left them in Mankato, where a jeweler's family had taken them in. In that instance, she surely was referring to Charles Otto, the jeweler and justice of the peace who in reality had married her and Andrew at the Mankato jail.[6]

However, no evidence showed that Otto ever had custody of the two girls.

In effect Caroline whitewashed her Minnesota past. She did so with good reason, if she wished a better life in Wisconsin. Her one attempt, with the affidavit of 1876, to clarify the events of the past few years was likely a great expression of love for Andrew as well as a conscience clearing act on her part. Yet that cost her dearly and may even have helped force her out of Watonwan County. The bitter consequences of that act in Minnesota offered her little incentive to repeat the same story in Wisconsin. In her "revised" version, all the events of the previous eight years had taken place in or around Mankato. Watonwan County was excluded entirely from her story. The move to Kansas Lake, the domestic turmoil (including Lars's spousal abuse and her own possible adultery), Lars's violent death, the harsh winter of 1872-1873, Caroline's leaving her two daughters behind with Hogan and the interlude in Omaha with Andrew, Caroline's own arrest and temporary incarceration in Mankato, her jailhouse wedding and later escape from the county sheriff's home, Andrew's trial, his murder conviction, her own confession of guilt in 1876, her life at Andrew's parents' farm, and the neighbors she knew all disappeared, in her retelling, into the mists of the past.

While she lived in Wisconsin, Caroline expunged, or tried to expunge, the trauma of her years in Minnesota. Yet at the very heart of her emotional life lay an intense but profoundly sad love story between her and Andrew. The fact that she was willing to exchange wedding vows with him under such unusual circumstances was an illustration of their deeply felt relationship. In between Caroline's turbulent experience with Lars and the colorless qualities of her time with Tingom came her passionate romance with Andrew. In the long run, however, those strong feelings of love for Andrew had to be denied, at least publicly.

The idea that Caroline could have returned to live in Madison without unburdening more of her past to her sister was unusual. Regardless of what Caroline neglected to tell Anna Maria about Lars and Andrew, she could not write off her two daughters by Lars, since Anna Maria knew of both girls. Annie and Isabel were still in Mankato, Caroline said, and could be brought to Wisconsin. Gilbert Tingom doubtless resented the girls' existence. Nevertheless he promised to travel to Minnesota himself and bring the girls back, but it was a promise he never fulfilled.[7] In the end, it was Tingom and Caroline together who failed to return Annie and Isabel to their mother and their brother and half-sister. All the outward evidence indicated that Caroline lived out her life in silence about Kansas Lake and without ever making any attempt to find her daughters or even to tell people in Wisconsin the truth of their whereabouts. Most likely, she feared that if the daughters came to her home in Wisconsin they would tell people in Wisconsin the truth of her Minnesota past and reveal the secrets she guarded so diligently. In Dane County, Caroline was respected as a wife and mother. She tended to her farmland and let the outside world go by.

So during the years after 1876 when Andrew went on with life in Minnesota state prison, Caroline assumed a different guise in Wisconsin. She joined a church, raised five children, and managed to earn a living from her farm, an ambition that had failed for her in Watonwan County. Her new life after 1876 brought her what she came to America to achieve, that is, financial security. Yet those years of outward respectability constituted only a fragment of her life story. Her mindset was also important, and the fabric of her thought processes started building bit by bit over many years preceding her Wisconsin experience.

Caroline's origins in Sweden were important to her mental history. From her father's bad example she learned the positive traits of valuing money and the proper care of a farm. Anders Nilsson's other qualities impacted Caroline more negatively. It would have been consistent with her father's character if he placed the burden of running the household on his children. It would also have been part of a pattern if Caroline married Lars partly in hopes of escaping the difficulties of life with her father, just as she later found Gilbert Tingom in Madison when she sought refuge from her troubles in Minnesota. She seems to have been attracted to men with habits similar to (or even worse than) her father's. Andrew was surely the first man who showed an interest in Caroline for her own qualities and could view her relationship with Lars — and her father — as unfair to her. Yet even in Andrew Caroline found a man whose situation was destined to bring her discontentment and place her in a desperate position.

Before 1868 Caroline could not have imagined the trauma to come in Minnesota. When it came, her response was to prevaricate. Very likely she found herself feeling alone and scared in 1874 and let the exigencies of the moment and her need to protect her children dictate her story to the district court. In short, fear, confusion, and a strong drive for self-preservation could account for her mindset in the early 1870s.

Caroline may have been a fabulist or practiced storyteller. Early in life she could have discovered she might "get away with" her more outlandish actions by denying their reality, much as her father likely did. Therefore she described her actions in a way that made her morally acceptable to others. Seen in that light, she would have been able to repent of her misdeeds or transgressions, but only to meet social needs. Caroline could assure her loved ones in Wisconsin that Annie and Isabel were safe in Minnesota, while she described a foster home for them there that did not exist. Likewise, she could admit that Lars and Andrew had indeed existed but that they merely "went away" or "left" at some unspecified point in time. With the years, that time receded into the increasingly distant past, which made it easier to bear the painful memory of it or to live in denial of it. Thus she created a history for herself that fit a chronological scheme but omitted events she perceived as a challenge to her social acceptance and respectability. In the long run, unfortunately, that tendency could pose as many problems as it enabled her to avoid.

In Watonwan County Caroline had had every reason to feel herself a victim of circumstances, which converged on her in a sequence she had no capacity to foresee or control. What followed was her sensation of being caught in a wildly spinning vortex, from which the only escape seemed to be the invention of new accounts of her life in the 1860s and 1870s. Her many conflicting stories about some events and her revised personal history spoke clearly of a primitive survival response that led her to dissemble. Keeping silent about Watonwan County created for her a sense of psychic space from the trauma at Kansas Lake.[8] Surely she felt it was her only choice in seeking a path toward respect in the eyes of the Wisconsin community and her newly acquired friends there. By dissembling, she was able to work and live respectably in Dane County without running the risk of being judged because of her questionable past in Minnesota.

Caroline would not have been human had she not at times wondered about the last years of her father's life, the way Andrew's years in prison turned out, or the well-being of Annie and Isabel. It could not have been other than clear to her that she salvaged some parts of her family at the expense of others. She had reason to remind herself of the extent to which she was the cause of Andrew's and her two daughters' abandonment to their fates — or at least to ask where her responsibility in that respect began and ended. If she found an answer to that question, she failed to share it with others.

For much of her life, Caroline lived in several different physical worlds, which became mutually exclusive, blocked off, as it were, from one another. In the early years of her immigration, she lived her life in Minnesota and Wisconsin in an environment that was largely cut off from mainstream Sweden and America alike. Then came the division between her two lives in Minnesota and Wisconsin. In Dane County, Caroline exhibited an apparent ability to compartmentalize her life in Minnesota into a separate mental file, which was never opened publicly after 1876. She could not possibly have forgotten people at Kansas Lake such as Andrew's parents, Peter and Catherine Olson, or Charles Johnson, but she kept them in a secret part of her consciousness, which could come forward only in her solitary reflections. Then came the violence of Lars's death and the dramatic events following it. The task of living with that past and processing it psychologically, while also keeping it secret, was guaranteed to place an enormous strain on Caroline's mental resources. At times her sense of place must have reached nearly schizophrenic proportions.

At the same time that Caroline had a psychological foot in two different states, she was also anchored in three different families. Remaining in Watonwan County after 1876 were her two daughters by Lars. With Caroline in the move to Wisconsin went John Albert and Christine, whom she claimed as Andrew's. Finally were the three sons with Gilbert Tingom. Here Caroline faced another choice. Despite the fact that all three of those families were her own flesh and blood, she could choose to keep the individual sibling groups as separate, or only minimally connected, parts of her mental existence. In that case she kept them apart from one another physically as well. Conversely, Caroline might also choose to reveal and share each individual family group's whereabouts and life history with the other groups. If she followed that latter path, Caroline disclosed the information so vaguely or obliquely that those she told it to never understood her message. By all indications she chose the former of the two paths. Its long-term effects were less than happy.

If studied up close, the photograph Caroline had taken of herself in Madison in 1868 showed a woman with intelligence in her eyes, a sensuous quality about her lips, and a strong chin. She looked straight out from that photo, young and dressed in her best clothes. The stopover in Madison was a respite. The poverty of Sweden was behind her, the arduous ocean voyage accomplished, and the nightmare at Kansas Lake yet to happen. The photograph showed the face of a survivor. (Figure 17)

But a survivor at what cost? The task of living with her past and processing it psychologically, while also keeping it secret, was guaranteed to place an enormous strain on Caroline's mental resources. Though she resided in one place in Wisconsin, her mental life there was one of multiple realities, which had to be kept separate from one another. Potentially the situation was laden with anguish. Publicly she kept Andrew's memory alive only by claiming him as the father of John Albert and Christine. Later in life, John Albert followed his mother's description of events in her life and traveled to Minnesota to find his lost sisters and traces of Andrew, but he got no farther than Mankato. He searched there in vain, of course. It was the wrong city in the wrong county.[9] That Caroline lied to her own son, who was seeking the truth, defied common sensibility, but her dissemblance pointed, once again, to the depth of shame and regret she carried about her life in Minnesota. In more than one instance, she sacrificed the psychic well-being of her closest loved ones in order to maintain her own respectability in the community.

With the events of 1872, a process of inner conflict and psychic splintering, which had already begun in Caroline's mind before Lars's death, was set in full motion. Caroline's inability to bring clarity to the happenings of November 8 and repair her own divided consciousness exacerbated the damage. As a result, she cannot have escaped living out her life in Wisconsin as a lonely woman, separated — at the deepest psychological level — from most all that was dearest to her. It never became clear just what Caroline Andersdotter Nilsson Johannesson Holm Johnson Tingom's feelings were. Those feelings may have been as many as the names she bore. She lived on in Wisconsin year after year with closely guarded, unuttered secrets. Those secrets prevented John Albert from finding his long lost sisters. They also kept Christine from meeting her biological father Andrew or even knowing that he was alive and so close nearby that he could have attended her wedding in 1893, thus reuniting her family.

Chapter XX
Returning Home

In 1893 Andrew returned to Kansas Lake after nearly twenty years away. At first glance things must have appeared unchanged to him. The landscape stretched off to the horizon in all directions. Coming from St. James and looking across from the northeast end of the lake, he could spy the opposite shoreline, beyond which all the Johnsons lived. There was the creek where Lars's body floated ashore in 1873, and beyond the bank were the earthen rises into which the Swedes had built their first dwellings, in the lee of the incessant wind. Missing, however, was Caroline. Whether she had been forced out by Andrew's parents or by the weight of public opinion or had chosen to leave of her own accord, the Swedish settlement bore no traces of her any longer, except for the continued presence of Annie and Isabel in South Branch township.

In 1893 Andrew might stand at the old familiar Kansas Lake spots and think back on what happened to all of them there, so long ago. In that frame of mind, he could easily remember the farm life he had known in the 1870s. The Swede Alexander Swanson, a Watonwan farmer of that bygone era, later gave an idea of the kinds of memories

Andrew would have had. Swanson remembered how farmers lived on the Kansas Lake prairie in those early days:

> *They had homesteads but there were no houses, no stables,*
> *no [farm]fields, no groves, no roads, no churches, no school*
> *houses, and no money, or at least very, very little of it. He was*
> *rich who had a team of oxen, a cow, a hog, a wagon, and a*
> *breaking plow and no debts.*[1]

Sharing was both common and necessary.[2] Alexander Swanson recalled:

> *Neighbors would willingly lend to each other not only*
> *agricultural implements and household goods but articles*
> *of food as well. Thus, flour was such an article to be*
> *borrowed and loaned, giving occasion to the saying that*
> *each family has its own household, but the flour is common.*[3]

Thinking back on those habits, Andrew could recall his own fateful trip to Charles Johnson's for a bag of flour over two decades earlier and reflect on how something so ordinary had radically changed his life forever.

Alexander Swanson remembered that work on the prairie was everlasting. The children tended the cattle "day in day out, Sundays and week days, in cold and rain, heat or hail, with no shelter but their clothing," while their parents worked the fields.[4] Food was often scarce and the comforts of communities back East even rarer. Swanson commented: "The greatest amusement of all was work; just plain hard work and seeing things grow."[5] The problem was that things did not always grow. In the early 1880s, the farmland failed to yield sufficient crops, and settlers feared the locusts had sapped the land of its productivity. A major farm crisis occurred, which threatened to destroy many lives. In its wake, a general malaise set in. There was a loss of optimism and a lessening of faith in the future, which Andrew missed during his years at Stillwater but which he could see traces of when he came back home again.

Decades later Reverend F. M. Eckman looked back on those years. The son of P. J. Eckman of the Sveadahl and Kansas Lake churches, he recalled the feeling among the settlers that a curse, of almost Biblical proportions, hung over the land after the grasshoppers left. F. M. Eckman explained that his father helped solve the problem:

> *It soon became evident that the crop failures were due more to*

> *misuse of the land than anything else. Many lacked proper tools*
> *for farming: others were lacking in will-power and information.*
> *Many "sowed in the stubble," and those who plowed seldom did*
> *it at the right time. My father, who was an old experienced farmer,*
> *tried to persuade them to plow both earlier and deeper and not to*
> *lose hope. That helped.*[6]

Despite those difficulties, Alexander Swanson remembered that people felt happiness and a nearness to the earth.[7] Unfortunately, the contentment he recalled was hardly universal. Bankruptcies, mental stress, marital discord, abandonment, suicides, and even killings could interfere with the sense of well-being, as people brought with them to the prairie the problems of their past. That was a complication Andrew could have seen clearly, as he looked back so many years later.

Whatever degree of romance he, Lars, and Caroline felt as they started out across America in 1868 soon clashed with the reality of jealous love and strident emotions. Frontier life worsened their troubles and led them to a series of tragic events, whose wellsprings the three of them surely understood only in part during the 1870s. They were still only in their thirties at that time, living in a new landscape far from home, governed (at least in part) by their emotions, and prey to their passions. From his new perspective in the 1890s, Andrew could realize that. He could also see that he and Caroline were the fortunate ones. They escaped with their lives and got a second chance, which could lessen, if not fully erase, their sufferings.

Compelling as they were, such memories could not lay claim to all of Andrew's energies. The Watonwan County he returned to also existed in the here and now with its palpable realities and everyday concerns. He came back to a world that had changed immensely. Some of his former acquaintances, such as Charles Johnson and J. W. Seager, remained in Watonwan County, but others had died or moved away. By the 1890s, a new generation had grown up, gotten children of their own, and adjusted to the prairie. They moved from sod houses and crude cabins into white frame farm homes.[8] As one observer wrote, a great transformation of pioneer life took place. In addition to new buildings and fenced-in fields, farmers bought more acres, replaced oxcarts with lighter vehicles, purchased organs, and their daughters learned to play and sing. They worked to get ahead, each farmer striving to outdo his neighbor.[9]

Andrew soon found he had returned to a mutable world. Not long after the 1874 trial, Charles Johnson's parents died.[10] In 1875 Charles married Kate Henrickson of one of the oldest Kansas Lake families, and they kept ownership of his parents' homestead. Soon Charles took a job in a St. James general store run by a Norwegian immigrant named Thomas Veltum. Veltum then purchased the former Kansas Lake farm of Charles's parents from Charles and Kate. Veltum, in turn, sold the farm three years later to Kansas Lake Pastor P. J. Eckman and his wife.[11]

In the early 1880s Charles's fortunes continued to shift. He clerked in general stores and in grocery and clothing businesses. On February 6, 1886, The St. James Journal reported that Charles had developed a "hankering for California," only to announce a week later that he had decided to stay and open a general store of his own in St. James. In the years following Charles struggled with alcoholism. His drinking grew increasingly worse. In time he even repeated several lesser aspects of the domestic abuse he had once so strongly objected to in Lars during the 1870s. Some of Charles's own children grew to fear his harsh manners and began leaving home.[12] By the time Andrew returned from prison, Charles's behavior had caused him to fall into near bankruptcy.

In 1880 Lars and Caroline's original farm passed into the hands of others. It was first taken over by John Peter Johnson, who had been at the lake since the early 1870s. John Peter then saw it go over to a Norwegian settler.[13] With that second tract sale, Andrew's family saw the land in the immediate vicinity of the lake — where the dramatic events of 1872 took place — pass on to a newcomer with no first-hand memory of those happenings.

Some things at Kansas Lake resisted change, however, at least for a while. Hogan and his parents stayed on as farmers. In 1877 Hogan took out a new mortgage on his eighty acres.[14] Later that year he took out yet another mortgage, this time on a promissory note co-signed, or marked, by his father. The note was issued to "Hawkin Jensin a single man."[15] Hogan's affairs then took a sudden turn for the worse. In 1883 he defaulted on his payments. The county sheriff delivered a notice of foreclosure and an announcement of the public sale of Hogan's land. The announcement was made to his father, who by that time was in possession of the premises. The original mortgage owner bought the property back from the sheriff for $512.00.[16]

With that sad transaction Hogan vanished without a trace from Watonwan County. He may have been one of those farmers who failed to diversify. Many settlers stubbornly tried for years to make a go of their farms by cultivating wheat. W. A. Chapman, the editor of The St. James Journal throughout the 1880s, was a native of the central Illinois prairie districts, where he had seen the bounteous corn harvests of that region. Chapman continually reminded farmers of Watonwan County that theirs was land made for corn. Only by switching crops could they end their farming troubles.

In the summer of 1881, Chapman made an informal survey of local wheat farmers. The overwhelming majority reported (July 30, 1881) that, in general, "wheat is a failure." Though a few farmers expected a good crop, their experience was the exception that proved the rule, in Chapman's mind. On March 1, 1884, he wrote that 1883 had been a poor year for crops; frosts made the wheat harvest "a total failure" that season. "This is corn country," he insisted, and it is "bad for wheat." Perhaps Hogan was one of those who remained devoted to wheat and lost his acreage as a result.

Neither is it far-fetched to imagine that Hogan, like others on the frontier, fell victim to alcohol. Indeed liquor flowed as freely in rural Minnesota as in Sweden. M. J. Severance and others like him argued throughout the 1880s for more and better measures to combat the drinking problem.[17] Interestingly, men of Hogan's father's age group seem to have fallen victim to this drinking habit less often than did men of the younger generations. The parents clung to the land, while their children all left it in time, as did Hogan. By the mid-1880s he had already given up and abandoned Watonwan County, or died, either as a result of poor farming techniques, inadequate finances, or drink.[18]

By way of contrast, the elder Johnsons stayed on in Long Lake township. In 1884 John and Christine sold a parcel of their land to the Kansas Lake Swedish Lutheran Church Cemetery Association. The sale came about when the congregation failed in an attempt to procure two acres for a church cemetery as a gift from the railroad company that owned land in the area. Instead John Johnson came to the rescue and offered three of his acres.[19] From that point on, John and Christine lived quietly on their farm until after Andrew's release from prison. The only change came on October 17, 1893, twenty years to the day from the birth of Andrew and Caroline's daughter Christine. Andrew's parents sold their farm to their daughter Petronella and her husband John Olson for $1.00.[20]

Even in that arrangement the Johnsons remained true to their Swedish traditions. John and Christine were allowed to continue living on the farm in agreement with Petronella's promise to use the earnings from the land as her parents' retirement income. Petronella agreed, in essence, to grant an *undantag* arrangement to her aging parents. That was similar to the agreement John had made with his own parents sixty years earlier in Sweden, on the Attavara farmstead of the 1830s. Petronella offered to "support, maintain and care for" her parents in their remaining years.[21] The family owned eighty acres in a burgeoning agricultural market. That promised a relief from want. Missing from the records of the family's finances, however, was any mention of Andrew. He was invisible in all the land negotiations involving John, Christine, and Petronella.

As John and Christine grew old, the Kansas Lake church granted them special privileges. They were exempted, for example, from paying the yearly membership dues to the congregation.[22] Then in 1894 came a brief notice about John's death. The St. James Journal reported that "John Johnson of Long Lake" who was "about 80 years of age and has suffered from ill health and been nearly blind for a number of years" committed suicide on May 12 of that year by drowning himself in the South Branch of the Watonwan River, just south of his farm. Ill and infirm, John Johnson was said to have thrown himself into the swollen river, which was in spring flood at the time.

On May 5, 1895, John's widow "Kristi Jenson," eighty-two, also died. The cause of death was given simply as "old age," but a deep longing for her husband of sixty-two years was surely an important contributing factor. Records said only that she was a "farmer[']s wife" and died without the care of an attending physician. Surely she subsided slowly at the family farm with Andrew and Petronella at her side.[23]

John and Christine's gravestones were placed near each other at a literal stone's throw from their farmhouse. (Figure 11 & 12) Only a fragile fence separated the cemetery from their property. Their tombstones bore silent witness to their long lives and the bravery they showed in starting over again in a new land. Since he committed suicide, John was buried at the edge of the cemetery, his epitaph facing westward away from the church building. Christine's grave, only a few feet distant, was decorated with the tender image of a lamb and a Bible verse.[24]

The day of Christine's passing coincided with the date for the opening of Andrew's trial twenty-one years earlier, that is, May 5. John died on the exact date that his first daughter Botilla was buried in Sweden and on the same date that Andrew's trial ended in 1874, that is, May12. It followed that while Botilla's funeral was held on John's thirtieth birthday in 1844, Andrew was sentenced to life in prison on his father's sixtieth birthday in 1874. It was surely difficult for those close to him to believe it a mere coincidence that John Johnson took his life on a May 12. As his birthday rolled around each year, that date must have awakened excruciatingly painful memories. By 1894 those memories and his infirmity became too heavy and the elder Johnson chose suicide. He drowned, just as his first daughter had done fifty years earlier. Perhaps she and Andrew were in his thoughts to the very end.

Chapter XXI
Moving On

Andrew stood with his sister at the graveside of his parents as they were buried. He likely returned there many times afterward. He must have reflected on the family's shared experiences and the life he remembered with them, both before and after prison. Though not without numerous and distressing complications, that life was a simple one at heart. On both sides of the Atlantic, they followed a steady course centered on work and helping others. The Nordic setting the Johnsons lived in allowed them to remain Swedish to the core, despite all their years in America.

John and Christine often traveled to St. James to shop or walked across the fields near Kansas Lake to visit neighbors. As they sold their property toward the end of their lives, they rode in to the Watonwan County courthouse with Andrew and Petronella and carried out those transactions. The Recorder's Office wrote down the details of the sales and even the time of day when the papers were finalized. John and Christine surely stopped at Charles Johnson's grocery store, where they could use Swedish, or greeted neighbors who also were in town.

At Andrew's trial in 1874, Hogan told of leaving Kansas Lake in the fall of 1872 to earn extra cash at a temporary job. He returned to spend Christmas with his parents. With their family and Caroline's together, they could celebrate in traditional Swedish fashion. An adult male disguised as a Christmas goat (*julbock*) gave gifts to Caroline's children. On Christmas Day, Halland families by tradition attended early morning church services with glowing lanterns (*julottan*). After church, families had dinner at home and played Christmas games. Adults often indulged in a customary draught of liquor.[1]

At the end of the century, Reverend P. J. Eckman wrote of the isolation at Kansas Lake, when the earliest immigrants sat forlornly in their huts on the wide-open prairie "without Christmas, Easter and Pentecost, without Sundays and a church."[2] Yet Christmas was the one season when even the poor splurged in Sweden, and the Johnsons surely did the same at Kansas Lake, to the best of their ability. Another tradition was the fall potato dig. Christine told of going to Hogan's farm in the fall of 1872, just before Lars disappeared. There she dug potatoes and visited with her older son. They had coffee and discussed Hogan's wife and daughters in Halland. Their talk was commonplace and intimate.[3]

While Andrew's mother openly showed her caring side, his father was, in his humble way, knowledgeable but reticent. As far back as the 1830s, the Swedish pastor in Veinge noted that John Johnson understood the written words of the scriptures and could understand and explain the catechism well. Christine, on the other hand, got a mark of "well" on the first task, but the clergyman judged her understanding of the catechism as "weak."[4] Still, at Andrew's trial in 1874, Christine was the only witness whose testimony showed any expression of emotion. When replying under oath if she had ever heard Caroline say that she wished Andrew would kill Lars, Christine let the court know she was indignant at such questioning and rejected it immediately as a fabrication. She exclaimed: "For God's sake, don't talk that way!"[5]

In the 1890s Andrew could reflect on his family's long custom of nurturing and caring. John and Christine aided the poor at Attavara in the 1830s. John, Christine, Hogan, and Andrew helped Caroline in the 1870s. The family stood by Andrew through all his years in prison. The grandparents took in Nels Peter and August in 1882. And Petronella and John Olson fostered her nephew Aaron, when Nels Peter and Augusta temporarily left him behind in the mid-1880s.

At his parents' graveside Andrew surely realized that an era was at an end. He and Petronella were the last of his kin who still called Kansas Lake home. As he gazed out over the vast fields surrounding him, his thoughts could easily drift back to Halland and the farmlands there. Nearly thirty years had gone by since Andrew pulled up stakes and found his way to Kansas Lake. During that time the simple patterns had often been terribly interrupted. Life had taken many unusual turns, for which logical cause-and-effect sequences were not always the sole apparent explanations. Most of the answers were somewhere inside him, but the process of finding them was long and complex.

Andrew stayed at Kansas Lake as long as his parents were alive. He was on good terms with his sister and brother-in-law, but his relations with some in the community were less solid. That applied, above all, to the Kansas Lake Church. Though Petronella and John Olson remained loyal members of the congregation, Andrew did not join the fold. He also kept his distance from Annie and Isabel. His acquaintance with Charles Johnson was never quite the same again either. Andrew and Charles could not avoid meeting from time to time. However, their lives had taken different turns by the 1890s. The mental distance was too great for them to bridge over totally and they seem to have kept a comfortable distance from each other.

A month after his mother's death, Andrew moved to St. James and took his carpenter's skills with him. In the beginning he boarded with attorney J. W. Seager.[6] Seager's spacious home functioned as a "center of hospitality" for visitors, young schoolteachers, and others in need of lodgings or help.[7] In 1895 Andrew rented a room at Seager's and stayed there long enough to get a foot back in the job market.

St. James was thriving in the 1890s. Railroads and shops were doing lively business as the farm crisis came to an end. In addition, St. James had become the county seat in 1878, replacing Madelia. Local newspapers boasted of a strong economy. A new mill, a schoolhouse, a church, several stores, and numerous family homes were being built. In a vein of local patriotism, The St. James Journal boasted (May 17, 1890): "St. James is going to boom this summer. St. James is the banner town. All classes of workmen find plenty of employment." The largest construction project of all was a new county courthouse, and Andrew could easily find work there. The courthouse was finished in

1898. The next year he left Watonwan County for good.[8]

By the end of the 1890s, Andrew, Petronella, and John Olson had all begun thinking about moving on.[9] Petronella and John decided it was time to go back to Minneapolis. They sold her parents' land to another Swedish immigrant. He was John Albert Moody, from Småland. Moody took out a mortgage on the property and moved his family into the farmhouse, thus marking the definitive end of Andrew and his family's fateful thirty-four year saga at Kansas Lake.[10]

Going to Minneapolis became a family affair. As Andrew, Petronella, and John prepared to leave for the city, only one matter clouded their last days at home. In 1899 news arrived from Sweden that Andrew's sister-in-law, Hanna Andersdotter, had died in Veinge, at age sixty-eight. Hanna outlived her daughter Bothilda, who died in childbirth in 1897. Of Hogan's family in Sweden, only Anna Johanna was left. Frail and ill, she was given her mother's tiny cottage and left to support her three fatherless children with menial day labor.[11]

Andrew received the news from Veinge in November and could think back on Hanna's years with Hogan and the fact that both were now gone, but it did not change his own life. Soon thereafter he boarded a passenger train heading north to Minneapolis. In doing so, he distanced himself from public scrutiny in Watonwan County once and for all. He may have felt a tinge of sorrow over all that had happened there. He surely also knew a definitive change was on its way. Each of his major moves in life had been a voyage into the unknown and the uncertain. Now, as a man nearing sixty, he faced yet another decisive transition. That was the task of adjusting to a metropolitan area. Like moving out onto the prairie years earlier, going to Minneapolis offered a new challenge.

Chapter XXII
A New Life

In Minneapolis Andrew found himself in the center of a burgeoning industrial city, whose population increased ten-fold between 1875 and 1900. The promise of jobs drew thousands of workers. They all had the hard facts of economic necessity in common. Andrew, Petronella, and John moved to the city's Sixth Ward, the so-called Seven Corners area, located in the heart of Minneapolis. The population of the Ward was 15,000, and the core amenities of urban life were all within walking distance.[1]

The Swedes knew what they were looking for when they chose the area. Sixty percent of the Sixth Ward was Scandinavian-American. John and Petronella bought a house and rented one of the rooms to Andrew. Andrew and John found day labor there, while Petronella worked as a housekeeper at the Augustana Home. Andrew's background as a carpenter allowed him to fit in easily with the employment opportunities. Nearly seventy percent of the workers in the Sixth Ward were skilled or unskilled laborers, and carpentry and woodworking were the most commonly advertised male occupations.[2] In 1900 Andrew was fully employed the entire year, while John Olson, twelve years his junior, was out of work for several months in a row.[3]

Inside Seven Corners, Scandinavian Americans could conduct their lives as if they lived in any middle-sized Nordic community back home. All the needs of ethnic life could be met. As Andrew went off to his day jobs or Petronella crossed over to the Augustana Home each day, they passed along block after block filled with shops and businesses where the use of English was unnecessary. Parks, schools, theaters, churches, and even hospitals catered to the Scandinavian population. Neighborhood features also included, of course, bars and a lively street culture.[4] It is not certain exactly how much Andrew partook of the social life, but it was a comfortable setting. Possibly he had changed mentally after all his years at Stillwater. If the routine of prison had saved him, it could also have dulled his response to the world around him. Judging from his work record, however, his physical vitality was still with him. It is safest to assume that he fit into his new surroundings without a hitch.

Despite the seeming decisiveness of his move to Minneapolis, Andrew did not stay long. He was a farm boy at heart. After two years in Minneapolis, he accepted a job in Superior, Wisconsin, and went back to the land. Once again he boarded a train and headed north. His new employer was a Norwegian named August Simons, who owned a dairy operation in Superior. Andrew arrived there around 1901. He lived at Simons's farm and did handy work, cared for the farmstead, and tended to the dairy herd.[5]

Like Caroline, Andrew kept up the eternal search for a place that resembled home, although he had now been gone from Halland for thirty-five years. In Superior he found an environment that came as close to resembling Veinge parish as any spot in North America. Superior was, like Halmstad, a thriving middle-sized harbor town. The Scandinavian presence was strong; over sixty percent of Wisconsin's Swedish-born residents lived in that northwestern corner of the state.[6] In the center of town stood the imposing Pilgrim Swedish Lutheran Church. The surrounding countryside featured farmland and forests. As in Halland, a mixed economy of crop farming and dairy herding was common. Many men worked in the harbor, built ships, did railroad work, and farmed, all in a combined effort to make ends meet. Andrew settled in on the south side of Superior, just three miles from the lakeshore.

Despite the intensity of his time with Caroline, Andrew's ties with Johanna Persdotter proved more lasting. He and his sons continued receiving letters from her and her second husband, until the news arrived from Sweden in the spring of 1903 that Johanna had passed away. She died at Bölarp at age seventy-two of what was described as "nervous instability."[7] There was no mistaking that the poverty and hard work she endured — after Andrew left her and she remarried — had taken their toll. Raising two small sons alone especially had taxed her resources. Perhaps as a result of her death, Andrew grew ever closer to his and Johanna's sons. The process was made easier with Nels Peter living just across the border from Wisconsin. Nels Peter thrived in Minnesota until the early 1900s, when he began feeling the first symptoms of lung disease. To escape the stone dust, he switched to farming outside of Sandstone, but he soon succumbed again to his passion for stonecutting. In 1905 he was back at the quarries once more.[8]

In the first years after Johanna's death, Andrew's life at Simons's dairy farm remained quiet. He had been there close to ten years when, unbeknownst to him, events farther south in Wisconsin took a turn for the worse. Caroline grew gravely ill with tuberculosis. She had fared badly, in fact, since the early 1900s. In the latter stages of her illness, she moved to John Albert's home in Madison, where her son and his wife cared for her. By 1907 she was close to death. The only surviving first-hand account of those days came from John Albert's daughter Ragnhild. She described standing in the doorway of Caroline's bedroom as a small child in 1907 and viewing her sick grandmother from a distance. Caroline lay wrapped in blankets in a far corner of the room. No one could go forward to her bed "because tuberculosis was so contagious."[9]

Even on her deathbed, Caroline was distanced from her family. Though her Wisconsin relatives tended to her, she told them nothing about the truths she had concealed for so long. The only tangible object she retained from her time in Minnesota was the wooden sewing box that Andrew had sent her from prison over thirty years earlier and that she had often displayed with affection to her Wisconsin family. Caroline died on September 30, 1907. (Figure 26) Her family said only that she was "very sick" in her last months. She lived sixty-five years, nearly forty of those in America.[10] She bore eight children with three different partners.

Caroline was buried at the Burke township Lutheran Church, a fitting place of rest. The countryside there consisted of rolling hills and heavily wooded valleys, reminiscent of parts of Värmland. The gravestones at the church spoke of a vibrant Norwegian presence. Secure in that environment, Caroline had removed herself for the last thirty years of her life from the physical reminders of Kansas Lake. In death she and her son Andrew shared the same headstone. They were laid to rest as close together as possible without actually being in the same grave. The name on his stone surely symbolized all that was psychologically closest to Caroline — that is, her father Anders, her second husband Anders-cum-Andrew, and her beloved American son Andrew.

In early October of 1907, Gilbert Tingom stood at Caroline's grave and listened to the minister's final words over her body. Then he packed up and left the area. Though Tingom lived another nineteen years after Caroline, he made no attempt ever to contact Annie, Isabel, or any others close to Caroline, except for his own sons, who were close at hand.[11]

During the last seven years of her life, Caroline and Andrew remained unaware of, or unconcerned about, the fact that they and their daughter Christine lived in the same state, only a few hours apart. Andrew never learned of Caroline's death. As sad as that fact was, he had other worries in those years, most notably about his older son. When Nels Peter's illness worsened yet again — just at the time when Caroline was nearing death — he gave up on the quarries at Sandstone for good. Andrew found forty acres of Homestead land outside of Superior at a spot called Copper Creek and convinced his son to move there. Augusta hoped the fresh air there would cure Nels Peter's illness. So instead of putting up an earth cabin such as the Swedes had used on the prairies years earlier, Andrew looked for a lot open to the wind and the elements.

Andrew and Nels Peter set about building a house at Copper Creek, but it turned out to be scarcely better than the one Andrew had at Kansas Lake in the 1870s. One of his grandchildren called it "only a shack of a house," with two rooms downstairs and drafty double rooms in the attic. (Figure 22) Only two weeks after the house was finished, Nels Peter left Augusta to run the farm and went off to St. Paul to work on government buildings under construction there.[12] Even as a sick man, he was unable to stay away from stone work.

Nels Peter spent the next years wandering from site to site. In his brief intervals at home, he worked with Andrew at building a second and larger house at Copper Creek, but it was never finished. Mortally ill and coughing up blood, he came home for good in 1913 and spent the next year in bed. In June of 1914, Nels Peter died in the unfinished second house, a victim of pulmonary tuberculosis and what the recording physician described as "Stone Cutter dust."[13] He was only fifty. His was an especially sad ending. Nels Peter came to America to escape the destitute lot of a Swedish farmhand but ended up suffering under equally bad, or even worse, working conditions in America. He died, quite literally, of suffocation.

Chapter XXIII
The Waning Years

After the loss of Nels Peter, Andrew's closest remaining relatives were August and Petronella. And time passed, even for Petronella, the baby of her family. She and John Olson stayed at home in Minneapolis. By 1901 Nels Peter and Augusta's son Aaron moved to their house and found work in the city as a mechanic. Three years later he married. In the period that followed he worked at four different jobs in Minneapolis. He and his wife lived at just as many addresses in south Minneapolis, until she succumbed to the Spanish flu in her early twenties.[1]

While Petronella observed her foster son's attempts to get settled, she also watched as her husband fell ill. In 1915 John Olson died of cancer.[2] He was buried in historic Layman's Cemetery, just to the south of the Seven Corners neighborhood.[3] In 1918 Petronella herself grew ill. She was stricken with heart disease and phlebitis, the result of her many years of strenuous housecleaning jobs. Alone and without help, she finally went to the Augustana Home, her old workplace, in December of 1918.[4] Sister Bothilda Svenson, the deaconess, signed Petronella into the care center with the explanation that she was "sick and unable to care for herself."[5]

Petronella was never to leave the Augustana Home. She died there in its nursing department on January 17, 1919.[6] Sister Bothilda knew much about the dead woman. She filled out the death certificate and got it right that Petronella was born in 1848 and lived for seventy years.[7] Bothilda was close to her in other ways as well, too close, in fact, in some people's opinion. She sat at the bedside and influenced the sick and dying woman as she made out her will only a week before passing away. Petronella left her house to her old employer, the Augustana Home, and the Augustana Swedish Lutheran Church, which she and John had joined twenty years earlier.[8] Her other assets amounted to just over $2,000. She bequeathed "to my brother Andrew Johnson, the sum of Five Hundred (500) Dollars in cash."[9]

On receiving news that his sister had left him so little, Andrew hired a lawyer to contest the outcome. Petronella's will went slowly through Probate Court in Minneapolis, with Andrew and the Augustana Church both arguing for possession of her property. Andrew explained his rights as her next of kin, and the church claimed its share as the only caregiver in her final hour of need. In the end, the Court saw it the church's way and declared in its favor. Thus Andrew lost in the Minnesota court system for the second and last time. The Augustana Church then sold Petronella's house to an Irish immigrant for $3,000.[10] If Andrew had received the house, he could have realized the profit himself, but that was not to be. In time he was granted the $500.00, but by then it surely felt like short shrift.

After 1914, Andrew had left off living full-time at the Simons dairy farm and moved to Copper Creek. (Figure 27) His relatives remembered him from those days as a very strong man, who — regardless of his age — kept on working in town or on nearby farms. He also did his best to improve the Copper Creek farm. He and Augusta kept a few horses, cattle, chickens, and pigs there. They grew potatoes, oats, and wheat. Augusta sold the produce at market in Superior, much as Caroline had done in Madison with the products of her Dane County farm.[11]

Those years offered scattered glimpses of Andrew at home. He chopped firewood, did carpentry work, saw his small grandchildren off to school, or helped them cross over dangerous streams in the woods. He never spoke of his days at Kansas Lake or the years in prison. With time, he developed a strong religious faith, though he seems never to have joined a church. On May 12, 1910, thirty-six years to the day after his sentencing in 1874, Andrew bought a Bible in Superior and recorded his name in it the following day.[12] That was his sole surviving testament to the suffering and losses he experienced and the introspection he surely had carried within himself since the early 1870s. The last view of Andrew alive came from the summer of 1920. A visitor who met him at Copper Creek described him simply as a seventy-nine-year-old farm worker, a widower, and Augusta's father-in-law.[13]

On November 6 of that year, Andrew suffered a stroke. He had just finished working at one of August Simons's dairy farms in Billings Park, just west of downtown Superior. He sat down to eat with the Simons family before taking the train back to Copper Creek. The first sign of trouble occurred during the meal. In confusion, he reached for a slice of meat on his plate and started eating it with his hands, thinking it was a slice of bread. Sensing the problem, Simons rushed him to St. Mary's Hospital in Superior, where he stayed for five days in intensive care. On November 11, 1920, Andrew's story, which began nearly a century earlier with his parents' wedding in Breared, came to an end. At five o'clock in the afternoon, he passed away, just short of eighty.[14]

Andrew fell ill and died in the same week in November as Lars disappeared forty-eight years earlier. Like Caroline, he lived the rest of his life after 1874 without saying a word in public concerning the death of Lars. After the middle of the twentieth century, his grandson Aaron was the only family member still alive who knew the close details of Andrew's early life, but he remained quiet about them. Some of Andrew's other relatives were vaguely aware that he once did time in prison, but no one knew when, where, or why. By the beginning of the twenty-first century, that memory had been diluted to an even foggier family recollection that some unnamed Johnson relative had once spent a year in prison, on unknown charges, but "was later declared innocent."[15] Of all those directly involved in Andrew's 1874 trial, only Annie Johnson, Charles Johnson, and J. W. Seager were still alive in 1920. After Andrew died, Augusta told authorities that he was a laborer, and they entered that on his death certificate. Concerning his Kansas Lake past there was only silence.[16]

"Laborer" was the designation Andrew himself had given authorities in Watonwan County fifty years earlier, in 1870, when he and his family were struggling settlers there. Like his sister who cleaned floors and his sons who joined labor unions, Andrew remained true to the working-class heritage. At his death, he left little behind. When his estate was finally settled in 1922, it amounted to $770.28, which included the $500.00 from Petronella. In the end, Augusta received the $695.00 that were left over from paying bills. She was also given Andrew's personal effects and belongings. Only the Bible he bought in 1910 still remains.[17] (Figure 15)

In the end, there were no eulogies published over Andrew. He lived out the last twenty-eight years of his life in freedom, and simplicity. Gone, but not forgotten, were the famines in Sweden, the ocean voyage to America, the toil on the railroads, the trauma of the 1870s, his two wives, both his parents, and his older son. He never remarried. The Simons dairy farm was a benign environment, located on the gentle plain between downtown Superior and the forest. The calm setting reflected the quiet tenor of his last years.

Andrew was buried in Graceland Swedish Cemetery, owned by the Pilgrim Swedish Lutheran church. (Figure 13) The cemetery lies just outside South Superior and near the border between Wisconsin and Minnesota, the two states where his American drama was played out. Graceland is located at the top of a long sloping hill. Thick stands of cedar trees cover the graveyard. Across the road is a cluster of birch trees. On the other side of the valley stands a deciduous forest. On a summer day, the late afternoon sun casts a checkerboard spectacle of shadow and bright sunlight. All is quiet except for the chirping of songbirds.

Beyond the valley lie the Superior plain and the great inland sea, Lake Superior. When Andrew buried Nels Peter at Graceland in 1914, he stood on that spot himself and could have imagined he was back in Veinge, with the North Sea just over the horizon and the woods surrounding him. Unmistakably Swedish names dominate on the Graceland headstones. Nels Peter and Andrew lie there side-by-side, among friends and kinfolk. Nothing in his epitaph or his final years distinguished Andrew. His job was an ordinary one among the masses of common workers before World War I. Even his name underscored his status as just another among many Swedish immigrants. He is one of eight Andrew Johnsons buried in Graceland Cemetery.

After Andrew's death, Nels Peter and Augusta's youngest daughter, Anna, took up residence in Eau Claire. In the 1920s John Albert Johnson also moved to Eau Claire and continued to search in Minnesota for traces of Annie, Isabel, and Andrew. John Albert would have been astonished to learn that Andrew, the man he and his sister Christine thought was dead, had lived for twenty years only two hours north of Eau Claire and that one of his granddaughters lived in the same community as John Albert himself. Anna Johnson and John Albert resided in Eau Claire County at the same time for nearly twenty years without knowing of each other's existence. Their paths must have crossed countless times during those years.

In Minnesota, meanwhile, Annie Johnson lost track of her mother. Along with Isabel, she waited for years to hear from Caroline, until at last she gave up all hope and resigned herself to never knowing the fate of either Caroline or her siblings John Albert and Christine. Annie stayed in Watonwan County, married William Barge, and raised two sons. (Figure 18) Like her mother, she assumed a silent approach about events in the Kansas Lake community of her childhood. Even with her own children, she was tight-lipped about her parents. When talk of them came up at home, she sent her children and grandchildren out of the room.[18] Annie failed even to tell the exact location of her father's gravesite.

To the very last, Andrew's and Caroline's lives were defined by a trend that began with their emigration and grew ever more pronounced after the death of Lars. The extreme closeness they experienced to many of their loved ones contrasted to the remarkable distance from others. Therein lay a profound sadness, which time never fully erased. While many of the family members on both sides of their marriages lived through the years in close proximity to one another, the ties and harmony between them grew increasingly more tenuous or were broken altogether. The separation caused a breach in the bonds of affection, which Andrew, Johanna Persdotter, and Caroline could never make whole again.

Numerous of the immigrants' descendants lived out their lives wondering about the fate of family members. In some cases they traveled the countryside searching for missing relatives and keys to severed connections that were far closer at hand than they imagined. Though the Johnson family members eventually found their places in America on a material level, for many of them peace of mind proved a more elusive commodity.

Chapter XXIV
The Pioneer Past

By the early years of the twentieth century, a curtain slowly began descending over the events and people at Kansas Lake. It was a shroud of misinformation, half-told tales, silenced voices, and unsolved riddles. As the years added up, a residue of fragmentary information remained, rather than forthright discussions, concrete details, and lessons learned. In that half-light, later descendants of the early Swedish settlers groped for answers to their questions. Among those were the following: Why were there so few first-hand recorded details about the people involved in the calamity at Kansas Lake? What knowledge, now lost, did the Scandinavian communities and congregations possess about Lars's death, and how long did they guard that knowledge? What did the residents say among themselves concerning Andrew's trial and its repercussions? Were details of Lars's, Caroline's, and Andrew's lives purposefully suppressed through the years and, if so, why?

One reply to those questions was suggested in the pages of The Madelia Times and The St. James Journal. Those publications stated that, as the years passed, newcomers to the area, with no knowledge of events in the past, replaced the old settlers. As a result, memories faded as the nineteenth century neared its end.[1] No doubt this happened to an extent, but it cannot be taken as an all-inclusive explanation. A case in point was John Albert Moody, who bought Andrew's parents' farm in 1902. He was said by Kansas Lake residents in the twentieth century to have arrived in the area nearly a decade after John and Christine Johnson died and a few years following Andrew's final departure from Watonwan County. According to that account, John A. Moody failed ever to meet Andrew and his parents and knew little about their history, even if he briefly met Petronella and John Olson when he bought the Johnson farm.

Such an explanation was misleading. Ledgers from the Kansas Lake Swedish Lutheran Church of that era show that John A. Moody resided in the area and was active in the Kansas Lake congregation throughout the 1890s.[2] John A. Moody and his father were paying congregation dues as early as 1891, and John A. Moody served as the church's recording secretary in 1897-1898. He knew Andrew, his parents, and John and Petronella Olson personally, attending church alongside John and Christine and John and Petronella for the better part of a decade. Moody was present when John and Petronella moved to the area (1890), when Andrew came home from prison (1893), and when the elder Johnsons died (1894 and 1895).[3] Nevertheless in the long run the stories that were passed down from John A. Moody, and others like him, which they had experienced first-hand, survived at Kansas Lake in fragmentary form, as part truth and part folklore.

Later on in the twentieth century, some people related, for instance, that John A. Moody heard about a man fitting the description of Andrew's father, who drowned himself in the creek flowing through his own property, not in the South Branch of the Watonwan River, as reported in the Watonwan County press. Lacking, however, was any proof of the drowned man's identity, according to that story.[4] In reality, reports that John Johnson took his life in the creek, not the river, amounted to information that John A. Moody knew for a fact. As a neighbor and fellow congregation member with John Johnson, he was privy to the details of the elder Johnson's death and was surely present at his burial in 1894.

Another case in point concerned those individuals who signed the petition for Andrew's commutation of sentence. They were said to be latecomers to the area, who knew little, if anything, about the legal proceedings of 1873-1874. That may be partly true. In all likelihood, however, such an explanation concealed the fact that the majority of people in Long Lake township during the 1890s, even newcomers, knew much about the Lars Johnson case. They likely agreed to sign the petition based on real information they had from long-time residents still in the area. Chief among them was George P. Johnston, who circulated the petition in 1892, explaining the details of the case as he went to potential signers asking for signatures.

In short, much accurate knowledge about the case and its aftermath existed in Long Lake township well into the twentieth century. Only gradually thereafter did that knowledge begin eroding. At Kansas Lake the greatest preserver of tradition was the Swedish language. Only as the twentieth century wore on and the language was used less and less did the erosion of knowledge accelerate. As the language disappeared, so did the tales told in it.

Another explanation for the lack of transmission of direct information existed. Stated briefly, an aura of repression is discernible in the written files. The early Swedes in their rural Minnesota settlements were unable to exorcise the effects of governmental oppression in Sweden. That made the majority of them compliant followers. In district court in Minnesota in 1874, they were able to discuss what they knew of events, since State authorities were conducting the questioning. That led them to respond candidly, as they were conditioned to do in authoritarian Sweden. Yet on their own they were unable to carry on a frank discussion of the causes and effects involved in the case, in an open community setting.

To a significant degree the stringent controls remindful of those of the Church of Sweden were transferred to the immigrants' church life in America. The wishes of the ministers serving Swedish-American congregations were powerful and their views influenced congregation members strongly. The most prominent pastor of the Kansas Lake and the East and West Sveadahl congregations in the early period was P. J. Eckman. He came from Småland in 1866 and began as a farmer. He was ordained as a Lutheran minister when he was forty-five.[5] Pastor Eckman was a man of rules and regulations. He insisted congregation members be dutiful and faithful to the decisions of their pastors and church councils. One writer described him as "a man who could not be moved a hair's breadth from that which was right."[6]

"That which he thought was right" might have been a more fitting description. In Eckman's view, traditional orthodox ministers in America were locked in a deadly struggle against liberal attitudes. The Lord's truths were absolute and not subject to relativist interpretations. Church discipline involved a strict adherence to that belief. Pastors with orthodox views girded themselves against new developments, such as Darwinism, empiricism, and the discipline of Biblical criticism, not to mention the mounting temptations of worldly life.[7] P. J. Eckman adamantly demanded that his parishioners follow what he considered the pure teachings of Christian doctrine.

In 1897, P. J. Eckman described the naiveté of the charter members of the Kansas Lake Swedish Lutheran Church, who met in 1871 to found the congregation. Lacking an ordained minister, the laymen decided that the church would follow the Evangelical Lutheran doctrine and be part of the Augustana Synod. While Eckman could pardon that action given the primitive circumstances of the time, he saw the members as having overstepped their boundaries on an ethical plane. The importance of P. J. Eckman's position of authority, as he saw it, shone through when he wrote of himself and pioneer ministers before him as coming to the prairies to gather and organize the scattered sheep and lambs and lead them to the right pasture.[8] His was a paternalistic stance.

On occasion Pastor Eckman could praise the Kansas Lake congregation for its regular attendance and faithful observance of communion. His most powerful tones were reserved, however, for warnings against spiritual waywardness. In his yearly reports to the Kansas Lake church, he expressed his distress at seeing how individuals neglected the means of grace or turned away from grace when it was offered and surrendered themselves to eternal perdition and damnation.[9]

Given the rigidity of such an attitude, it did not take long for P. J. Eckman to gain enemies. He refused, however, to back down on his opinions. One of the greatest fears he shared with other conservative Scandinavian-American clergy was that congregation members would lose their Scandinavian ways and adopt the habits of what they saw as rampant American materialism. Locked in that mindset, Eckman was faced with the unwelcome task of developing a balance between two opposing forces — differentiation and accommodation.

Differentiation emphasized the maintenance of Scandinavian language and culture in America and separation from Yankee social customs. Accommodation gave immigrants the freedom to expand their lives and work into the broader avenues of American culture and the use of English.[10]

In the differentiated group there was space only for conformity to received opinion from within the immigrant culture. That conformity offered comfort, but it also limited the settlers' horizons. It was easier to ignore ambiguous moral issues or to assign direct blame for disturbing situations than to confront and assess them in terms of their broad societal context and complexity. If an open discourse had taken place at Kansas Lake in the 1870s, more than one truth would doubtless have emerged, resulting in a situation that could have been viewed as a threat to absolutist moral values. First was that Lars, Caroline, and Andrew were all, to some degree, the guilty parties in the happenings at Kansas Lake. That was true of Lars for his abusive habits and of Caroline and Andrew for their suspect behavior, which incensed Lars and led Caroline to abandon two of her children permanently. Likewise, the community as a whole, whose members saw the trouble brewing, bore the guilt for not taking firmer steps to prevent the calamitous events of 1872.

Another aspect was that all the parties involved could be seen as victims. As a target of discrimination in Sweden, Lars carried complexes and inner tensions that were bound to explode at some point. Caroline, in turn, suffered domestic abuse. From their past in Sweden, the other settlers were unaccustomed to taking affirmative, proactive steps in helping society or preventing trouble. Even efforts to disarm Lars or send him for mental treatment ended in indecision and disarray. The immigrants were the victims of generations of oppression. That situation silenced them and debilitated the community, leaving it incapable of confronting and analyzing the multiple causality involved in the happenings leading up to Lars's death. Aside from rumor and gossip, the original settlers had no voice, but relied on the opinions and utterances of their ministers and church councils.

Against that background, a crisis of conscience eventually erupted in the Kansas Lake church. It simmered for well over a decade before boiling to the surface in the 1890s. During that time, P. J. Eckman carried on a vigorous campaign against two cardinal sins, as he saw them.

The first was the increasing tendency of his congregation members to join secret societies, such as the Free Masons and the Woodmen.[11] Eckman argued that the more devoted the Swedish Americans were to American secularism, the less they remained Scandinavian. The second perceived transgression was the church members' increasing belief that they could use private worship and reflection as a substitute for (or a complement to) services conducted by the Lutheran clergy.[12] P. J. Eckman retained that attitude even though the Conventicle Decree in Sweden had been abolished nearly half a century earlier. Pastor Eckman minced no words with his congregation in describing their sins in that regard.[13]

The eventual explosion of discontent against P. J. Eckman was unstoppable. On August 7, 1900, a special open meeting was called at the Kansas Lake church to air out the differences between P. J. Eckman and his church council and those who chafed under their leadership. Outside representatives of the Minnesota Conference attended the meeting. Most dissatisfied were some of the younger members of the Kansas Lake church, the very youngest of whom were already in their mid or late twenties. Many were born in America and all were educated in American public schools. A few raised a tumult from the outset. They made their presence felt by clapping loudly and stomping their feet. They then presented the outside observers with a list of forty names of congregation members who were unhappy with Pastor Eckman. They addressed the matter of his inflexible behavior, his rejection of ideas that did not fall in line with his own, and his reluctance (or inability) to use English.

Other dissenting members stated their belief in Darwinism. Reconciling Darwinism and empiricism with traditional Christian teachings was a necessity, in their minds. The meeting was stopped before chaos broke out, but not before some in the congregation made it clear that they were calling for a greater accommodation to the views of liberal Christianity and the broader English-language world around them. Their insistent tone had its bitter repercussions. Out of the approximately 200 congregation members at the time, fifty were dropped from the Kansas Lake church membership list. While some quit the church in protest, P. J. Eckman and his church council summarily expelled most of them from the congregation on the grounds of insubordination.[14]

P. J. Eckman tried stubbornly to hold back the wave of new thought, but that attempt placed him at a moral crossroads in more than one sense. His home was the very farmstead on which Charles Johnson and his parents lived in 1872 and which Andrew visited on November 8 of that year to borrow a sack of flour. The pathway to Eckman's house was the same one that Caroline claimed she trod on that morning to escape Lars's domestic abuse. Above all, it was the path on which Lars was believed to have met his violent death. That so unbending an upholder of conventional morality as Pastor Eckman lived for nearly a quarter of a century so close to the scene of such cloudily defined happenings was only one of the ironic reminders of the early1870s, which filled the lives of those at Kansas Lake for more than two generations thereafter. To P. J. Eckman's credit, he was aware of the difficult position he was in, and soon after the 1900 uproar, he resigned his call at Kansas Lake.[15]

In the early twentieth century P. J. Eckman's successors in the pulpit at Kansas Lake likely bothered to learn relatively little about the congregation's past. Even the early settlers who stayed on in the area labeled the topic of Lars, Caroline, and Andrew as taboo in general conversation outside their own circles. Included in that group were Peter Olson, the Westman family, and Charles and Kate Johnson. They feared that controversy would damage the respectability of their ethnic settlement, and so they remained reticent in the broader community about that which could cast a negative light on their reputation as a law-abiding group.

There were written records of the Kansas Lake congregation, however. The members began keeping detailed accounts of church activities as early as 1871. Those records from the 1870s, all written in Swedish, were eventually lost, but P. J. Eckman had access to them in 1897. When he honored a request that he write a brief overview (*historik*) of the Kansas Lake congregation for its twenty-fifth anniversary celebration (1871-1896), Eckman had his first-hand experience of life in the congregation (1880-1897) and the early texts pertaining to the church to work with.

In his overview, the pastor wrote as though the events of the early and mid-1870s were far back in time. He assumed that stance to impress on his listeners the venerable qualities of those earliest settlers. P. J. Eckman asked aging parishioners how old the Swedish settlement was and concluded that it seemed to have started between 1868 and 1870. In that way he emphasized the nearly mythical nature of that first settlement period. By placing it at a reasonably indefinite time in the past, he made it sound even more epochal and heroic. P. J. Eckman borrowed Pastor Mikael Sandell's diary from the early 1870s and also had the ledger book, now lost, containing records of Kansas Lake's church meetings from 1871-1877. Eckman described that latter volume as "the little old book of minutes."[16] No mention of Lars, Caroline, or Andrew occurred in those meetings, at least according to Eckman's recounting of the contents of the ledger.

Open Kansas Lake church council meetings were held twice in 1873, during the period when Andrew and Caroline were first arrested, when Lars's body was found, and after Andrew and Caroline were brought back from Omaha and charged with murder.

Comments on the case were missing from the church minutes even then. A hiatus in church meetings occurred from 1873 to 1876, but meetings resumed in 1877. However, P. J. Eckman left off reciting what took place then. In contrast to the early books, records of the meetings between 1891 and 1908 are still extant. Those minutes contain only a single fleeting reference to Andrew's parents and none at all to Andrew himself.

John and Christine Johnson lived barely an eighth-of-a-mile from the Kansas Lake church. They attended services there regularly and perhaps even had Caroline in their company at worship services for a few years in the 1870s. Still no comments about them entered the church's written record. In addition, when Andrew returned from prison at the beginning of January in 1893, his family had reason to rejoice. Here one of the scattered sheep Eckman wrote of in 1897 had been returned to the flock at Kansas Lake. Yet Pastor Eckman's report to the congregation, made only a week after Andrew's return, failed to mention that joyous event in one church family's life, and a charter member's at that. This omission was especially noticeable because P. J. Eckman had married Andrew's son Nels Peter in the Kansas Lake church only nine years earlier, he lived just four doors away from Nels Peter and Augusta at Sveadahl in 1885, and he later gave confirmation lessons to their son Aaron. So memories were fresh.

In only the most general of terms, P. J. Eckman, in his 1893 report, turned his parishioners' thoughts back to the days of the mid-1870s and the trials of the past, which Andrew had played a central role in:

> *This congregation was started only 20 years ago, and, thanks*
> *to God's unchangeable qualities, has remained in existence*
> *and developed despite many shades of light and darkness,*
> *personal weaknesses and shortcomings that are contained*
> *within those 20 years.*[17]

If personal comments about Andrew were made in the church at all, P. J. Eckman omitted them from his summary and from his own reports to the church members. In short, the Kansas Lake congregation showed a reluctance to commit to paper information about the shocking and ambiguous events surrounding Lars, Caroline, and Andrew, which were a significant, if also controversial, part of the church group's history.

In the early 1870s nearly all the settlers at Kansas Lake wished to be free of Lars and the problems he posed. His death enabled neighbors to carry on with their everyday affairs more smoothly. Later a sense of collective guilt surely set in, as people reflected on the course of events leading to his death and their role in those events. One historian has described what likely transpired: "Such a judgement [of collective guilt] spreads the burden so thinly that it becomes, in effect, a collective absolution." Collective guilt, in other words, can discourage individuals "from seeking to understand a complex and transformative period" in the group's history. "Among a wider populace, collective guilt can engender collective amnesia."[18]

In the nineteenth century, the Kansas Lake settlers, with their ministers in the lead, could feel it easier to wish the full implications of Lars's case away rather than face up to them in public. If they all shared guilt and let it be diluted across the congregation, no one need have it weighing too heavily on his or her individual conscience alone. Such a response offered all the more reason not to discuss the controversial happenings of the 1870s, or those that came later, for the public record. That response made it possible for the local community to dismiss Caroline's claim of guilt in 1876. It was easier to ignore her affidavit than to delve into its potentially uncomfortable moral complications. In brief, at some point Caroline (and perhaps to some extent Andrew as well) lied about what happened between herself, Andrew, and Lars, but how and why were questions no one dared ask aloud and pursue to the end.

People who suffer trauma have difficulty expressing the damage to their psyche, even though they remember the traumatic experience vividly for a long period afterward and constantly rework it in their thoughts. The Scandinavians in Long Lake township came from an Old World background in which open discourse was not encouraged (or was even forbidden) among the common people. Acts of extreme physical violence were also foreign to them. Even if Lars's death initially cleared the air of conflict, the violence said to be involved in it and the shock waves it sent through the ethnic colonies was guaranteed to remain with people for many years. The trauma hit home hardest after the first sensational aspects wore off and left a residue of personal anguish and introspection.

As late as 1893, the anonymous informant told a St. James newspaper, as reported above, that he and others remembered the death of Lars as especially violent. The visceral aspects of the case did not quickly disappear from people's minds. Therefore, the settlers kept their own counsel and maintained a tight lid on their emotions, refusing to let challenging opinions leak out. If the long-term effects of the case resembled a pressure cooker, the local pastors played a significant role in holding the lid tightly in place until the boil passed its peak and left only a tepid cooling down of emotion. That process equated, in the long run, with repression. The result was doubly sad. It deprived the immigrants' children of open access to vital details of their family heritage. At the same time it denied to those children's children an intimate acquaintance with essential parts of their community's history.[19]

From that situation a paradox arose. While news of Lars's death, Caroline's puzzling actions, and Andrew's trial initially spread rapidly and created a sensation, the community members later kept the details within their own circles and excluded them from the broader public discourse. That exclusionary tendency added to the loss of traditions. By the time the Swedish language eventually died out in the area, there had been little transference of those traditions to the English-speaking descendants. The resultant loss fell heavily, once again, on present-day observers who would know the truth. Therein lay the damage that secrecy could do to the fabric of an otherwise tight-knit community.[20]

Conversely, the bright side of the Johnson story was that through the years a few caring individuals had the courage to keep the flame of conscience and free discourse alive, search for the truth, and fight for Andrew's cause. They included M. J. Severance, J. W. Seager, and George P. Johnston. Their actions resulted in the successful petition of 1892, which was signed by newer members of the community and which helped facilitate Andrew's release from Stillwater. That drive to get signers was a victory for the younger generation of Kansas Lake Swedes, raised in Minnesota and educated in American public schools, who insisted on exercising their right to free speech, in both secular and church life. It spoke highly as well about the others in Watonwan County who refused to relinquish their strong humanistic values and flexible religious beliefs.

Andrew's release from prison was one concrete result of the loud call to lessen the reliance on the conservative past and to accommodate a new era of tolerance and broad community concern. The even more tangible result was the chance it gave Andrew to live out his life in a productive civilian environment. He made the best of that opportunity.

Chapter XXV
The Legacy

The long story of Lars, Caroline, and Andrew was filled with many ifs. A few stand out prominently. If society in the 1870s had understood domestic abuse better, it could have taken steps to lessen Lars and Caroline's troubles. If authorities then had seen the potentially injurious effects of ethnic stereotyping, Andrew's trial might have been conducted differently. If officials and the public had investigated the assertions in Caroline's affidavit of 1876, they might have reinterpreted Lars's death and Andrew's involvement in it. If the Scandinavian settlers who supported Caroline before November of 1872 had been as vocal on her behalf after that time, she and her four children might have stayed together. If M. J. Severance and J. W. Seager had left documents telling how they assisted Andrew between 1872 and 1895, the record would be complete. Or if George P. Johnston had written down what he knew about Andrew and Lars, details of their behavior might have become more obvious.

With those ifs, society's encounter with Lars, Caroline, and Andrew reached a roadblock. The local legal community and the people of Watonwan County failed to carry on a discourse about the moral and social questions suggested by the Johnsons' history both before after 1872. Those were strong indicators of nineteenth century society's inability to come to grips with issues of such importance. At the same time, the shortcomings of society in that era resonate loudly of our own age's continued concerns about questions such as domestic abuse, ethnic stereotyping, and gender equality, which we are slow to resolve completely.

In some respects our cup of knowledge about the Johnsons is half empty. The precise details of Lars's demise will forever remain a mystery, just as the exact manner in which Andrew lived out his life mentally after prison or how Caroline dealt with her divided loyalties psychologically may never come to light. In this connection the words of the Swedish novelist Vilhelm Moberg are apt. While visiting the nearly forgotten graves of nineteenth-century Swedish pioneers in Minnesota in 1950, Moberg wrote: "We know so little about how the great majority of these kinsmen of ours lived; we know so little about how they died."[1]

Lars, Caroline, and Andrew passed away in a state of emotional anonymity. It shall never become fully clear what thoughts they carried to the grave. Buried with them were vital facts that would aid in answering questions about the daunting dilemmas they — and others of their era — struggled with. It was members of the younger generation of Swedish Americans after them who first showed a willingness to approach such questions. Even then, those who remained quiet in the community were at least as numerous as those who spoke out on the ticklish issues of individual and group psychology.

In other respects the cup is half full. Valuable truths emerged from the Johnson story. The most obvious ones concerned the historical process. Like thousands of their countrymen, Lars, Caroline, and Andrew fled Sweden and followed an epochal path. Their move was part of family migration and a systematic search for economic opportunity. They arrived in the Midwest, helped build the rail lines linking the coasts, and later settled among the many ethnic groups on the new Homestead Lands. Along the way the three Swedes and their relatives experienced some of the momentous events of Swedish and American history. Those included the Great Famine of the 1860s, mass immigration, railroad expansion and the westward movement in America, the momentous blizzards, the grasshopper plagues, the

Hinckley fire, the labor movement, and the growth of urbanization in the Upper Midwest.

What went wrong in their lives was a personal story. The exhilarating mix of peoples and the feeling of entitlement the immigrants experienced were mixed with culture shock. Freedom from Old World oppression was empowering, but it could also be puzzling. Despite the injustices in their homelands, they had already crossed the important social and cultural thresholds there. In America they were starting over. That situation held a potential for considerable misunderstanding and confusion, which became a reality for the three Johnsons. They learned how American mythmaking might collide with the realities of everyday life. Their path from Sweden to America was one that necessitated constant adjustment to ever-changing social and cultural barriers.

While America provided the Johnsons with homes and work, the material comforts came at a heavy price in personal suffering and separation. The process of cultural adaptation took its toll. At various times the newcomers found it necessary to dissemble, conceal their whereabouts, or bury their true feelings below the surface of everyday living, all in order to have a chance at carrying on as successful participants in American life. Though they transferred much of their Swedish culture and heritage to the United States, they also found it necessary to abandon loved ones and sacrifice essential aspects of their emotional lives in order to carry on with the New World experience. In that respect, the Promised Land functioned in their existence as a "shadow kingdom," dispersing family members far and wide across oceans and continents and placing many forever out of touch with one another and their native birthright.[2]

For modern generations, Lars, Caroline, and Andrew might now appear only as obscure figures in a distant drama. Lars's death, Andrew's conviction, Caroline's stay in Watonwan County, and their lives in Wisconsin all passed like a flash of lightning and may seem eminently forgettable. Yet their immigration and the hard work and suffering they and their descendants put into life in America is worthy, in its own way, of being remembered.

In the end, the fertile soil of the Midwest received the immigrants for their final repose. While Caroline lies next to her beloved son near Madison, Andrew is buried beside his son and daughter-in-law in

Superior. The same soil has hidden the remains of Lars, showing complete indifference to posterity's search for his burial site. Above his grave, in some unknown field at Kansas Lake, bloom now only the wildflowers of oblivion.[3] Of Lars himself, the man who walked out into the darkness on that ill-fated morning in 1872, only fading memories and lingering questions remain.

Postscript

The separation of Lars, Caroline, and Andrew's families once seemed wholly irreparable. By the beginning of the twenty-first century, Caroline's story especially had resulted in a situation among her descendants that was remindful of the multiple realities she herself felt in her own lifetime. Caroline's descendants in Minnesota knew nothing of her life after 1876, while the family members in Wisconsin were equally in the dark about her history in Minnesota between 1868 and 1876. Though neighboring states, Minnesota and Wisconsin seemed, in this case, worlds apart.

That broken connection was repaired to an extent in 2003, when the sundered Minnesota and Wisconsin branches of Caroline's families discovered each other and were reunited for the first time in 130 years.[1] As their descendants could see, Lars, Caroline, and Andrew's story was one of oppression, strong passions, puzzling psychological motives, isolation, violence, and abandonment. Still, the three were not alone. Others played significant roles in their saga as well. Following are details about several individuals who were closely connected with the three main figures in the story:

Annie Johnson stayed in South Branch township. She and William Barge farmed near Kansas Lake. Annie lived for seventy-six years after 1874 but never again spoke of Lars and Caroline in public. Through the years she passed by the site of Lars and Caroline's Kansas Lake farm hundreds of times without ever talking about it. So silent was she, in fact, about Lars and Caroline that her own sons were unable to give their grandparents' names for Annie's death certificate. Annie died in South Branch on April 10, 1950, at eighty-seven, carrying with her what she remembered of Lars, Caroline, and Andrew.[2] (Figure 20)

Isabel Johnson stayed in South Branch until her twenties. She then married a Watonwan County man and left Minnesota. She died in Great Falls, Montana, in 1951. Isabel, too, failed throughout her adult life to talk about her parents.[3]

Hogan Johnson faded into oblivion. The sole written information on his fate was the Swedish pastor's official church reports from Veinge, which stated cryptically in 1890 that Hogan was "In America. Dead." However, no records of his death have emerged in the United States. From the 1880s to 1916, a Swede named Hogan Johnson lived near Andrew in Superior, Wisconsin, but his date of birth did not match with that of Andrew's brother. Anna Johanna Håkansdotter, Hogan's younger daughter, never married. She stayed in Halland until she died in 1942, at age seventy-eight. She outlived Hogan, her mother, and her sister by well over four decades. Despite the exploitation and poverty she experienced, Anna Johanna lived her life with dignity and bravery.[4] (Figure 19)

Charles Johnson stayed for many years in St. James and eventually overcame his alcoholism, but only after his children fled from his home and moved to the West Coast. Early in the twentieth century, Charles and his wife followed their daughters to Seattle. Charles later moved to Great Falls, Montana, the same town as Isabel Johnson lived in. He died there in 1928. He left no descendants in Watonwan County.[5]

John Wesley (J. W.) Seager remained in St. James and continued on as one of the county's most prominent citizens. He practiced law there until the 1930s. He died while on vacation in Missoula, Montana, in 1933, at the age of ninety-one. Though he met Annie occasionally through the years, he never spoke with her about Lars, Caroline, or Andrew and left no record of his experiences with them.[6]

Martin J. (M. J.) Severance stayed in Mankato after he retired from the district court in 1900. He was one of the most influential men in southern Minnesota and a champion of the common people. However, he left no personal papers and the exact details of his efforts through the years to help Andrew were never made public. He had no known contact with Andrew after the mid-1890s. Severance died in Mankato in 1907. His family later left Minnesota.[7]

George P. Johnston had a checkered career. Three years after helping with Andrew's release, Johnston died, tragically. His end began in 1894, when he was stricken with mental problems. His illness progressed rapidly.

In the summer of 1894, Johnston instructed workers to tear down his house in St. James while his wife was on vacation. He was stopped by trade union members and then examined by medical doctors and declared insane. Committed to the state mental facility in St. Peter, he was diagnosed as manic-depressive and shown to have drinking problems. Claiming he was God, Johnston wandered the fields by the hospital and threatened to burn the buildings down and kill employees and patients alike. Doctors reported he had suffered three such bouts of mental distress in the past. The first came in 1872, the same year Lars disappeared.

Soon after his release from the hospital in 1895, Johnston was found dead outside his home. He died from repeated blows to the head with a claw hammer. The injuries, described as ghastly wounds, were incurred in his house, in a neighbor's barn, and inside his own backyard shed. The death sequence left a copious trail of blood across the two lawns. The head injuries were identical to those that killed Lars twenty-three years earlier. Despite that fact, the coroner ruled out foul play and declared Johnston's death a suicide.

In private, Johnston was pursued by demons. His father died in 1876 leaving the family insolvent. His mother suffered various periods of insanity. Long before her son's commitment, she was confined for several years to the St. Peter mental treatment center. George P. Johnston himself was a man of extremes. As the clerk of district court, he had countless friends. He was beloved by the rank-and-file of his trade union, the Ancient Order of United Workmen. Indeed union members cared for him in his final illness and hundreds attended his funeral. He also had numerous enemies. Among them was J. W. Seager. Highly respected people in Watonwan County charged Johnston with collusion in politics, jury tampering, packing of caucuses, intimidation of voters, and venality. In 1883, eighty local Republican Party members, including Seager, signed a petition denouncing Johnston for alleged unethical professional behavior.

Though a favorite of humble workers, Johnston was an extrovert and braggart. He repeatedly spread stories around town about the most trivial events in his personal life. He was especially fixated on money. At St. Peter, he claimed to have a bag containing $100,000, which he imagined hospital employees were stealing cash from. He also argued that treatment center workers had taken money from mail sent to him at the hospital. In St. James, Johnston boasted of get-rich projects, and he made extensive real estate purchases in the county, claiming to be able to make others rich from them.

It never became clear how much Johnston knew about Lars. Possibly he encountered Lars on one or another of Lars's begging ventures in the early 1870s, during Johnston's period of mental instability and paranoid concern about money. Lars conceivably attempted to beg cash from him. Such an incident would have caused Johnston to react strongly against the beggar and denounce him. Likewise, it is possible that Johnston wandered the fields of the county during his 1872 bout of mental distress (as he did incessantly on the grounds of the mental treatment center in St. Peter in the 1890s) and observed Lars and his strange behavior or heard tales of them. As a result, Johnston may have carried information about Lars that he never revealed to legal authorities or law officers. If such information existed, it might have shed light on the allegations presented at Andrew's trial.

During the years, Johnston may well have had some secret knowledge on his conscience about Andrew's trial and incarceration. If so, he had good reason to continue working on Andrew's behalf. The urging of Judge M. J. Severance also influenced him, of course. In the final result, the fact that Lars and George P. Johnston met their deaths in similar violent ways raised questions, but there were no firm answers to them. When Johnston died in 1895, Andrew was living in St. James and could not have escaped noticing the immense commotion and shock Johnston's death caused in town. Sadly, there is no way of judging Andrew's relationship to Johnston either before or after his prison days. Neither is it clear how Andrew responded to Johnston's death.[8]

August Johnson, Andrew's younger son, settled in Mankato in

the mid-1880s and stayed there for fifty-eight years. He lived quietly, worked as a laborer, and was a faithful labor union member. In 1899 he married a Swedish-American woman and had two daughters with her. August died in Mankato in 1944, at the age of seventy-eight. He passed on two years after his cousin Anna Johanna Håkansdotter in Halland. He recorded nothing about his family history and apparently learned nothing of Anna Johanna's death in Sweden. His older daughter, Mae Fleming Smith, lived in Mankato until her death in 1983 at age eighty-three. She was twenty when Andrew died and was the last living relative who had known him personally. She left no personal papers or reminiscences.[9]

Augusta Johnson survived Nels Peter by twenty-seven years. After Andrew died, she moved to South Superior. She functioned as the backbone of her family until her death in November of 1941. She was buried at Graceland Cemetery in Superior.[10]

Gilbert Tingom sold the last of his and Caroline's property near Madison in 1909. Tingom was never well liked by his family or in-laws. After 1907 he moved in with his oldest son until the son's wife unceremoniously booted him out. Tingom lived thereafter with John Albert Johnson in Eau Claire, Wisconsin. He remained a passive bystander until the end. Tingom died in January of 1926, at the age of eighty.[11]

Christine Johnson, the daughter of Andrew and Caroline, lived out her life in southern Wisconsin. For her Wisconsin relatives, she was the main source of information on Caroline's doings after 1880. Christine died in 1970, at the age of ninety-seven. Sadly, she lived her entire life in the mistaken and tragic belief that her father Andrew had died in 1873. Andrew never set eyes on her again after 1874, when she was an infant. Her brother John Albert Johnson died in 1936. He recounted the story of his unsuccessful searches for Annie and Isabel and traces of Andrew to his family members until the end of his life.[12]

Aaron Johnson was the last of Andrew's family who had lived at Kansas Lake and knew their story first-hand. He held the key to the history of all the Swedish Johnsons longest and best. He praised his mother Augusta but disliked his father Nels Peter, calling him "a mean drunk." Aaron also knew Andrew well. He was nine at Kansas Lake when Andrew returned from prison in 1893, and the two were personally acquainted up until Andrew's death twenty-seven years later.

In the 1970s Aaron told his younger siblings that he had many family stories to relate that would surprise and shock them all and explain many mysterious events and personalities. Unfortunately, he died in 1979, at age ninety-five, before revealing what he knew. When Aaron's voice fell silent, the final curtain descended on the drama of Lars, Caroline, and Andrew Johnson. Their secrets died with him.[13]

Endnotes

Chapter I
The Emigrants' Dilemma

[1] Byron J. Nordstrom, <u>The History of Sweden</u> (Westport, Connecticut & London, England: Greenwood Press, 2002), p. 64.

[2] Ibid., pp. 63-85.

[3] Ibid., p. 74.

[4] <u>Prisma's Swedish-English Dictionary</u>, third edition (Minneapolis: University of Minnesota Press, 1989), p. 575. See also: Sten Malmström and Iréne Györki, <u>Bonniers svenska ordbok</u> [Bonnier's Swedish Dictionary] (Stockholm: Albert Bonniers Förlag AB, 1980), p. 369. <u>Bonniers svenska ordbok</u> defines *undantag* as "a benefit, as for example a free dwelling or certain foodstuffs, which the seller of a farm property could lay claim to from the new owner." Translation by the present author.

[5] c:\Snöstorp\Snöstorp text\Torp och gårdar i Snöstorp.doc. Computer generated text by Håkan Håkansson, Halland Genealogical Society, Halmstad, Sweden.

[6] Franklin Scott, <u>Sweden: The Nation's History</u> (Minneapolis: University of Minnesota Press, 1978), p. 353; Nordstrom, <u>The History of Sweden</u>, p. 85.

[7] Scott, pp. 340, 437, and 441-444.

[8] Lars Ljungmark, <u>Swedish Exodus</u>, tr. Kermit Westerberg (Carbondale & Edwardsville: Southern Illinois University Press, 1979), p. 31.

[9] Nordstrom, <u>The History of Sweden</u>, pp. 81-83.

[10] This act was known in Swedish as *Konventikelplakatet*. Lars M. Andersson and Lena Amurén, <u>Sveriges historia i årtal</u> [Sweden's History Year by Year] (Lund, Sweden: Historiska Media, 2003), p. 126.

[11] Household Examinations were known in Swedish as *husförhör*. Records of parishioners' movements in and out of their parishes were called *inflyttningslängder* and *utflyttningslängder*.

[12] The Universal Education Act of 1842 went by the Swedish name *1842 års folkskolestadga*. Andersson and Amurén, p. 159.

[13] Christian Flor, a Danish educator, visited Sweden in 1866 and made the observation on rural Swedes and political affairs. See: Margaret Forster, <u>School for Life: A Study of the People's Colleges in Sweden</u> (London: Faber and Faber Ltd., 1944), p. 22.

Chapter II
The Värmland Background

1 Frequent travels in search of work were called in Swedish *arbetsvandringar*. For details, see: Lar-Göran Tedebrand, <u>Värmlandsundersökningen</u> [The Värmland Study] (Karlstad, Sweden: Emigrantregistret i Karlstad och Värmlands Hembygdsförbund, 1975), pp. 23-26.

2 Gösta von Schoultz, <u>Värmland</u> (Stockholm: Almqvist & Wiksell/Gebers, 1982); <u>Värmland, Vallfartsmål och vildmark</u> [Historic Sites and Wilderness] (Malmö: Allhems förlag, 1966).

3 The wording in Swedish read: "Anmäld för förargelse af Signeri. Varnad 3/10/[18]38 af N. H. att därmed uppehöra." Bro, Värmland, Husförhörslängder 1836-40. Micro-fiche #53200, 2 of 6, p. 55. Svenska Emigrantinstitutet, Växjö, Sweden. This information was also included in the Bro, Värmland, Husförhörslängder for 1841-45, 1846-50, 1851-55, and 1856-60.

4 The local healers were known in Swedish as "kloka gummor" and "kloka gubbar," or "wise old women" and "wise old men."

5 Bengt af Klintberg, <u>Svenska trollformler</u> [Swedish Charms and Spells] (Stockholm: Wahlström & Widstrand, 1965), p. 21. Information on "games of the powerless" from a personal communication from Bengt af Klintberg to the author, October 17, 2003.

6 The titles in Swedish were: *klockare, kyrkvärd*, and *nämndeman*. Information from Carl-Johan Ivarsson in a personal communication to the author, July 18, 2003.

7 Lars Fredrik was described in Swedish as being taken *ur mantal*. Bro, Värmland, Husförhörslängder 1851- 55. Micro-fiche #53203, 3 of 10, p. 57. Svenska Emigrantinstitutet, Växjö.

8 Lars Fredrik's military duty was called *beväring* in Swedish. For his military discharge, he was described as being *casserad*. The wording of his discharge added: "Dvärg, befriad." See: Bro, Värmland, Husförhörslängder 1851-55.

9 Kila Kyrkoarkiv. Husförhörslängder, Kila AI:14. Värmlandsarkiv, Karlstad, Sweden.

10 Governors' Files Folder, vol. 2, Sibley to Stassen (1856-1943). State of Minnesota against Andrew Johnson, trial testimony, p. 8b. Open file. Location #111.F.5.9B. Minnesota State Archives, MHS, St. Paul.

11 "Skolhuset," <u>Djupvikens hemman i Kila socken. En beskrivning av människorna och deras bosättning från 1600-talet till 1900-talet</u> [The Schoolhouse. Homesteads in Djupviken in Kila Parish. A Description of the People and Their Settlement from the 1600s to the 1900s] (Kila, Sweden: Kila Östra Bygdegårdsförening, Forskargruppen, 1989), pp. 113-115.

12 Kila, Värmland, Husförhörslängder 1861-65. Micro-fiche #514743, 2 of 6, p. 28. Svenska Emigrantinstitutet, Växjö.

13 Ibid.

[14] Quotation from Carl-Johan Ivarsson in a personal communication to Pat Henke, October 18, 2000. Source: Näs häradsrättsarkiv. Näs härads dombok 8/10 1852-1867. Värmlandsarkiv, Karlstad.

[15] On Anders Nilsson's estate, see: Näs häradsrättsarkiv. Näs häradsrätt, bouppteckningar. Värmlandsarkiv, Karlstad. Issued yearly.

[16] Julius Ejdestam, "Tiggarna," De fattigas Sverige [The Beggars in The Poor People's Sweden] (Stockholm: Rabén & Sjögren, 1969), pp. 123-131. See also: Fritiof Bengtsson, ed., Halländska emigrantöden 1860-1930: Drömmen om Amerika — Vision och verklighet [The Emigrants of Halland and Their Destinies. The Dream of America — Vision and Realitiy] (Halmstad, Sweden: Bokförlaget Spektra, 1976), pp. 52-54.

[17] Ejdestam, "Tiggarna," De fattigas Sverige, pp. 123-131. Beggars' passes were called *tiggarpass* in Swedish. Beggars' badges were called *tiggarbrickor*. Beggars' benches were called *tiggarbänkar*.

[18] State of Minnesota against Andrew Johnson, trial testimony, p. 8a.

[19] Beata Losman, "Okända kvinnors röst: Landsbygdskvinnor i 1800-talets Värmland" [The Voice of Unknown Women: Rural Women in Värmland in the 1800s], Forum för kvinnliga forskare och kvinnoforskning, Rapport 1983:1. Göteborg, 1983, pp. 4-5.

[20] Theodore C. Blegen, Minnesota: A History of the State (Minneapolis: University of Minnesota Press, 1985), p. 305.

[21] Hans Mattson, Reminiscences: The Story of an Emigrant (St. Paul: D. D. Merrill Company, 1892), p. 110.

[22] Scott, p. 373.

[23] Mattson, p. 110 ff.

[24] Pat Henke, Karolina Andersdotter, p. 2. Unpublished manuscript, April 2000, updated May 2002.

[25] For details on the numbers of Swedish emigrants, see: Lars Ljungmark, Den stora utvandringen: Svensk emigration till USA 1840-1925 [The Great Migration: Swedish Emigration to the United States, 1840-1925] (Stockholm: Sveriges Radio, 1965), pp. 69, 73, and "Tabeller" [Tables], pp. 178-198. English edition: Swedish Exodus. On page 47, the 1979 English edition gives slightly different figures for the number of emigrants from the Swedish provinces than did the 1965 Swedish edition.

[26] State of Minnesota against Andrew Johnson, trial testimony, p. 9a.

[27] Christiania Politikontroll, Emigrant Protokoll 2 1867-68, Oslo, Norway, p. 169; and Bro kyrkoarkiv AI:23. Värmlandsarkiv, Karlstad.

[28] Pat Henke, Karolina Andersdotter, p. 2.

[29] Personal communication from Pat Henke to the author, July 28, 2003.

[30] State of Minnesota, County of Watonwan, Long Lake Township, Register of Births 1871-1900, vol. A, p. 1, l. 9. Minnesota State Archives, MHS, St. Paul.

Chapter III
Anders Johannesson: The Halland Beginnings

¹ Johannes Jönsson and Kjerstin Håkansdotter were born in 1814 and 1813 respectively. They were married on January 1, 1833, in Breared parish, Halland. Of their two sons, mentioned below in the text, Håkan Johannesson was born on October 2, 1833; Anders Johannesson was born on September 13, 1841. For details of the 1833 wedding, see: Kyrkoarkiv, Hallands län, Breared. Vigde 1820-60. Landsarkivet, Lund, Sweden. For details of the sons' births, see: Födelse och Dop bok år 1820-1852, pp. 148 and 227. Kyrkoarkivet. Hallands län, Breared. Landsarkivet, Lund.

² The Attavara farm originated in the 1600s when the Swedish crown awarded it to a Finnish soldier named Atte, who fought for Sweden in the Thirty Years War. See: Personer bosatta på Attavara åren 1867-1900 [Residents of Attavara, 1867-1900]. Unpublished text by Nils Alexandersson, Halland Genealogical Society, Halmstad, 2003.

³ At Attavara, Johannes Jönsson assumed the title of *åbo*, a southern Swedish variant of the more common term *hemmansägare*. *Åbo* could refer to a farmer who had the inherited right to use another's land, often a parcel of Crown land. By the nineteenth century, it more commonly designated a small freeholder, who owned his own farm. Johannes fit the second category of farmer. Kari Marklund, ed., NationalEncyklopedin: Ett uppslagsverk på vetenskaplig grund utarbetat på initiativ av Statens Kulturråd [National Encyclopedia: A Reference Work Based on Scientific Methods and Funded by Sweden's National Cultural Commission]. 20 volumes. (Stockholm: Bokförlaget Bra Böcker, 1989-1996), vol. 20, pp. 320 and 322.

⁴ Breared, Hallands län, Husförhörslängder 1838-1842, 1842-1845. Filmade svenska kyrkoböcker. Micro-fiche #412425 and #412426. Svenska Emigrantinstitutet, Växjö.

⁵ Veinge kyrkoarkiv. Döde och Begrafne i Weinge 1844. Micro-fiche C:7, #41101, 1 of 6. ForskarCentrum, Kyrkhult, Sweden. The girl's death was recorded thus in Swedish: "26 april 1844 drunknade[;] 12 maj begrovs flickan Botilda från Skaftaberget."

⁶ Attavara I. Unpublished text in possession of Håkan Håkansson, Halland Genealogical Society, Halmstad, 2003.

⁷ Ibid.

⁸ Cora V. Eckstrom, Kansas Lake Lutheran Church 1871-1971: A Century of God's Grace (Butterfield, Minnesota: Kansas Lake Lutheran Church, 1971), p. 5.

⁹ The Jönssons' place was actually called by three different names in Swedish: Skaftaberget, Skaftabygget, and Skaftahus. The names meant, roughly, Shaftmountain, Shaftsettlement, and Shafthouse. For the sake of simplicity, the name has here been regularized throughout to Skaftaberget.

¹⁰ Attavara I. Unpublished text in possession of Håkan Håkansson, Halland Genealogical Society, Halmstad, 2003.

¹¹ The record of Petronilla's stillborn sister says in Swedish: "Döfödde flickebarnet/twillingen — från Skaftaberget." Veinge kykoarkiv. Födde och

Döpte i Veinge 1848. Guns GID: 1861.44.12800. From Håkan Håkansson and Birgitta Wiman, Halland Genealogical Society, Halmstad.

[12] The records of Johannes and Kjerstin's deceased daughters are found in: Veinge kyrkoarkiv. Födde och Döpte i Veinge 1845. Micro-fiche D:7, #41101, 2 of 6; Döde och Begrafne Veinge 1845. Micro-fiche D:7, #411011, 2 of 6; Födde och Döpte i Weinge Församling År 1850; and Döde och Begrafne i Weinge Församling 1850. Micro-fiche C:7, #411011, 3 of 6. All from: ForskarCentrum, Kyrkhult. The stroke was called *slag* in Swedish.

[13] Losman, "Okända kvinnors röst," p. 32.

[14] "Alsingska skolan" [The Alsing School] in Ivar Knutsson, ed., <u>Veinge och Tjärby genom sekler</u> [Veinge and Tjärby through the Centuries] (Halmstad: Veinge Hembygdsföreningen, 1986), pp. 54-59. Quotation, p. 56.

[15] Veinge, Hallands län, Husförhörslängder 1855-1862, p. 59. Svenska Emigrantinstitutet, Växjö.

[16] Ibid., p. 57. See also: Veinge kyrkoarkiv. Vigde Veinge 1842-64. Micro-fiche C:7, #411011, 6 of 6. ForskarCentrum, Kyrkhult; Veinge Födde 1860-1865 (1862), Utdrag ur 1862 års födelsebok för Weinge moder församling i Laholms prosteri, Hallands län, Götheborgs stift, blad 5, #30. ForskarCentrum, Kyrkhult.

[17] For Anna Johanna's birth record, see: Veinge kyrkoarkiv. Veinge Födde 1860-65 (1864), blad 6, #74. ForskarCentrum, Kyrkhult.

[18] For details on tenant farming, see: Ivar Knutsson, ed., <u>Veinge och Tjärby genom sekler</u>, p. 100.

[19] Ejdestam, <u>De fattigas Sverige</u>, p. 24.

[20] Ivar Knutsson, ed., <u>Veinge och Tjärby genom sekler</u>, p. 100.

[21] Information from Håkan Håkansson, Halland Genealogical Society, Halmstad.

[22] On Anders's wedding, see: Veinge kyrkoarkiv. Micro-fiche C:7, #411011, 1 of 6. Vigde Weinge 1842-1864 (1862). ForskarCentrum, Kyrkhult. On Johanna's youth: Veinge, Hallands län, Husförhörslängder 1855-62, p. 44. Svenska Emigrantinstitutet, Växjö.

[23] Ann-Sofie Kälvemark, "Att vänta barn när man gifter sig. Föräktenskapliga förbindelser och giftermålsmönster i 1800-talets Sverige" [Being Pregnant When You Get Married: Pre-Marital Relationships and Marital Patterns in Nineteenth-Century Sweden], <u>Historisk tidskrift</u>, 2: 1977, pp. 181-199.

[24] Information taken from Johanna Persdotter's divorce suit against Anders Johannesson: Utdrag af Domboken hållen vid Lagtima Sommartinget med Höks Härad i Tjerby år 1880. Äktenskapshandlingar 1880-1882, Höks Härad, Hallands län. Landsarkivet, Göteborg, Sweden.

[25] Ivar Knutsson, ed., <u>Veinge och Tjärby genom sekler</u>, p. 284.

[26] On Anders's children: Veinge kyrkoarkiv. Veinge Födda 1860-1865. Utdrag ur 1862 års Födelsebok, blad 5, #81; Veinge Döda, Utdrag ur 1863 års Dödbok, blad 3, #37; Veinge Födda 1860-1865. Utdrag ur 1864 års Födelsebok, blad 6, #8; Veinge Födda 1865-1870. Utdrag ur 1866 års

Födelsebok, Lex blad, #56. All from ForskarCentrum, Kyrkhult.

27 Emigrantlistor 1868, Hallands län t. o. m. Norrbottens län. År 1868, reel #7123, 31 December, 1868. Genealogical Society Utah, LDS. The minister's comments appeared thus in Swedish:

> *Ingen förändring med Socknen har under året skett. Inga*
> *märkeliga naturtilldragelser hafva under året hänt. För*
> *de flesta nära missväxt, för flere total å både säde och hö,*
> *genom den ovanliga hettan och torkan under sommaren.*

28 Ejdestam, De fattigas Sverige, p. 85.

29 Veinge, Hallands län, Husförhörslängder 1861-1869, Särskild Förteckning 1869. Svenska Emigrantinstitutet, Växjö.

30 Ibid. Svenska Emigrantinstitutet, Växjö.

31 Johanna Persdotter's divorce suit, 1880. Landsarkivet, Göteborg.

32 Attavara I; Veinge, Hallands län, Husförhörslängder 1861-1869, Särskild Förteckning 1869-1870. Svenska Emigrantinstitutet, Växjö.

33 Ibid. The phrase "former farm owners" was written in Swedish as *förra åboen*.

34 Johanna Persdotter's divorce suit, 1880. Landsarkivet, Göteborg.

35 Veinge, Hallands län, Husförhörslängder 1870-1879. Micro-fiche #411495, 5 of 5, pp. 139 and 148. Svenska Emigrantinstitutet, Växjö. The Swedish record says the following about Håkan: "rest t[ill] Amerika '67" (traveled to America, [18]67).

36 Tracking the family between 1866 and their appearance in the American Midwest in 1868 has proven difficult. Repeated searches in the archives of port cities in Sweden and other northern European countries have failed to uncover the exact date the Jönssons left Sweden or the route they took to America.

37 One British ship of the early period of emigration reported that seven babies were born on board during the Atlantic crossing. All the mothers died, and all the babies but one. Duane Meyer, The Highland Scots of North Carolina (Raleigh, North Carolina: The Carolina Charter Tercentenary Commission, 1963), p. 17.

38 Per Esbjörnsson släktmatrikel arbetsmaterial, 2004-03-20 [Per Esbjörnsson family tree research materials, March 3, 2004], pp. 1-3. From Håkan Håkansson and Birgitta Wiman, Halland Genealogical Society, Halmstad.

39 Johanna Persdotter's divorce suit, 1880. Landsarkivet, Göteborg.

40 The Swedish term *Amerikaänkor* was used for "America widows." Ann-Sofie Kälvemark, "Utvandring och självständighet. Några synpunkter på den kvinnliga emigrationen från Sverige" [Emigration and Independence. Some Views on Female Emigration from Sweden], Historisk tidskrift, 2:1983, p. 167.

41 Fritiof Bengtsson, ed., Halländska emigrantöden 1860-1930. Drömmen om Amerika — Vision och verklighet, p. 36; Ljungmark, Den stora utvandringen, p. 183.

42 State of Minnesota against Andrew Johnson, trial testimony, p. 40a.

Chapter IV
Settling In: Kansas Lake

[1] William Watts Folwell, A History of Minnesota, vol III (St. Paul: Minnesota Historical Society, 1926), p. 62.

[2] Richard V. Francaviglia, "The Historic and Geographic Importance of Railroads in Minnesota," in Anne J. Aby, ed., The North Star State: A Minnesota History Reader (St. Paul: Minnesota Historical Society Press, 2002), pp. 181-182.

[3] Information on bunk cars from Craig Pfannkuche, Chicago & North Western Historical Society, May 4, 2004; John C. Luecke, The Chicago and Northwestern in Minnesota (Eagan, Minnesota: Grenadier Publications, 1990), p. viii.

[4] Luecke, pp. 27-28.

[5] 1873-1923. Minnesalbum utgivet av Svenska Lutherska West Sveadahls Församlingen i Watonwan Co., Minn. med anledning av dess femtioårs-jubileum den 24, 25 juni 1923 [1873-1923. Memory Book Issued by the West Sveadahl Swedish Lutheran Congregation in Watonwan County, MN, on the Occasion of its Fiftieth Anniversary Celebration, June 24-25, 1923] (Rock Island, Illinois: Augustana Book Concerns Tryckeri och Bokbinderi, 1923), p. 36. Translation by the present author.

[6] Ibid., p. 8.

[7] Theodore Blegen and Philip D. Jordan, ed., With Various Voices: Recordings of North Star Life (St. Paul: The Itasca Press, 1949), p. 260.

[8] By the 1880s fully one-third of all available farmland in Watonwan County was owned by the St. Paul & Sioux City Railroad Company. In the 1860s and 1870s other sizable portions of land were United States Government Homestead acreage. The St. James Journal, August 5, 1882.

[9] Andrew signed the land over to his father the same day he bought it. See: Reception Record Watonwan County Minnesota, Book A, p. 226. Recorder's Office, Watonwan County Courthouse, St. James, Minnesota. Records indicate Andrew was naturalized on June 9, 1869, and his father on October 21 of that year. Those taking out naturalization papers were required to supply their date and place of arrival in the United States, but Andrew and his father failed to give those details. That omission fits the pattern of their clandestine departure from Sweden. See: Watonwan County District Court Naturalization Records 1872-1945. SAM, vol. [A]-B 1867-1906, Declarations; vol. A-E 1872-1906, Final Papers. Minnesota State Archives, MHS, St. Paul.

[10] The Anglicizing of the Swedes' names was evidenced by notes in: Minnesota Federal Population Census Schedules, 1870, Watonwan County, Long Lake Township, p. 2, l. 38. Minnesota State Archives, MHS, St. Paul.

[11] In 1880 Petronella was serving in the household of Andrew Horberg, thirty-six, a married farmer from Sweden, whose farm was in Nicollet County, Minnesota. See: 1880 US Census, Family History Library Film 1254627, NA Film Number T9-0627, p. 97c. Genealogical Society Utah, LDS.

[12] "History of St. James," St. James Herald, February 14, 1873.

¹³ Luecke, p. 71.

¹⁴ For a description of living conditions on the prairie, see: Blegen, Minnesota: A History of the State, p. 203.

¹⁵ Jens Torson died in Watonwan County in 1881. The St. James Journal, August 6, 1881.

¹⁶ As cited in Luecke, p. 70.

¹⁷ As the noted biologist Richard Dawkins has pointed out, our forebears' first-hand acquaintance with the land exceeded ours because they lived closer to the soil and had to survive on it, but they also used their intimate knowledge of the land to exploit and even overexploit it. Richard Dawkins with Yan Wong, The Ancestor's Tale: A Pilgrimage to the Dawn of Evolution (Boston and New York: Houghton Mifflin Company, 2004), p. 28.

¹⁸ Blegen, Minnesota: A History of the State, pp. 195-197.

¹⁹ John A. Brown, ed., "Reminiscences," History of Cottonwood and Watonwan Counties Minnesota: Their Peoples, Industries and Institutions, vol. 1 (Indianapolis: B. F. Bowen & Co., 1916), pp. 586-587.

²⁰ 1873-1923. Minnesalbum utgivet av Svenska Lutherska West Sveadahls-Församlingen i Watonwan Co., Minn., p. 8. Translation by the present author.

²¹ 1870-1920. Minnesalbum utgifvet af Svenska Lutherska Öst Sveadahls-Församlingen i Watonwan County, Minn. [1870-1920. Memory Book Issued by the East Sveadahl Swedish Lutheran Congregation in Watonwan County, MN] (Rock Island, Illinois: Augustana Book Concerns Tryckeri, 1920), p. 27.

²² State of Minnesota against Andrew Johnson, trial testimony, pp. 5b and 6a.

²³ Ejdestam, Svenskt Folklivslexikon [Dictionary of Swedish Folk Life] (Stockholm: Rabén & Sjögren, 1992), p. 78. As geographer John Rice has pointed out, the Scandinavians had no more experience of the prairies than did other ethnic groups, but they were willing to accept the challenge of living there, often out of sheer necessity since land elsewhere was already occupied. John Rice, "The Swedes," in June Denning Holmquist, ed., They Chose Minnesota: A Survey of The State's Ethnic Groups (St. Paul: Minnesota Historical Society Press, 1981), p. 258.

²⁴ State of Minnesota against Andrew Johnson, trial testimony, p. 35a.

²⁵ Ibid., p. 7b.

²⁶ Blegen and Jordan, ed., With Various Voices: Recordings of North Star Life, pp. 260-261.

²⁷ For details of Charles Johnson's family's emigration, see: Utflyttningslängden för Örs församling år 1857; also Husförhörslängden från Örs församling 1850-1855 and 1856-1861, Älvsborgs län. For Peter Olson and Catherine Olson, see: Husförhörslängden för Råggärds församling 1861-1865 and Utflyttningslängden, Starlanda by, Råggärds församling, Älvsborgs län 1861-1865. Both in Svenska Emigrantinstitutet, Växjö.

²⁸ For details of the Kansas Lake church buildings, see: Cora V. Eckstrom, "The Houses of Worship," Kansas Lake Lutheran Church 1871-1971: A Century of God's Grace (Butterfield, Minnesota: Butterfield Advocate,

1971), pp. 5 and 6. An earlier, more detailed description is in: <u>Seventy-fifth Anniversary 1871-1946 July 7-14, 1946</u> (Butterfield, Minnesota: Kansas Lake Lutheran Church, 1946), pp. 4-10. The Kansas Lake Swedish Lutheran Church was officially incorporated on July 18, 1872, before Justice of the Peace J. R. McLean in St. James. See: Certificate Book and Estray Notices and Miscellaneous Documents. Recorder's Office, Watonwan County Courthouse, St. James, Minnesota.

²⁹ The text that appeared in the January 6, 1888, edition of <u>The Madelia Times</u> was entitled "Telephone Polson's Legislative Experience." It told the humorous and brief fictional tale of a Scandinavian at the Minnesota State Legislature. Its author remained anonymous.

³⁰ Kansas Lake Secretary's Book 1891-1908. Kansas Lake Församlings Protokoller 1891, p. 92. In possession of Kansas Lutheran Church, Long Lake township, Watonwan County, Minnesota. Translation by the present author.

³¹ <u>Seventy-fifth Anniversary 1871-1946 July 7-14, 1946</u>, p. 5.

³² State of Minnesota against Andrew Johnson, trial testimony, p. 17a.

³³ Andrew and Hogan's mother's last name of Håkansdotter was rendered by a puzzled clerk of district court in 1874 in Madelia as "Hagan." He began by trying to record her entire last name but clearly gave up halfway through the name. Her first name was given variously as: Christine, Kersti, Cristi, Chesty, Chersti, and Chrestena. See: The district court for the county of Watonwan and State of Minnesota: The State of Minnesota vs. Andrew Johnston [sic], February 14, 1874. Open File. Location #119. K. 19. 7(B). Minnesota State Archives, MHS, St. Paul.

Chapter V
Lars and Caroline at Kansas Lake

¹ State of Minnesota against Andrew Johnson, trial testimony, pp. 25a and 25b.

² Ibid., p. 36b.

³ Wm. Bracher, engineer, <u>The Plat Book of Watonwan County</u> (Philadelphia, Pennsylvania: Interstate Publishing Co., 1886), p. 8. Lars and Caroline's house was in the southwest quarter of section 8, township 105, and Charles Johnson and his parents lived in the northwest quarter of section 8, township 105.

⁴ 1880 US Census, Long Lake, Watonwan, Minnesota. FHL Film 1254637. National Archives Film T9-0637, p. 430A. Caroline's third child in America, John Albert Johnson, was born on March 11,1871. State of Minnesota, County of Watonwan, Long Lake Township, Register of Births 1871-1900, vol. A, p. 1, l. 9. Minnesota State Archives, MHS, St. Paul.

⁵ State of Minnesota against Andrew Johnson, trial testimony, p. 9a.

⁶ <u>The Plat Book of Watonwan County</u>, p. 2.

⁷ For descriptions of prairie fires, see: Blegen and Jordan, ed., <u>With Various Voices: Recordings of North Star Life</u>, p. 253; Eliza St. John Brophy, <u>Twice a Pioneer</u> (New York: Exposition Press, 1972), pp. 99-100; C. P. Hunstad, "A Prairie Fire," in <u>Odin, Minnesota Centennial 1899-1999: 100 Years</u> (Odin,

Minnesota: Odin Centennial Society, 1999), p. 4.

[8] State of Minnesota against Andrew Johnson, trial testimony, p. 33b.

[9] Ibid., pp. 14a; 15a and 15b. The St. James Herald repeated the use of the term "Little Lars" in its April 4, 1873, issue.

[10] State of Minnesota against Andrew Johnson, trial testimony, p. 17b.

[11] Ibid., p. 18a.

[12] Ibid. John Johnson's comments quoted here appear at various points in his testimony between pages 20b and 23b, in reply to attorneys' queries.

[13] Blegen and Jordan, ed., With Various Voices: Recordings of North Star Life, p. 255.

[14] State of Minnesota against Andrew Johnson, trial testimony, pp. 29b and 30; 9a.

[15] Ibid., pp. 28a; 9b and 10a.

[16] Ibid., p. 40a.

[17] Ibid., p. 36a.

[18] Ibid., p. 10b.

[19] Ibid., pp. 3a; 10b.

[20] Ibid., p. 26a.

[21] Ibid., pp. 14a; 8a; 14a.

[22] Ibid., p. 14a.

[23] Ibid., p. 22a.

[24] Ibid., pp. 29b and 30.

Chapter VI
Conflict

[1] State of Minnesota against Andrew Johnson, trial testimony, p. 9a.

[2] Ibid., pp. 24a and 24b.

[3] Stillwater State Prison Folder, Inmate Record Book, vol. A, p. 300. Minnesota State Archives, MHS, St. Paul.

[4] State of Minnesota against Andrew Johnson, trial testimony, p. 9a.

[5] Ibid., pp. 9b and 10a.

[6] Ibid., pp. 10a; 42a and 42b.

[7] Ibid., pp. 17a and 17b.

[8] Svenska Nybyggaren used the Swedish terms "den halftokige" and "sinnessvaghet."

[9] Translations of the quotations are by the present author.

[10] State of Minnesota against Andrew Johnson, trial testimony, p. 14a.

[11] Annette Atkins, Harvest of Grief: Grasshopper Plagues and Public Assistance in Minnesota, 1873-1878 (St. Paul: Minnesota Historical Society

Press, 1984), p. 41.

[12] David Arill and Edvard Olsson, <u>Värmländska folkminnen</u> [Folk Memories from Värmland] (Karlstad, Sweden: Hjalmar Pettersson & Co. Bokhandel, 1932), p. 26.

[13] State of Minnesota against Andrew Johnson, trial testimony, p. 6a.

[14] Ibid., p. 11b.

[15] Ibid., pp. 11b; 16b.

[16] Ibid., pp. 2b and 3a; 7b.

[17] Ibid., p. 3a. Caroline added: "Doctor Neill came to our house some days after this. There were several people at our house when Dr. Neill came there. One Charles Johnson, Andrew and others were there. I don't remember what was said at this time. I was in the house all the time the doctor was there. He came to see if my husband was crazy and if so to have him sent to the Insane Asylum."

[18] Ibid., p. 3a.

[19] Ibid., p. 17a.

[20] Ibid., p. 17a.

[21] Ibid., p. 29b.

[22] Ibid., pp. 29b and 30.

[23] Ibid., p. 24b.

[24] Ibid., p. 10a.

[25] Lawrence M. Friedman, <u>A History of American Law</u> (New York: Simon & Schuster, 1985), p. 502.

[26] Ibid., pp. 498-501.

[27] Ibid., p. 501.

[28] Marriage Record. Watonwan County Recorder's Office. Watonwan County Courthouse, St. James, Minnesota.

[29] Barbara Lois Zust, "The role of the abusive partner," in <u>The Meaning of INSIGHT Participation Among Women Who Have Experienced Intimate Partner Violence</u>. Ph. D. dissertation, University of Minnesota, August 2003, p. 71. See also: "Ecological Assessment of Men," in Jeffrey L. Edleson and Richard M. Tolman, <u>Intervention for Men Who Batter: An Ecological Approach</u> (Newbury Park, California: SAGE Publications, 1992), pp. 26-51; "The Violent Male," in Joy M. K. Bussert, <u>Battered Women: From a Theology of Suffering to an Ethic of Empowerment</u> (New York: Lutheran Church in America, 1986), pp. 41-53.

[30] Zust, p. 71.

[31] Ibid., p. 74.

[32] State of Minnesota against Andrew Johnson, trial testimony. Hogan Johnson's comments are on p. 14b. John Johnson, Charles's father, reported hearing Andrew comment on separating Lars and Caroline, p. 21b.

[33] Ibid., p. 5b.

[34] Ibid., p. 6a.

[35] Ibid., p. 6b.

[36] Ibid., p. 35a.

[37] Ibid., pp. 17a and 17b; 35a.

Chapter VII
Missing Lars

[1] State of Minnesota against Andrew Johnson, trial testimony, p. 21b.

[2] History of Cottonwood and Watonwan Counties Minnesota: Their Peoples, Industries and Institutions, vol. I, p. 585.

[3] State of Minnesota against Andrew Johnson, trial testimony, p. 7a.

[4] Ibid., p. 17b. The description of the storm is from: "Severe Storm," Mankato Herald, November 23, 1872.

[5] State of Minnesota against Andrew Johnson, trial testimony, p. 26b.

[6] Ibid., pp. 38b and 39a.

[7] "Mrs. Sophia Graf Recalls Terrific Snowstorm of 1873," Madelia Times Messenger, June 20, 1930, p. 1. The 1873 storm was also described in "Winter of 1872-3," and "Great Storms," in History of Cottonwood and Watonwan Counties, Minnesota: Their Peoples, Industries and Institutions, vol. 1, pp. 81, 576, and 585.

[8] History of Cottonwood and Watonwan Counties, Minnesota: Their Peoples, Industries and Institutions, vol. I, pp. 321-322.

[9] Folwell, A History of Minnesota, vol. III, pp. 71-72.

[10] Blegen and Jordan, ed., With Various Voices: Recordings of North Star Life, pp. 305-309.

[11] "Mrs. Sophia Graf Recalls Terrific Snowstorm of 1873," p. 1.

[12] The St. James Journal reported at length on the storm. An excerpt reads thus:

> All roads leading into town are effectively blockaded and
> such a thing as getting to town with a team is an impossibility.
> In the country people live at some distance from one another,
> and unless well supplied with fuel and provisions, there are
> many hardships, if not suffering, to undergo. We very much
> fear that such has been the case in many localities the past two
> weeks. With the country roads blockaded the loss is greater
> than in getting to trains. Our country people have been unable
> to visit town and dispose of their butter, eggs, potatoes, etc., and
> get in exchange family supplies. People have been compelled to
> come to town on foot, the past two weeks, after flour, groceries, etc.,
> and hauling it home on hand-sleds.

Chapter VIII
New Problems

[1] Details of this story from Carol Bratland in a personal communication to the author, November 29, 2003.

[2] Philip Moody related this version of the story in a personal communication to the author, May 27, 2003.

[3] State of Minnesota against Andrew Johnson, trial testimony, p. 33a.

[4] Ibid., pp. 31a and 31b.

[5] Ibid., p. 25a.

[6] Translation by the present author.

[7] State of Minnesota against Andrew Johnson, trial testimony, p. 13b.

[8] Ibid., p. 9a.

[9] Ibid., p. 4b.

[10] Ibid., pp. 3b and 4a.

[11] Ibid., p. 12b.

[12] Ibid., p. 38a.

[13] Ibid., p. 4b.

[14] Ibid., p. 13a.

Chapter IX
Finding Lars

[1] For information on Swedish settlement in Omaha, see: O. M. Nelson, The Swedish Element in Omaha: A Historical Record of the Cultural and Commercial Activities of Swedish-born Residents of Omaha and Their Descendants, with 500 Biographies (Omaha, Nebraska, 1935); Louise Bloom Baumann, The Swedes in Omaha and South Omaha (Omaha: Swedish Cultural Committee, 2005).

[2] State of Minnesota against Andrew Johnson, trial testimony, p. 21a.

[3] According to local reports, there were once six unmarked graves at the Kansas Lake Lutheran Church cemetery. Lars was reportedly buried in one of those graves. All traces of any such graves have long since disappeared. Information from Carol Bratland in a personal communication to the author, April 20, 2002.

[4] State of Minnesota against Andrew Johnson, trial testimony, p. 15b.

[5] Ibid., p. 12b.

[6] Ibid., p. 13b.

[7] Ibid., p. 29a.

[8] Ibid., pp. 28b and 29a.

[9] Ibid., p. 16a.

[10] Ibid., p. 34b.

[11] The State of Minnesota Against Andrew Johnson and Caroline Johnson. The State of Minnesota[,] County of Watonwan, In Justice Court. July 11, 1873. Open file. Location #119. K. 19. 7(B). Minnesota State Archives, MHS, St. Paul.

[12] Evolution of the Blue Earth County Court House and Jail, pp. 1-2. Unpublished text by Blue Earth County Historical Society, Mankato, Minnesota.

[13] State of Minnesota against Andrew Johnson, trial testimony, p. 34b.

[14] On the occurrence of respiratory diseases among Minnesota prisoners in the nineteenth century, see: W. C. Heilbron, <u>Convict Life at the Minnesota State Prison Stillwater, Minnesota</u> (Stillwater, Minnesota: Valley History Press, 1996), p. 54. Updated and expanded edition of 1909 original.

[15] Marriage License, August 20, 1873, State of Minnesota, District Court for Blue Earth County. Contained in: Marriage Record, Blue Earth County, Book C, p. 593. Records Division, Blue Earth County Courthouse, Mankato.

[16] Watonwan County Folder, State of Minnesota, County of Watonwan, State of Minnesota against Andrew Johnston [sic], February 14, 1874. Watonwan County Civil and Criminal Cases. Open file. Location #119.K.19.7b. Minnesota State Archives, MHS, St. Paul.

[17] Register of Births, Watonwan County, Minnesota, Book A, p. 18, l. 23. Recorder's Office, Watonwan County Courthouse, St. James, Minnesota.

Chapter X
Early Trial Reports

[1] <u>History of Cottonwood and Watonwan Counties, Minnesota: Their Peoples, Industries and Institutions</u>, vol. I, pp. 556-557.

[2] <u>The St. James Journal</u>, May 12, 1874; <u>Madelia Times</u>, May 5, 1874; <u>St. James Herald</u>, May 9, 1874.

[3] US Federal Population Census 1870 Minnesota, Madelia Township. Film T132, Roll #12. Svenska Emigrantinstitutet, Växjö.

[4] Watonwan County Folder, Criminal Cases, State of Minnesota, County of Watonwan against Andrew Johnson. No. A120. Summary of sixth district trial proceeding, May 12, 1874. Six pages. Open File. Location #125. F. 18. 4(F). Minnesota State Archives, MHS, St. Paul.

[5] Ibid., p. 5.

[6] Translation by the present author.

[7] Translation by the present author.

Chapter XI
On Trial

[1] "Memorial to Judges," <u>Mankato Free Press</u>, November 22, 1907.

[2] Governors' Files Folder, vol. 2, Sibley to Stassen (1856-1943), J. S. Pillsbury

Administration, Applications for Pardon. State of Minnesota against Andrew Johnson, trial testimony. Minnesota State Archives, MHS, St. Paul. The trial testimony is recorded in eighty-seven pages of handwritten text. The copy now extant is not quite complete. The last two pages are truncated. Except for page 30, the sheets have writing on both the front and back sides; the front sides are labeled a. and the back sides are labeled b. Included in the Pillsbury folder is Caroline's affidavit of 1876. As noted, another source of information on the Johnson case testimony is Svenska Nybyggaren, a Swedish-language newspaper in St. Paul during the 1870s. On eight different dates it reported on Lars's disappearance and Andrew's and Caroline's subsequent actions: April 17, 1873; June 5, 1873; July 17, 1873; July 24, 1873; September 4, 1873; September 11, 1873; May 14, 1874; and May 21, 1874. All reports were on page two of the respective editions.

[3] US Federal Population Census 1870 Minnesota, Madelia township. Film T132, Roll #12. Svenska Emigrantinstitutet, Växjö.

[4] State of Minnesota against Andrew Johnson, trial testimony, p. 10a.

[5] Personal communication from Judy Klee to the author, December 28, 2002.

[6] State of Minnesota against Andrew Johnson, trial testimony, pp. 32a; 18b; 36b; 23b.

[7] Ibid., p. 9b and following.

[8] Ibid., p. 22b.

[9] Ibid., p. 22b.

[10] Ibid., p. 35a.

[11] Ibid., p. 26a.

[12] Ibid., pp. 31a and 31b.

[13] Ibid., p. 25a.

[14] 1880 United States Census. South Branch, Watonwan, Minnesota. FHL Film #1254637. National Archives Film T9-0637, p. 410C. The 1880 census listed Daniel Barge, sixty, as a farmer; his wife Elisabeth, sixty-two, as a housekeeper; Anna Johnson, seventeen, also as a housekeeper. For a history of the Barge family, see comments in: Susan Hewitt Pierson, Pennsylvania Roots and Spreading Branches: Genealogy of Allied Lines Keller-Leckenton-Page (Barge) 1721-1980 (St. James, Minnesota: Watonwan County Shoppers Guide; Blue Earth, Minnesota: Central Graphics, 1980).

[15] State of Minnesota against Andrew Johnson, trial testimony, p. 25b.

[16] A principal reason for the belief in such sightings among Swedish commoners traced back to the calendars formerly in use. Between the older Julian and the newer Gregorian calendars there existed a two-week discrepancy, which was known as Division Time. It was believed that during a period each autumn, which coincided with the two-week gap in the calendars, it was possible for the dead to return (often in crippled or headless form) to have concourse with the living. For a brief discussion of such sightings, see: "Spöktips för hela landet" [Tips about Ghosts for the Whole Country], Svenska Dagbladet, June 24, 2002, p. 17. A longer discussion is in: Åke Ohlmark, "Historiska svenska slottsspökerier" [Historic

Swedish Stories about Haunted Castles], <u>Spökhistorier från alla länder och tider</u> [Ghost Stories from All Countries and Ages] (Stockholm: Tidens förlag, 1980), pp. 219-264.

[17] State of Minnesota against Andrew Johnson, trial testimony, pp. 25a and 25b.

[18] Ibid., p. 25a.

[19] Ibid., pp. 25b and 26a.

[20] Ibid., pp. 26b and 27a.

[21] Ibid., pp. 26b and 27a.

[22] Ibid., p. 25b.

[23] Ibid., pp. 2b; 36b; 17b; 14b; 35b.

[24] Ibid., p. 7a.

[25] Ibid., p. 10b.

[26] Ibid., p. 17b.

[27] Ibid., p. 32b.

[28] Ibid., pp. 20b; 30.

[29] Ibid., p. 21b.

[30] Ibid., p. 40b.

[31] Ibid., p. 23a.

[32] Ibid., p. 37a.

[33] Ibid., p. 16b.

[34] Ibid., p. 35b.

Chapter XII
The Verdict

[1] State of Minnesota against Andrew Johnson, trial testimony, p. 29b.

[2] State of Minnesota, County of Watonwan against Andrew Johnston [sic]. No. A210, Summary of district court trial proceeding, May 12, 1874, p. 6. Minnesota State Archives, MHS, St. Paul.

[3] Ibid., p. 6.

[4] M. J. Severance, Appeal to Minnesota Supreme Court, June 28, 1875. Contained with: State of Minnesota, County of Watonwan against Andrew Johnson. See also: State of Minnesota, County of Watonwan, District Court. The State of Minnesota vs. Andrew Johnson. Notice of Appeal. M. J. Severance, Attorney for Defendant. June 28, 1875. Watonwan County Folder, Civil and Criminal Cases. Both are Open Files. Location #119. K. 19. 7(B). Minnesota State Archives, MHS, St. Paul. The full text of Severance's appeal is no longer extant.

[5] District Court, Sixth Judicial District, Watonwan County, State of Minnesota, 1874, Minutes, p. 45. Open File. Location #114. C. 15. 7(B). Minnesota State Archives, MHS, St. Paul.

[6] State of Minnesota against Andrew Johnson, trial testimony, p. 40a.

[7] Ibid., p. 40a.

[8] Fredrik Ström, "Halländska historiegubbar" [Tales of Halland], in Olof Christiansson, ed., <u>Hallandshistorier</u> [Halland Stories] (Stockholm: Wahlström & Widstrand, 1946), pp. 5-7. For cunning and clever, Ström used the Swedish words *knepig* and *illmarig*.

[9] Kenneth L. Karst, <u>Belonging to America: Equal Citizenship and the Constitution</u> (New Haven and London: Yale University Press, 1989), pp. 95-96.

[10] David A. Harris, <u>Profiles in Injustice: Why Racial Profiling Cannot Work</u> (New York: The New Press, 2002), p. 29.

[11] Jeffrey B. Bumgarner, <u>Profiling and Criminal Justice in America: A Reference Handbook</u> (Santa Barbara, California: ABC-CLIO, 2004), pp. 37-38.

[12] Harris, p. 29.

[13] Harris, p. 29.

[14] <u>The Wells Atlas</u>, November 11, 1870, and June 16, 1871.

[15] <u>Svenska Nybyggaren</u>, May 12, 1874, in comments written before Andrew's trial began but published on the day of the verdict.

[16] Harris, p. 26.

Chapter XIII
The Response

[1] State of Minnesota against Andrew Johnson, trial testimony, cover sheet.

[2] Governors' Files (II), J. S. Pillsbury Administration, Caroline Johnson affidavit, June 30, 1876, State of Minnesota, County of Blue Earth, 2 pages. Minnesota State Archives, MHS, St. Paul.

[3] Whether Caroline herself affixed the signature or someone else did so for her is not certain. Comparing the handwriting of the signature with that of M. J. Severance in the text of the affidavit shows, at any rate, that the signature writer's hand was not Severance's.

Chapter XIV
At Stillwater Prison

[1] "A Noble Girl. Miss Amanda E. Gustafson's Chosen Mission of Christian Charity and Love," <u>The Prison Mirror</u>. Stillwater, Minnesota, August 10, 1887, p. 2. Anniversary Supplement — A Report of the First Prison Mirror. Contained in <u>The Mirror</u>, Stillwater Prison, June 14, 1991.

[2] Ibid., p. 2.

[3] Ibid., p. 2.

[4] Ibid., p. 2.

[5] Ibid., p. 2.

[6] Lars Olsson, "Evelina Johansdotter, Textile Workers, and the Munsingwear Family: Class, Gender, and Ethnicity in the Political Economy of Minnesota at the End of World War I," in Philip J. Anderson and Dag Blanck, ed., Swedes in the Twin Cities: Immigrant Life and Minnesota's Urban Frontier (St. Paul: Minnesota Historical Society Press, 2001), p. 78.

[7] James Taylor Dunn, "The Minnesota STATE PRISON during the STILLWATER Era, 1853-1914," Minnesota History, vol. 37, nr. 4 (December, 1960), p. 138.

[8] Minnesota Correctional Facility — Stillwater Mission Statement 1989-1990 (Stillwater, Minnesota: Minnesota Department of Corrections, 1990), p. 4.

[9] Orville F. Quackenbush, The Development of the Correctional, Reformatory, and Penal Institutions of Minnesota: A Sociological Interpretation (Ann Arbor, Michigan: UMI Dissertation Services, 2001), p. 95. Reprint of Ph. D. dissertation, University of Minnesota, 1956.

[10] W. C. Heilbron, "Warden Henry Wolfer: The 'Modern' Warden," in Convict Life at the Minnesota State Prison: Stillwater, Minnesota, pp. 177-181.

[11] Heilbron, p. 11.

[12] Ibid., pp. 11-16.

[13] Details on the number of Swedish-American inmates before World War I are taken from Stillwater State Prison Folder. Stillwater Prison's Convict Register, vol. I-IV. Minnesota State Archives, MHS, St. Paul.

[14] Stillwater State Prison Folder. Convict Register.

[15] It is not certain if this judgement by prison officials on inmate drinking habits was based on factual knowledge or only on informal questioning.

[16] Quackenbush, p. 65.

[17] Ibid., pp. 114-115.

[18] Ibid., p. 70.

[19] Details from an official State of Minnesota report from Stillwater State Prison. See: "Minnesota State Prison," The Madelia Times, October 8, 1886.

[20] Pat Henke in a personal communication to the author July 28, 2003.

[21] John Carter, "Prison Life As I Found It," The Century Magazine, vol. 80 (September, 1910), pp. 752-758. Quotation from Carter, p. 753.

[22] Ibid., p. 753.

[23] Ibid., p. 755.

[24] Quackenbush, p. 146.

[25] Ibid., p. 115. For more on prison rules, see: Prison Rules, Good Time Law, Library Catalogue of the Minnesota State Prison, at Stillwater, Minnesota (Stillwater, Minnesota: The Prison Mirror, 1901).

[26] Dan Peterson in Convict Register, #1548. Stillwater State Prison Folder. Minnesota State Archives, MHS, St. Paul.

[27] Charles Burling in Convict Register, #2764. Stillwater State Prison Folder. Minnesota State Archives, MHS, St. Paul.

[28] Junior Danielson in Convict Register, #3373. Stillwater State Prison Folder. Minnesota State Archives, MHS, St. Paul.

[29] Stillwater State Prison Folder. Miscellaneous Records. Daily Prison Round, September 1882 – April 1884. Location #117.G.14.2(F); Miscellaneous Account Fund, 1874 - 1883. Location #117.G.14.2(F). Both in Minnesota State Archives, MHS, St. Paul.

[30] Stillwater State Prison Folder. Good Conduct Book 1874-1886, Monthly Statement of Disbursements, pp. 2, 7, 14, 19, 31, 33, 42, 99, 100. Minnesota State Archives, MHS, St. Paul.

[31] Ted Genoways, ed., Hard Time: Voices from a State Prison, 1849-1914 (St. Paul: Minnesota Historical Society Press, 2002), p. 20.

[32] Dunn, p. 148.

[33] Carter, p. 756.

[34] See: Library Catalogue section of Prison Rules, Good Time Law, Library Catalogue of the Minnesota State Prison, at Stillwater, Minnesota. For information on sharing of newspapers, see: Heilbron, pp. 120-123.

[35] Nels Hast was pardoned by the Minnesota Governor in 1883 for reasons not made clear in the records. See: District Court of Faribault. The State of Minnesota Against Nels Hast, June, 1871. Faribault County File, Criminal Cases. Open File. Location #119. D. 10. 9(B). Minnesota State Archives, MHS, St. Paul. His pardon was recorded under his name in the Convict Register.

[36] Carter, p. 753; Heilbron, p. 31.

Chapter XV
Caroline: A Riddle

[1] Kälvemark, "Att vänta barn när man gifter sig," pp. 181-186.

[2] Bernhard Granholm, "Okänd fader — men kanske inte okänd" [Father Unknown — But Maybe Not Unknown], in Håkan Skogsjö, ed., Släktforskarnas dagbok '98 [Journal of Genealogy '98] (Stockholm & Göteborg: Sveriges Släktforskarförbund, 1998), pp. 238-268.

[3] For an engaging discussion of such social practices, see: Vilhelm Moberg, "What the Provincial Laws Relate," A History of the Swedish People: From Prehistory to the Renaissance, tr. Paul Britten Austin (New York: Dorset Press, 1972), pp. 186-197; Moberg, "Life in the Villages," A History of the Swedish People: From Renaissance to Revolution, tr. Paul Britten Austin (New York: Dorset Press, 1973), pp. 191-205.

[4] Friedman, p. 497.

[5] Hunstad, "The Grasshopper Years," Odin, Minnesota 1899-1999: 100 Years, pp. 4-5.

[6] Briefly-Written Facts Regarding the Past and Present of St. James and Watonwan County, Minnesota (St. James, Minnesota: St. James Plaindealer, 1895), p. 8.

[7] It has proven impossible to ascertain how much Hogan's implements might have cost.

[8] Ole Danielson, "Pioneer History of Long Lake Township," in Shirley R. Knudson, ed., History of Watonwan County Minnesota (Dallas, Texas: Curtis Media, Inc., 1996), p. 65. Reprint of a text written by Danielson on September 1, 1941.

[9] Folwell, vol. III, p. 104.

[10] Hogan's claims court appearance is recorded in: State of Minnesota, County of Watonwan. District Court, Sixth Judicial District. David M. Osborne, John H. Osborne and Orrin H. Burdick. Partners as D. M. Osborne et al against Hogan Johnson. Watonwan County Folder. Civil and Criminal Cases. Open File. Location #119. K. 19. 7(B). Minnesota State Archives, MHS, St. Paul. J. W. Seager helped Hogan to "authorize [a] Judgment by Confession without action" to be entered against Hogan in favor of the plaintiffs. See also: D. M. Osborne & Co. against Hogan Johnson, State of Minnesota, County of Watonwan, District Court — Sixth District Court. Watonwan County Judgement Book, pp. 163-164. Open File. Location #119. K. 19. 7(B). Minnesota State Archives, MHS, St. Paul.

[11] Atkins, pp. 51 and 104.

[12] Ibid., pp. 33-34.

[13] Seventy-fifth Anniversary 1871-1946, p. 12.

[14] Atkins, p. 109.

[15] Glenda Riley, "In or Out of the Historical Kitchen?: Minnesota Rural Women," in The North Star State: A Minnesota History Reader, p. 218.

[16] Atkins, pp. 44-45.

[17] Blegen, Minnesota: A History of the State, p. 175.

[18] "Franklin H. Waite," Mankato Free Press, November 22, 1907.

[19] "Death Claims Martin J. Severance," Mankato Free Press, July 11, 1907.

[20] "Grand Old Man of This Community Passes Away at Age 91," Watonwan County Plaindealer, December 7, 1933.

[21] For a brief but well-balanced and nuanced survey of this question, see: Deborah Fink, "Gender," in David T. Wishart, ed., Encyclopedia of the Great Plains (Lincoln and London: University of Nebraska Press, 2004), pp. 319-323.

[22] Atkins, p. 9; Blegen, Minnesota: A History of the State, p. 197.

[23] The fictional writings of the Scandinavian immigrant authors Drude Krog Janson and Kristofer Janson bore witness to the existence of severe moral codes among Scandinavian Americans on the Minnesota prairie. The Jansons were prominent church leaders and social theorists who argued for the adaptation of new social concepts among Scandinavian Americans. Natives of Norway, they spent considerable time near Madelia in the 1880s. The Jansons used their own first-hand observations from their years of church service in Brown County and Watonwan County to depict what they perceived as the narrow moral horizons in the rural settlements there. Their

fictional writings reflected especially the difficult position of women in the patriarchal Scandinavian settlements of those times. An ordained minister, Kristofer Janson also wrote of the strict codes of behavior in the immigrant churches. In the Jansons' fictional works, ideas of women's rights are often introduced to Scandinavian immigrant women by female Yankee crusaders who come into the rural settlements from larger areas outside the farming districts.

Referred to here is Kristofer Janson's short story collection <u>Praeriens Saga: fortaellingar fra Amerika</u> [The Saga of the Prairies: Stories from America] (Chicago: Skandinavens bogtrykkeri, 1885). The lead story "Kvinden skal vaere manden underdanig" has been translated by Rudolf J. Jensen as "A Woman Must Obey Her Husband" (unpublished). See also Drude Krog Janson's novel <u>Saloonkeepers datter: fortaelling</u> (Minneapolis: C. Rasmussens forlagsboghandel, 1892). Drude Krog Janson's novel has appeared in English as <u>A Saloonkeeper's Daughter</u>, tr. Gerald Thorson, ed. Orm Øverland (Baltimore: The Johns Hopkins University Press, 2002). For the ideas on Caroline's choices, I am indebted to Anne Marie Rekdal's discussion of the fate of Nora in Henrik Ibsen's drama <u>Et dukkehjem</u> (<u>A Doll's House</u>). Striking similarities exist between the dilemma faced by Ibsen's fictional heroine in a patriarchal hierarchy and that of Caroline Johnson in Watonwan County. See: Rekdal, "The Female Jouissance: An Analysis of Ibsen's <u>Et dukkehjem</u>," <u>Scandinavian Studies</u>, vol. 74, no. 2 (Summer, 2002), pp. 159-180.

Chapter XVI
Veinge Revisited

[1] Information from Håkan Håkansson, Halland Genealogical Society, July, 2003. The Swedish term for destitute was *utfattig*. See also: Veinge, Hallands län, Husförhörslängder 1880-91. Micro-fiche #411497, 3 of 9, pp. 37 and 89. Svenska Emigrantinstitutet, Växjö. On Hogan, see: US Federal Population Censuses. Film T9. Roll #637. 1880 Minnesota. Long Lake Twp. Watonwan County. Minnesota State Archives, MHS, St. Paul.

[2] Veinge, Husförhörslängder 1861-69. Micro-fiche #411492, 5 of 7, p. 148; Veinge Husförhörslängder 1870-79. Micro-fiche #411495, 4 of 5, p. 119; Veinge Husförhörslängder 1880-91. Micro-fiche #411497, 3 of 9, 6 of 9, 7 of 9, 9 of 9, pp. 105, 78, 185, 223, 292. Svenska Emigrantinstitutet, Växjö. In their impoverished circumstances, Hanna's daughter Bothilda and her husband Nils had two sons, born in 1888 and 1890. Veinge, Hallands län, Veinge kyrkoarkiv 1888-1894, Utdrag ur 1893 års Födelsebok, #30. ForskarCentrum, Kyrkhult.

[3] Veinge, Hallands län, Husförhörslängder 1880-91. Nr. 4 Göstorp, p. 37. Svenska Emigrantinstitutet, Växjö.

[4] For information on unwed mothers who were abandoned, see: Granholm, "Okänd fader — men kanske inte okänd."

[5] Veinge, Hallands län. Husförhörslängder 1880-1891, 1891-1897, 1897-1902, 1902-1908. Micro-fiche film #00003 271. Landsarkivet, Lund. Also: Personal communication from Erik and Asta Berg to the author, Halland Genealogical

Society, Halmstad, January 24, 2004; Ivar Knutsson, ed., Veinge och Tjärby genom sekler, p. 156. On March 7, 1899, Anna Johanna gave birth to a boy, named Bernhard Julius Håkansson, and on August 15, 1902, came a second son, Johan Gottfrid Johansson. Anna Johanna's second son was troubled throughout his life with mental illness and lived part of his time with his mother and part in various mental institutions in southern Sweden.

⁶ Hälsingborgs Landsförsamling, Skåne, Husförhörslängder 1875-1884. Micro-fiche #42750, 6 of 13, p. 188, l. 13. Svenska Emigrantinstitutet, Växjö. Also: Veinge, Hallands Län, Husförhörslängder 1880-1891. Micro-fiche #411497, 3 of 9, p. 91. Svenska Emigrantinstitutet, Växjö.

⁷ Information from Håkan Håkansson, Halland Genealogical Society, Halmstad. See also: Johanna Persdotter's divorce suit, 1880. Landsarkivet, Göteborg.

⁸ Johanna Persdotter's divorce suit, 1880. Landsarkivet, Göteborg.

⁹ The phrase "malice and aversion" was expressed thus in Swedish: *af ondska och motvilja.*

¹⁰ Johanna Persdotter's divorce suit, 1880. Landsarkivet, Göteborg.

¹¹ Veinge, Hallands län, Veinge kyrkoarkiv 1880-1891. Utdrag ur 1883 års Vigselbok för Weinge, #9. Landsarkivet, Lund.

¹² Johanna Persdotter's divorce suit, 1880. Landsarkivet, Göteborg. "Against her will" appeared in Swedish as "mot min vilja."

¹³ Losman, "Förtryck eller jämställdhet? Kvinnorna och äktenskapet i Västsverige omkring 1840" [Oppression or Equality? Women and Marriage in Western Sweden Around 1840], Historisk tidskrift, 3:1982, pp. 294-295.

¹⁴ Johnna Persdotter's divorce suit, 1880. Landsarkivet, Göteborg.

¹⁵ Personregister till Göteborgs Poliskammares Emigrantlistor 1882, vol. EIX 19-21, A-E, pp. 1-434 (page number missing), and vol. EIX 19-21, A-E, pp. 1-434 (p. 162). Svenska Emigrantinstitutet, Växjö.

¹⁶ Stillwater State Prison Folder, Register of Correspondences, 1892, p. 106. Open File. Location #114. E. 14(B). Minnesota State Archives, MHS, St. Paul.

Chapter XVII
In a New World

¹ Nels Peter and Augusta took out their marriage license on May 22, 1884, and were married two days later. See: Marriage Record, Watonwan County, Book B, p. 53. N. P. Johnson to Augusta Johnson. Recorder's Office, Watonwan County Courthouse, St. James, Minnesota. Their first child was born in Long Lake township. See: Birth Record, Watonwan County. Book A 1870-1894, p. 102, l. 1. Recorder's Office, Watonwan County Courthouse, St. James, Minnesota.

² 1885 Census Schedule, State of Minnesota, Town of Nelson, County of Watonwan, p. 13. Minnesota State Archives, MHS, St. Paul.

³ Information on the Sveadahl tenant farm comes from a personal communication from Tom Anderson of Sveadahl to the author, January 28,

2005. A life-long resident of the area, Tom Anderson visited the site of the tenant farm as a youth with his father. They dug at the site and recovered shards of household utensils and pieces of farm implements from the tenant farm, all dating from the nineteenth and early twentieth centuries. At one time the location was also used as an *undantag* arrangement for a poor widow and her children. Information from a personal communication from Reverend Evelyn Weston, of the Sveadahl Lutheran Church, to the author, January 28, 2005.

4 Twelfth Census of the U. S. 1900. Schedule #1 — Population, Sheet #2. State of Minnesota. County of Pine. Sandstone township. Minnesota State Archives, MHS, St. Paul.

5 Donna Bieg in a personal communication to the author, March 30, 2005.

6 For a description of life in Pine County as Nels Peter and Augusta Johnson would have known it, see: "Sandstone Township," in Jim Cordes, Pine County ... and Its Memories (North Branch, Minnesota: Riverview Corporation, 1989), pp. 135-152.

7 Fifth Decennial Census of Minnesota. Population Schedule 1905. County of Pine. Sandstone township. Minnesota State Archives, MHS, St. Paul.

8 Cordes, pp. 135-152.

9 Wikopedia — www.answers.com/topic/hinckley-fire and www.hinckleymn.com/history.htm.

10 Blegen and Jordan, ed., With Various Voices: Recordings of North Star Life, pp. 315-316.

11 Information from Donna Bieg in a personal communication to the author, March 30, 2005.

12 Founded in the 1880s by Danish immigrants to Minnesota, Askov was primarily an agricultural settlement.

13 Minnesota State Population Census Schedules, 1865-1905, roll 103. Washington — Watonwan Counties, p. 78. Minnesota State Archives, MHS, St. Paul. Proof of Petronella and John's new location at Kansas Lake appears in the Minnesota census schedule from June, 1895, which lists the following persons: John Olson, a farmer, and his wife Nellie Olson. John Olson had then lived in Minnesota for fifteen years and had spent the past five years and two months in Long Lake township.

14 Minnesota State Population Census Schedules, 1865-1905, reel 103. Washington-Watonwan 1895, p. 78. Minnesota State Archives, MHS, St. Paul.

15 Stillwater State Prison Folder. Visitors and Correspondence Registers. Correspondence Register, 1892-1899, p. 106. Minnesota State Archives, MHS, St. Paul.

16 Stillwater Democrat, February 19, 1887; as cited in John Koblas, When the Heavens Fell: The Youngers in Stillwater Prison (St. Cloud, Minnesota: North Star Press, 2002), p. 84.

Chapter XVIII
Facing Freedom

[1] The 1892 petition for Andrew's pardon is no longer extant. Thus there is no way of knowing which persons signed it.

[2] "Memorials to Judges," <u>Mankato Free Press</u>, November 22, 1907.

[3] Henry Wolfer, "On Modern Prison Management," <u>The Century Magazine</u>, vol. 80 (December, 1910), pp. 317-318.

[4] Executive Documents of the State of Minnesota for the Fiscal Year Ending July 31, 1894, vol. III (St. Paul: The Pioneer Press Co., 1895), pp. 286 and 307. For comments on the granting of pardons, see: Dunn, p. 151.

[5] Stillwater State Prison Folder. Book of Murders, sheet 2. Minnesota State Archives, MHS, St. Paul.

[6] Stillwater State Prison Folder. Inmate Record Book, vol. A, p. 300. Minnesota State Archives, MHS, St. Paul.

[7] Stillwater State Prison Folder. Register of Correspondences, 1892, p. 106. Minnesota State Archives, MHS, St. Paul.

[8] Carter, p. 755.

[9] Heilbron, p. 45.

[10] <u>The St. James Journal</u>, December 30, 1892, and January 6, 1893.

[11] Stillwater State Prison Folder. Wardens' Correspondence and Miscellany 1889-1894, Book 2, Henry Wolfer to Geo. P. Johnson [sic]., Esq., January 6, 1893, p. 655. Open File. Location #109. F. 18. 5(B). Minnesota State Archives, MHS, St. Paul.

[12] Tollefson generations beginning with Teman's father. Family genealogy. Unpublished manuscript in possession of Pat Henke.

Chapter XIX
Caroline in Wisconsin: Reinventing Her History

[1] "Adam P. Johnsons Make Camp on Prairie in 1879," Newman Grove (Nebraska) <u>Reporter</u>, Seventy-fifth Anniversary Jubilee Edition, June 9, 1963.

[2] All of the above information is from: Pat Henke, Karolina Andersdotter, p. 2.

[3] Indentures, Dane County, Wisconsin, April 21, 1890, and September 28, 1909. Dane County Courthouse, Madison, Wisconsin.

[4] Pat Henke, Karolina Andersdotter, p. 2.

[5] Ibid., p. 2.

[6] Ibid., p. 1.

[7] Ibid., p. 2.

[8] My discussion here is based to a large degree on: Darlene Clark Hine, "Rape and the Inner Lives of Black Women: Thoughts on the Culture of Dissemblance," <u>Hine Sight: Black Women and the Deconstruction of American History</u> (Brooklyn, New York: Carlson Publishers, 1994), p. 41.

[9] Pat Henke, Karolina Andersdotter, p. 2.

Chapter XX
Returning Home

[1] "Reminiscences," <u>History of Cottonwood and Watonwan Counties, Minnesota: Their Peoples, Industries and Institutions</u>, vol. I, pp. 586-587.

[2] Rice, "The Swedes," <u>They Chose Minnesota: A Survey of The State's Ethnic Groups</u>, p. 258.

[3] "Reminiscences," <u>History of Cottonwood and Watonwan Counties, Minnesota: Their Peoples, Industries and Institutions</u>, vol. I, p. 583.

[4] Ibid., p. 587.

[5] Ibid., p. 588.

[6] <u>1870-1920. Minnesalbum utgifvet af Svenska Lutherska Öst Sveadahls-församlingen i Watonwan County, Minn.</u>, p. 29. Translation by the present author.

[7] "Reminiscences," <u>History of Cottonwood and Watonwan Counties, Minnesota: Their Peoples, Industries and Institutions</u>, vol. I, p. 588.

[8] Rhoda Gilman, <u>The Story of Minnesota's Past</u> (St. Paul: Minnesota Historical Society Press, 1991), p. 124.

[9] <u>1873-1920. Minnesalbum utgivet af Svenska Lutherska West Sveadahls-Församlingen i Watonwan Co., Minn.</u>, p. 27.

[10] Charles Johnson's father's death is recorded in: Register of Deaths, Town of Long Lake, County of Watonwan, State of Minnesota, Book A, p. 7, l. 21. Recorder's Office, Watonwan County Courthouse, St. James, Minnesota. For details on Christine Johnson's death, see: Register of Deaths, Town of Long Lake, County of Watonwan, State of Minnesota, Book A, p. 7, l. 34. Recorder's Office, Watonwan County Courthouse, St. James, Minnesota.

[11] See: Mortgage Record, Book B, p. 592, and Mortgage Book E, p. 144. Recorder's Office, Watonwan County Courthouse, St. James, Minnesota. Also: Legal Notices, <u>The St. James Journal</u>, February 26, 1881. Charles Johnson married Kate Henderson on October 29, 1875, in Madelia. See: Marriage Record, Watonwan County, Book A, p. 194. Recorder's Office, Watonwan County Courthouse, St. James, Minnesota. See also: Minnesota State Population Census Schedule, 1895, Watonwan County, p. 264, and 1905 Census of Minnesota, Population Schedule, County of Watonwan, City of St. James, reel 162, l. 78-79. Both in Minnesota State Archives, MHS, St. Paul.

[12] Personal communication from Judy Klee to the author, December 28, 2002.

[13] <u>The Plat Book of Watonwan County</u>, 1886. p. 8.

[14] 1880 United States Census, Long Lake, Watonwan County, Minnesota. FHS Film #1254737, National Archives Film T9-0637, p. 432B. See also: Reception Record, Book B, designation J (no page number). Recorder's Office, Watonwan County Courthouse, St. James, Minnesota.

¹⁵ Mortgage Record, Book F, p. 356. Recorder's Office, Watonwan County Courthouse, St. James, Minnesota. See also: Mortgage Record, Book B, p. 464. Recorder's Office, Watonwan County Courthouse, St. James, Minnesota. Hogan gave a $175.00 down payment to a land agent in Madison, Wisconsin.

¹⁶ Mortgage Record, Book E, p. 70; Sheriff's Foreclosure Record, Book 3. Certificate of Sales Record, p. 7. Both in: Recorder's Office, Watonwan County Courthouse, St. James, Minnesota. See also: The St. James Journal, January 6, 1883, for legal notice of the foreclosure on Hogan's land.

¹⁷ Blegen, Minnesota: A History of the State, p. 206.

¹⁸ While it is not impossible that Hogan stayed close to his parents' farm for a while after losing his land, by 1885 he had disappeared from Watonwan County altogether. Where he went and what fate awaited him is open to speculation.

¹⁹ Deed Record, Book J, p. 310. Recorder's Office. Watonwan County Courthouse, St. James, Minnesota. See also: Seventy-fifth Anniversary 1871-1946, p. 6.

²⁰ Deed Record, Book W, p. 633. Recorder's Office, Watonwan County Courthouse, St. James, Minnesota.

²¹ Mortgage Record, Book X, p. 59. Recorder's Office, Watonwan County Courthouse, St. James, Minnesota.

²² Kansas Lake Secretary's Book, p. 11. The church membership dues were known in Swedish as *kommunikantavgift*. In addition to John and Christine Johnson, several aged persons, mainly widows and widowers, received the benefit from the congregation of not having to pay membership dues in the 1890s.

²³ Andrew's parents' deaths were recorded in: Register of Deaths, Town of Long Lake, County of Watonwan, State of Minnesota, Book A, p. 30, l. 11, and in Book B, p. 46, l. 2. Recorder's Office, Watonwan County Courthouse, St. James, Minnesota.

²⁴ Christine Johnson's epitaph (from Luke 11:28) reads: "Saliga äro de som höra Guds ord och gömma det" (Blessed are they that hear the word of God, and keep it).

Chapter XXI
Moving On

¹ "Julfirande i Veinge på artonhundratalet" [Celebrating Christmas in Veinge in the Nineteenth Century], in Ivar Knutsson, ed., Veinge och Tjärby genom sekler, pp. 282-284.

² Kansas Lake Secretary's Book, pp. 92-93. Pastor Eckman's words in Swedish were: "utan Jul, Påsk och Pingst, utan Söndag och Kyrka."

³ State of Minnesota against Andrew Johnson, trial testimony, p. 42a.

⁴ The mark of "well" was given in Swedish as *väl*; "weak" was *svagt*. Veinge, Hallands län, Husförhörslängder 1818-1842. Micro-fiche film

#412425, p. 186. Svenska Emigrantinstitutet, Växjö.

[5] State of Minnesota against Andrew Johnson, trial testimony, p. 42b.

[6] Minnesota State Population Census Schedule, 1895, Watonwan County, p. 257. Minnesota State Archives, MHS, St. Paul.

[7] "Grand Old Man of This Community Passes Away at Age 91," Watonwan County Plaindealer, December 7, 1933, pp. 1 and 5.

[8] J. W. Seager remained active in St. James until his death in 1933. Once Andrew left Watonwan County, he seems to have lost all contact with Seager and other officials who had been involved in his trial, conviction, and release from prison.

[9] We have at least one indication that Andrew was looking for a new place to live in the 1890s. On November 8, 1895, The St. James Journal wrote: "Andrew Johnson is back from his trip to Arkansas. He says the country is no good and he don't [sic] want to live there." A note of caution is in order, however, in assuming that this notice referred to Andrew Johnson of Kansas Lake. There were three men named Andrew Johnson in Watonwan County at the time and a fourth named Andrew Jones. It was not uncommon for the identities of the four men to be confused in the columns of the newspaper.

[10] Mortgage Record, Book 41, p. 603; Mortgage Record, Book 53, pp. 241-242. Recorder's Office, Watonwan County Courthouse, St. James, Minnesota.

[11] Information from Håkan Håkansson, Halland Genealogical Society, Halmstad, and Pastor Sven-Olof Johansson, Pastorsexpeditionen, Veinge Parish, Halland, Sweden, November 27, 2003, and December 3, 2003. See also: "Från sockenstämma till storkommun" [From Small Parish to District Center], in Ivar Knutsson, ed., Veinge och Tjärby genom sekler, p. 76.

Chapter XXII
A New Life

[1] Byron J. Nordstrom, "The Sixth Ward: A Minneapolis Swede Town in 1905," in Nils Hasselmo, ed., Perspectives on Swedish Immigration: Proceedings of the International Conference on the Swedish Heritage in the Upper Midwest, April 1-3, 1976, University of Minnesota, Duluth (Chicago: The Swedish Pioneer Historical Society, 1978), p. 152.

[2] Ibid., p. 160.

[3] Census of the U. S. Schedule No. 1. Population, 1900. City of Minneapolis, p. 144, l. 132-134. Minnesota State Archives, MHS, St. Paul.

[4] Nordstrom, "The Sixth Ward: A Minneapolis Swede Town in 1905," p. 163.

[5] Simons's full name was August Lawrence Simons. He was born in Norway in 1864, and died in Superior in 1955. He arrived in Superior in 1888 and started his dairy operations there the following year. It is not clear how Andrew found employment with Simons, but the two men appear to have enjoyed a cordial relationship for the better part of two decades. See: "Retired Dairy Operator Dies," The Evening Telegram, Superior, Wisconsin, August 19, 1955. Also: Death Certificates, Book 39, p. 400. Register of Deeds, Douglas County Courthouse, Superior, Wisconsin.

[6] Frederick Hale, <u>Swedes in Wisconsin</u> (Madison: The Wisconsin Historical Society Press, 2002), p. 19.

[7] Information on Johanna Persdotter's death from: Pastor Sven-Olof Johansson, Pastorsexpeditionen, Veinge Parish, December 3, 2003. The cause of death was given in Swedish as *nervsvaghet*.

[8] 1895 Minnesota State Population Schedules, 1865-1895, roll 81. Ottertail — Pine. County of Pine, City of Sandstone; Twelfth Census of the U. S. 1900. Schedule #1 — Population. Sheet #2. State of Minnesota, County of Pine, Sandstone township; Fifth Decennial Census of Minnesota, Population Schedule, 1905. Schedule sheet 33. County of Pine, Village of Sandstone. Minnesota State Archives, MHS, St. Paul.

[9] Information from Ragnhild Preston in a personal communication to the author, August 28, 2003.

[10] Pat Henke, Karolina Andersdotter, p. 2; and Pat Henke in a personal communication to the author, April 10, 2003.

[11] Gilbert Tingom died on January 25, 1926, in Eau Claire County, Wisconsin. See: State of Wisconsin, Department of Public Health — Bureau of Vital Statistics, Eau Claire County 1926, Copy of Death Record #40. Eau Claire County Courthouse, Eau Claire, Wisconsin.

[12] Some of Nels Peter's stonework is in the Minnesota State Capitol building in St. Paul. His farm at Copper Creek was located twelve miles south of downtown Superior and just east of Wisconsin State Highway 35 leading southward.

[13] State of Wisconsin, Department of Health — Bureau of Vital Statistics. Copy of Death Record. June 15, 1914. Volume 4, p. 270. Register of Deeds, Douglas County Courthouse, Superior, Wisconsin. See also: "Nels P. Johnson," <u>The Superior Telegram</u>, June 16, 1914, p. 7.

Chapter XXIII
The Waning Years

[1] To follow Aaron R. Johnson's moves in Minneapolis, see: <u>Davison's Minneapolis City Directory</u>, (Minneapolis, 1905, 1908, 1910, 1915, 1917), 1905, p. 908; 1908, p. 806; 1910, p. 893; 1915, p. 1012; 1917, p. 1004.

[2] State of Minnesota, Department of Vital Statisitics. Death certificates 1915, roll 9, #17,700. Certificate of Death #1263. County of Hennepin, City of Minneapolis. Minnesota State Archives, MHS, St. Paul.

[3] For details on Layman's Cemetery, see: <u>Minneapolis Pioneers and Soldiers Memorial Cemetery, 1858-1936</u> (Minneapolis: Minneapolis Protective Cemetery Association, 1936).

[4] For a concise history of the Augustana Home, see: Patty Crawford et al, <u>Augustana Home: A Mighty Social Ministry, 1896-1996</u> (Minneapolis: Augustana Home of Minneapolis, 1995).

[5] Application to the Board of Directors, Mission Cottage, December 14, 1918. In: Admittance to the Augustana Home for Aged, p. 53. Augustana Nursing Home Archives, Augustana Care Corporation, Minneapolis.

6 Ibid., back side of first sheet.

7 MHS Death Certificates 1919. Roll 9, #16,707-19,029. Certificate of Death. County of Hennepin. City of Minneapollis. Petronella Olson. Minnesota State Archives, MHS, St. Paul.

8 Inventory of Swedish American Church Archives in the United States. Micro-film Roll #128. Augustana (1866) Minneapolis, Hennepin County, Minnesota. Receptions 1887-1899. 1899, p. 221. Bernadotte Memorial Library Archives, Gustavus Adolphus College, St. Peter, Minnesota.

9 Last Will and Testament of Petronella Olson. January 10, 1919. Copy in possession of Augustana Nursing Home Archives, Augustana Care Corporation, Minneapolis.

10 State of Minnesota, County of Hennepin. In the Matter of the Estate of Petronella Olson. Decree of Distribution. No. 21398. Hennepin County District Court. Probate-Mental Health Division. Hennepin County Government Center, Minneapolis.

11 Donna Bieg in a personal communication to the author, March 30, 2005.

12 Ibid., March 30, 2005.

13 1920 Federal Census of the United States. Township of Superior, County of Douglas, State of Wisconsin. Svenska Emigrantinstitutet, Växjö.

14 Information on Andrew's stroke from: Personal communication from Ida Johnson Walker to Donna Bieg, March, 1987. For details on Andrew's death, see: State of Wisconsin. Department of Health — Bureau of Vital Statistics. Copy of Death Record. Andrew Johnson. November 11, 1920. Vol. 8, p. 152. Register of Deeds, Douglas County Courthouse, Superior, Wisconsin.

15 Records of the family memory of a relative being sent to prison but then declared innocent are in possession of Donna Bieg.

16 See: Copy of Death Record. Andrew Johnson. November 11, 1920. In note 14 above.

17 State of Wisconsin, Douglas County, in County Court. In the matter of the Estate of Andrew Johnson. Executors' or Administrators' Final Account and Order, April 7, 1922. Probate Records. Register of Deeds, Douglas County Courthouse, Superior, Wisconsin.

18 Personal communication from Carol Bratland to the author, November 29, 2003.

Chapter XXIV
The Pioneer Past

1 As early as the 1880s, newspapers in St. James and Madelia began reporting that early settlers were leaving the St. James area. See, for example: "St. James Department," The Madelia Times, February 4, 1887.

2 The Treasurer's Book and the Secretary's Book were subtitled in Swedish: Räkenskaps — Bock för Kansas Lakes — Församling 1892 [Account Book for the Kansas Lake Congregation 1892] and Kansas Lake Församlings Protokoller 1891 [Minutes of the Kansas Lake Congregational Meetings

1891]. Those and other still extant Kansas Lake church books are now in the possession of the Kansas Lake Lutheran Church, Long Lake township, Watonwan County. In those books, John A. Moody and his father, Johan Moody, were referred to by various names, among which were "Johan Modig," "John Modig," and "John A. Modig."

3 John A. Moody came from Sweden to America with his parents. In 1895 they were living in Odin township, Watonwan County. At that time the family had lived in Odin township since 1883. In the late 1890s John A. Moody married. By 1902 he and his wife were living at Andrew's parents' former farmstead at Kansas Lake. See: 1895 Minnesota Census Report, County of Watonwan, township of Odin, State of Minnesota, p. 166, l. 18ff.; Fifth Decennial Census of Minnesota, 1905. Population Schedule, County of Watonwan, township of Long Lake, p. 101. Both in Minnesota State Archives, MHS, St. Paul.

4 Philip Moody related this version of the story in a personal communication to the author, May 27, 2003.

5 F. M. Eckman et al, <u>Minnesskrift 1858-1908 tillegnad Minnesota-Konferensens af Ev. Lutherska Augustana-Synoden 50-års Jubileum</u> [Festschrift, 1858-1908, Dedicated to the Minnesota Conference of the Evangelical Lutheran Augustana Synod on the Occasion of Its Fiftieth Anniversary] (Minneapolis: Hahn & Harmon Company, 1908), p. 145.

6 <u>1870-1920. Minnesalbum utgifvet af Svenska Lutherska Öst Sveadahls-Församlingen i Watonwan County</u>, p. 12. The quotation reads in Swedish: "Han var en man, som icke kunde rubbas ett hårsmån från det som var rätt."

7 For a detailed discussion of this conflict that is focused on Scandinavian-American church life in the final decades of the nineteenth century, see: Nina Draxten, <u>Kristofer Janson in America</u> (Boston: Norwegian-American Historical Association and Twayne Publishers, 1976), pp. 104-131.

8 Kansas Lake Secretary's Book 1891-1908, p. 97. Organizing the scattered sheep and lambs Pastor Eckman described in Swedish as: "samla och ordna de spridda fåren och lammen och föra dem på det rätta betit."

9 Ibid., pp. 36-37. For eternal perdition and damnation, Pastor Eckman used the Swedish words: "evigt förderf och fördömelse."

10 For a concise discussion of approaches to accommodation and differentiation, see: Crawford et al, <u>Augustana Home: A Mighty Social Ministry 1896-1996</u>, pp. 6-7.

11 In Swedish, Pastor Eckman referred to secular societies as "hemliga föreningar," that is, "secret societies."

12 Pastor Eckman termed private worship and reflection on religious matters "det enskilda bruket," that is, "private use [of religion]".

13 Kansas Lake Secretary's Book 1891-1908, pp. 123-128. Borrowing from some of the more vituperous parts of the Scriptures, Pastor Eckman described his congregation members as, among other things: arrogant ("högfärdige"), blasphemers ("försmädare"), ingrates ("otacksamma"), irreverent ("ogudaktige"), traitors ("förrädare"), covetous ("girige"), and as loving luxurious living more than God ("de der mer älska vällust än Gud").

[14] Seventy-fifth Anniversary 1871-1946, p. 16.

[15] Kansas Lake Church Board Meetings 1901 to 1940/Kansas Lake Församlings Kyrkoråds Prottokoller, år 1901 [-1940], p. 3. In possession of Kansas Lake Lutheran Church.

[16] Kansas Lake Secretary's Book 1891-1908, p. 96. Pastor Eckman referred to the book in Swedish as: "den lilla gamla protokollsboken."

[17] Ibid., p. 14. Pastor Eckman wrote in Swedish:

> *Denna församling räknar blott 20 år och har på den*
> *fasta grunden af Guds oföränderlighet ägt bestånd och*
> *utvecklats under många vexlingar af ljus och mörker,*
> *svaghet och brist som ligga innefattade uti dessa 20 åren.*

[18] Jason Lavery, "All of the President's Historians: The Debate over Urho Kekkonen," Scandinavian Studies, vol. 75, Nr. 3 (Fall, 2003), p. 381.

[19] One such descendant is Judy Klee, the great granddaughter of Charles Johnson. After reading the district court trial transcript from 1874, Judy Klee described her own response with these words:

> *Behind a 135-year-old curtain stood great grandfather*
> *Charles Johnson, great-great grandfather Johannes Johnson,*
> *and great-great grandmother Christine reporting in district*
> *court in 1874 their birthdates, where they lived, how they lived,*
> *who their neighbors were, that their closest neighbor may*
> *have been murdered, and the body washed up on the shore*
> *of their homestead. Why had this event been lost in our family?*
> *If I had said to my grandmother Mable Hansen, "Tell me*
> *about your father's Kansas Lake neighbor Lars Johnson,"*
> *what would she have said? Mable's mother Kate, Charles*
> *Johnson's wife, lived, as a girl, in the homestead next to*
> *Charles and his parents, and Charles and Kate married about*
> *a year after the Kansas Lake trial. In such a small community*
> *as Kansas Lake before the advent of radio or television and*
> *the daily volume of soul deadening violence, a neighborhood*
> *murder, even if only alleged, would result in a pitch of*
> *momentous concern, shaking the fabric of life and leaving a*
> *cavernous memory groove and etheric shame in all citizens*
> *but the most callous or mentally ill — or so I imagine.*

A personal communication from Judy Klee to the author, November 12, 2003, p. 2.

[20] That secrecy might not have been as great if all the Kansas Lake records from the earliest period had survived. The fate of the Kansas Lake church books, 1871 to 1891, remains an open question. Some reports indicated they reside even now among books in the nearby Sveadahl and Trimont Lutheran churches, but searches have not located them there. On June 19, 1904, the Kansas Lake church suffered extensive damage from a fire. Some of the books from the early years of the congregation, including Pastor Sandell's

diaries, were most likely destroyed in that fire. See: Cora V. Eckstrom, "The 1889 Church Burned," Kansas Lake Lutheran Church 1871-1971: A Century of God's Grace, p. 6.

Chapter XXV
The Legacy

[1] Moberg, The Unknown Swedes: A Book About Swedes and America, Past and Present, tr. and ed., Roger McKnight (Carbondale and Edwardsville: Southern Illinois University Press, 1988), p. 64.

[2] Rochelle Wright, "Vilhelm Moberg's Image of America," (Ph. D. dissertation, University of Washington, 1975), pp. 34-40.

[3] For the expression "wildflowers of oblivion" I am indebted to Vilhelm Moberg, who used the Swedish phrase "glömskans vildgräs" in describing the graves of forgotten immigrants in Minnesota. Moberg, Den okända släkten (Stockholm: Albert Bonniers Förlag, 1959), p. 71.

Postscript

[1] Descendants of Caroline's Minnesota and Wisconsin families met one another at a regularly scheduled Watonwan County Historical Society meeting in April of 2003 in St. James, Minnesota.

[2] Carol Bratland in a personal communication to the author, August 28, 2003. See also: Death Records, Watonwan County Minnesota 1946-1973, Book 1950, p. 90, l. 4. Recorder's Office, Watonwan County Courthouse, St. James, Minnesota. Also: "Rites Are Held for Mrs. Anna Barge, 87," St. James Courier, April 11, 1950.

[3] 1880 United States Census, Long Lake, Watonwan County, Minnesota, FHL Film 1254637, National Archives Film T9-0637, p. 430A. Isabel married Wilson B. Burley in 1887. The St. James Journal, February 19, 1887.

[4] The church ledger from Sweden said only the following in Swedish about Hogan: "Mannen i Amerika. Död." ([Hanna Andersdotter's] husband in America. Dead.) Veinge, Hallands län. Husförhörslängder 1880-91. Micro-fiche #411497, 3 of 9, p. 89. Svenska Emigrantinstitutet, Växjö. See also: State of Wisconsin. Department of Health — Bureau of Vital Statistics. County of Douglas. Copy of Death Record. Hogan Johnson. Register of Deeds. Douglas County Courthouse, Superior, Wisconsin. Also: "Aged Pioneer Passes Away," The Superior Telegram, December 13, 1916, p. 11. It is not altogether impossible that Hogan Johnson of Kansas Lake moved to Superior in the 1880s and fibbed about his age. The woman the Hogan Johnson who lived in Superior married came to America from Sweden in 1883, the same year Hogan relinquished his farm and disappeared from Kansas Lake. Neither the obituary nor the death certificate of Hogan Johnson in Superior made any reference to his parents' names or any mention of a brother living in the Superior area. As a result, theories about Hogan's fate can only be described as speculation.

[5] Judy Klee in a personal communication to the author, December 28, 2002.

[6] "Grand Old Man of This Community Passes Away at Age 91," <u>Watonwan County Plaindealer</u>, December 7, 1933, p. 1; personal communication from Carol Bratland to the author, November 29, 2003.

[7] "Death Claims Martin J. Severance," <u>Mankato Free Press</u>, July 11, 1907, pp. 5-6. See also: "Honorable Career," <u>Mankato Revue</u>, May 26, 1902.

[8] Johnston's encounters with mental health officials were recorded in: <u>The St. James Journal</u>, August 17, 1894; St. Peter State Hospital Folder. Admissions and Discharges, Minnesota Hospital for Insane, Book M. Male. June 1893-September 1899, pp. 5 and 22. Open File. Location #108.I.18.5(B-1); St. Peter State Hospital Folder. History Accompanying Patient, Examination on Admission, August 13, 1894, pp. 386-389. Open File. Location #108.I.18.5(B-1); and St. Peter State Hospital Folder. Case Book March 1894-March 1896, George P. Johnston, History Accompanying Patient and Examination on Admission, pp. 385-389. Open File. Location #108.I.18.5(B-1). All in Minnesota State Archives, MHS, St. Paul. On Johnston's political career, see: <u>The St. James Journal</u>, October 14, 1882; October 28, 1882, p. 5; November 18, 1882, p. 4; September 18, 1886; December 18, 1886; January 15, 1886. On Johnston's death, see: <u>St. James Plaindealer</u>, July 7, 1895, and July 11, 1895. George P. Johnston's death was recorded in: Register of Deaths. Watonwan County, Village of St. James, Book A 1870-1895, p. 94, l. 21. Recorder's Office, Watonwan County Courthouse, St. James, Minnesota.

[9] On August Johnson: Personal communication from Donna Bieg to the author, March 28, 2005. See also: "P. August Johnson, North Mankato, Dies at Age 73," <u>The Mankato Free Press</u>, May 29, 1944; "North Mankato," <u>The Saint Peter Herald</u>, June 2, 1944, p. 5; and Certificate of Death. Minnesota State Department of Health, Division of Birth and Death Records and Vital Statistics, 1944, #9124. Minnesota State Archives, MHS, St. Paul. Information on Mae Fleming Smith from: "Mae Fleming Smith," <u>The Free Press</u>, Mankato, November 18, 1983.

[10] Shirley Moriarity Christeson in a personal communication to Pat Henke, March 19, 2005. See also: "Mrs. Augusta Johnson," <u>The Evening Telegram</u>, Superior, Wisconsin, November 15-16, 1941; and Wisconsin State Board of Health. Bureau of Vital Statistics, November 14, 1941. Vol. 25. Register of Deeds, Douglas County Courthouse, Superior, Wisconsin.

[11] Pat Henke in a personal communication to the author, July 18, 2003. See also: State of Wisconsin, Department of Public Health — Bureau of Vital Statistics, Eau Claire County 1926. Copy of Death Record #40. Eau Claire County Courthouse, Eau Claire, Wisconsin.

[12] Pat Henke, Karolina Andersdotter, pp. 2-3.

[13] Donna Bieg in personal communications to the author, March 28 and 30, 2005. For information on Aaron Johnson's death, see: MHS Death Certificate Index. Certificate Identification #1979-MN-005763. Minnesota Department of Vital Statistics. Hubbard County. Minnesota State Archives, MHS, St. Paul; and Death Notice, <u>Park Rapids Enterprise</u>, Park Rapids, Minnesota, March 28, 1979.

Bibliography

Archives

Augustana Nursing Home, Archives, Augustana Care Corporation, Minneapolis

Admittance[Book] to the Augustana Home for Aged

Papers of Former Patients.

Blue Earth County Courthouse, Records Division, Mankato, Minnesota

District Court for Blue Earth County, Marriage Record, 1873.

Douglas County Courthouse, Superior, Wisconsin

Register of Deeds, Index to Deaths, Vol. I-IV

Register in Probate

Zoning Department.

ForskarCentrum, Kyrkhult, Sweden

Veinge, Hallands län, Veinge Kyrkoarkiv.

Genealogical Society Utah, Latter Day Saints, Family History Library

Emigrantlistor 1868, Hallands län t. o. m. Norrbottens län

1880 US Census, Family History Library.

Gustavus Adolphus College, Bernadotte Memorial Library Archives, St. Peter, Minnesota

Inventory of Swedish American Church Archives in the United States.

Hennepin County Government Center, Minneapolis

Division of Public Records, Abstract Tract Index Office, Records Section

Hennepin County District Court, Probate-Mental Health Division

Office of Deed Certificates.

Landsarkivet, Göteborg, Sweden

Äktenskapshandlingar, Höks Härad, Hallands län, 1880-1882.

Landsarkivet, Lund, Sweden

Hallands län, Breared, Kyrkoarkiv

Veinge, Hallands län, Veinge Kyrkoarkiv, 1880-1891.

Minnesota State Archives, Minnesota Historical Society, St. Paul

US Federal Population Census Schedules, 1870. Watonwan County, Long Lake Township

Governors' Files Folder, Vol. 2, Sibley to Stassen (1856-1943)

MHS Death Certificates Index, on-line

The 1875 Minnesota Census, Watonwan County, Long Lake township

Minnesota State Population Census Schedule, 1895. Pine County, Watonwan County

1905 Census of Minnesota, Population Schedule. Pine County, County of Watonwan

US Federal Population Census Schedules, 1880, 1900, 1910. Pine County, Watonwan County

St. Peter State Hospital Folder, Admissions and Discharges, June 1893-September 1899

St. Peter State Hospital Folder, Case Book, March 1894-March 1896

St. Peter State Hospital Folder, History Accompanying Patient, Examination on Admission, 1894

State of Minnesota, Department of Vital Statistics, Death Certificates (all counties)

Stillwater State Prison Folder, Book of Murders

Stillwater State Prison Folder, Convict Register, 4 volumes

Stillwater State Prison Folder, Good Conduct Book 1874-1886, Monthly Statement of Disbursements

Stillwater State Prison Folder, Hospital Register

Stillwater State Prison Folder, Visitors and Correspondence Registers, Correspondence Register 1892-1899

Stillwater State Prison Folder, Wardens' Correspondence and Miscellany 1889-1894

Watonwan County Folder, Criminal Cases

Watonwan County Folder, Judgement Book

Watonwan County Folder, Probate Court Records, 1870-1976.

Nicollet County Courthouse, Recorder's Office, St. Peter, Minnesota
Marriage Records, 1880-1890.

Pilgrim Lutheran Church, Superior, Wisconsin
Membership Book, 1890-1945.

State of Wisconsin – Bureau of Vital Statistics, Eau Claire County
Death Records 1926.

Superior Public Library, Superior, Wisconsin
Area Research Center for the State of Wisconsin Historical Society.

Svenska Emigrantinstitutet, Växjö, Sweden
Breared, Hallands län, Husförhörslängder, 1838-1842, 1842-1845, 1846-1850, 1851-1855, 1855-1862, 1861-1869

Bro, Värmland, Husförhörslängder, 1836-1840, 1841-1845, 1846-1850, 1851-1855, 1856-1860, 1865-1869

Kila, Värmland, Husförhörslängder, 1861-1865

US Federal Population Census 1870 Minnesota, Madelia Township

Veinge, Hallands län, Husförhörslängder, 1845-1850, 1850-1860, 1861-1869, 1870-1879, 1880-1891, Särskild förteckning 1869

Hälsingborgs Landsförsamling, Skåne, Husförhörslängder, 1875-1884

Personregister till Göteborgs Poliskammares emigrantlistor, 1882.

Swenson Swedish Immigration Research Center, Augustana College, Rock Island, Illinois
Inventory of Swedish American Church Archives in the U. S. A.

Värmlandsarkiv, Karlstad, Sweden
Bro och Huggenäs Kyrkoarkiv, Husförhörslängder

Kila Kyrkoarkiv, Husförhörslängder

Näs häradsrättsarkiv, Näs härads dombok, 1852-1867

Näs häradsrättsarkiv, Näs häradsrätt, bouppteckningar.

Watonwan County Courthouse Recorder's Office, St. James, Minnesota

Certificate Book and Estray Notices and Miscellaneous Documents

Death Record, 1871-1973

Deed Record, Book J

Marriage Record, Book A, Book 41, Book 53

Mortgage Record, Book F, Book X

Reception Record

Register of Births, Book A

Register of Deaths, Book A.

Articles (scholarly)

Clark Hine, Darlene. "Rape and the Inner Lives of Black Women: Thoughts on the Culture of Dissemblance." <u>Black Women and the Reconstruction of American History</u>. Brooklyn, NY: Carlson Publisher, 1994. Pp. 37-47.

Dunn, James Taylor. "The Minnesota STATE PRISON during the STILLWATER Era, 1853-1914." <u>Minnesota History</u>. Volume 37, Number 4 (December, 1960). Pp. 137-150.

Francaviglia, Richard V. "The Historic and Geographic Importance of Railroads in Minnesota." <u>The North Star State: A Minnesota History Reader</u>, Anne J. Aby, ed. St. Paul: Minnesota Historical Society Press, 2002. Pp. 181-187.

Granholm, Bernhard. "Okänd fader - men kanske inte okänd." <u>Släktforskarnas dagbok '98</u>, Håkan Skogsjö, ed. Stockholm & Göteborg: Sveriges Släktforskarförbund, 1998. Pp. 238-268.

Kälvemark, Ann-Sofie. "Att vänta barn när man gifter sig. Föräktenskapliga förbindelser och giftermålsmönster i 1800-talets Sverige." <u>Historisk tidskrift</u>, 2: 1977. Pp. 181-199.

_____. "Utvandring och självständighet. Några synpunkter på den kvinnliga emigrationen från Sverige." <u>Historisk tidskrift</u>, 2: 1983. Pp. 140-174.

Lavery, Jason. "All of the President's Historians: The Debate over Urho Kekkonen." <u>Scandinavian Studies</u>, Vol. 75, Nr. 3, (Fall 2003). Pp. 375-398.

Losman, Beata. "Okända kvinnors röst. Landsbygdskvinnor i 1800-talets Värmland." Forum för kvinnliga forskare och kvinnoforskning. Göteborg. Rapport 1983:1. Pp. 1-52.

_____. "Förtryck eller jämlikhet? Kvinnorna och äktenskapet i Västsverige omkring 1840." <u>Historisk tidskrift</u>, 3: 1982. Pp. 291-318.

Nordstrom, Byron J. "The Sixth Ward: A Minneapolis Swede Town in 1905." <u>Perspectives on Swedish Immigration: Proceedings of the International Conference on the Swedish Heritage in the Upper Midwest, April 1-3, 1976, University of Minnesota, Duluth</u>. Nils Hasselmo, ed. Chicago: The Swedish

Pioneer Historical Society, 1978. Pp. 151-165.

Olsson, Lars. "Evelina Johansdotter, Textile Workers, and the Munsingwear Family: Class, Gender, and Ethnicity in the Political Economy of Minnesota at the End of World War I." Anderson, Philip J. and Blanck, Dag, ed. Swedes in the Twin Cities: Immigrant Life and Minnesota's Urban Frontier. St. Paul: Minnesota Historical Society Press, 2001. Pp. 77-90.

Peterson, Harold F. "Early Minnesota Railroads and the Quest for Settlers." Minnesota History. Vol. 13. (March, 1932). Pp. 25-44.

Rekdal, Anne Marie. "The Female Jousissance: An Analysis of Ibsen's Et dukkehjem." Scandinavian Studies, Vol. 74, nr. 2 (Summer 2002). Pp. 149-180.

Riley, Glenda. "In or Out of the Historical Kitchen?: Minnesota Rural Women." Anne J. Aby, ed. The North Star State: A Minnesota History Reader, St. Paul: Minnesota Historical Society Press, 2002. Pp. 213-225.

Articles (popular)

"A Noble Girl: Miss Amanda E. Gustafson's Chosen Mission Of Christian Charity and Love." The Prison Mirror. Stillwater, Minnesota. August 10, 1887.

"Adam P. Johnsons Make Camp on Prairie in 1879." Newman Grove (Nebraska) Reporter, 75th Anniversary Jubilee Edition, June 9, 1963.

Carter, John. "Prison Life As I Found It." The Century Magazine. Vol. 80. (September, 1910). Pp. 752-758.

Danielson, Ole. "Pioneer History of Long Lake Township." Shirley R. Knudson, ed. History of Watonwan County Minnesota. Dallas, Texas: Curtis Media, Inc., 1995. P. 65. Text of article written on September 1, 1941.

"Death Claims Martin J. Severance." Mankato Free Press. July 11, 1907. Pp. 5-6.

"Death of Peter Olson." St. James Plaindealer, February 8, 1919.

"Grand Old Man of This Community Passes Away at Age 91 [death of J. W. Seager]." Watonwan County Plaindealer, December 7, 1933. P. 1.

"History of St. James," St. James Herald, February 14, 1873.

"Mrs. Sophia Graf Recalls Terrific Snowstorm of 1873." Madelia Times-Messenger, June 20, 1930.

"Rites Are Held for Mrs. Anna Barge." St. James Courier, April 11, 1950.

"Spöktips för hela landet." Svenska Dagbladet, June 24, 2002. P. 17.

Wolfer, Henry. "On Modern Prison Management," The Century Magazine. Vol. 80 (December, 1910), pp. 317-318.

Books

Aby, Anne J., ed. The North Star State: A Minnesota History Reader. Foreword by Paul Gruchow. St. Paul: Minnesota Historical Society Press, 2002.

Andersson, Lars M. and Amurén, Lena. Sveriges historia i årtal. Lund, Sweden: Historiska Media, 2003.

Arill, David and Olsson, Edvard. Värmländska folkminnen. Karlstad, Sweden: Hjalmar Pettersson & Co. Bokhandel, 1932.

Atkins, Annette. Harvest of Grief: Grasshopper Plagues and Public Assistance in Minnesota, 1873-1878. St. Paul: Minnesota Historical Society Press, 1984.

Barton, H. Arnold. A Folk Divided: Homeland Swedes and Swedish Americans, 1840-1940. Carbondale and Edwardsville: Southern Illinois University Press, 1994.

Baumann, Louise Bloom. The Swedes in Omaha and South Omaha – 1889. Omaha: Swedish Cultural Committee, 2005.

Bengtsson, Fritiof, ed. Halländska emigrantöden 1860-1930: Drömmen om Amerika – Vision och verklighet. Halmstad, Sweden: Bokförlaget Spektra, 1976.

Blegen, Theodore C. Minnesota: A History of the State. Minneapolis: University of Minnesota Press, 1985.

_____ and Jordan, Philip D. With Various Voices: Recordings of North Star Life. St. Paul: The Itasca Press, 1949.

Bodenhamer, David J. Fair Trial: Rights of the Accused in American History. New York and Oxford: Oxford University Press, 1992.

Bracher, William, engineer. The Plat Book of Watonwan County. Philadelphia, Pa: Interstate Publishing Co., 1886. Reprint Justina Ebeling et al. Madelia, MN: Watonwan County Historical Society Board of Directors [no date given].

Briefly-Written Facts Regarding the Past and Present of St. James and Watonwan County, Minnesota.... An Illustrated Souvenir. St. James, MN: St. James Plaindealer, 1895.

Brophy, Eliza St. John. Twice A Pioneer. New York: Exposition Press, 1972.

Brown, John A., ed. History of Cottonwood and Watonwan Counties, Minnesota: Their Peoples, Industries and Institutions. 2 vol. Illustrated. Indianapolis: B. F. Bowen & Co., 1916.

Bumgarner, Jeffrey B. Profiling and Criminal Justice in America; A Reference Handbook. Santa Barbara, California: ABC-CLIO, 2004.

Bussert, Joy M. K.. Battered Women: From a Theology of Suffering to an Ethic of Empowerment. New York: Lutheran Church in America, 1986.

Christiansson, Olof, ed. Hallandshistorier. Stockholm: Wahlström & Widstrand, 1946.

Cordes, Jim. Pine County ... and Its Memories. North Branch, Minnesota: Riverview Corporation, 1989.

Crawford, Patty et al. Augustana Home: a Mighty Social Ministry, 1896-1996. Minneapolis: Augustana Care Corporation, 1995.

Davison's Minneapolis City Directory, 1900 – A-G. Vol. XXVII. Minneapolis: Minneapolis Directory Company, 1890. Also volumes for: 1900, 1905, 1908, 1910, 1915, 1917.

Dawkins, Richard, with Yan Wong. The Ancestor's Tale: A Pilgrimage to the Dawn of Evolution. Boston & New York: Houghton Mifflin Company, 2004.

Djupvikens hemman i Kila socken. En beskrivning av människorna och deras bosättningar från 1600-talet till 1900-talet. Kila, Sweden: Kila Östra Bygdegårdsförening, Forskargruppen, 1989.

Draxten, Nina. Kristofer Janson in America. Boston: Norwegian-American Historical Association and Twayne Publishers, 1976.

Eckman, F. M. et al. Minnesskrift 1858-1908 tillegnad Minnesota-Konferensens af Ev. Luterska Augustana-Synoden 50-ars Jubileum. Minneapolis: Hahn & Harmon Company, 1908.

Eckstrom, Cora V., ed. Kansas Lake Lutheran Church 1871-1971: A Century of God's Grace. Butterfield, MN: Butterfield Advocate, 1971.

Edleson, Jeffrey L. and Tolman, Richard M. Intervention for Men Who Batter: An Ecological Approach. Newbury Park, California: SAGE Publications, 1992.

Ejdestam, Julius. De fattigas Sverige. Stockholm: Rabén & Sjögren, 1969.

_____. Svenskt Folklivslexikon. Stockholm: Rabén & Sjögren, 1992.

Executive Documents of the State of Minnesota for the Fiscal Year Ending July 31, 1894. Vol. III. St. Paul: The Pioneer Press Co., 1895.

Folwell, William Watts. A History of Minnesota. Vol. III of IV. St. Paul: Minnesota Historical Society, 1926.

Forster, Margaret. School for Life: A Study of the People's Colleges in Sweden. London: Faber and Faber Ltd., 1944.

Friedman, Lawrence M. A History of American Law. New York: Simon & Schuster, 1985.

_____. American Law: An Introduction. New York and London: W. W. Norton & Company, 1998.

Genoways, Ted, ed. Hard Time: Voices from a State Prison, 1849-1914. St. Paul: Minnesota Historical Society Press, 2002.

Gilman, Rhoda. The Story of Minnesota's Past. St. Paul: Minnesota Historical Society Press, 1991.

Gotsch, Phil et al. Kansas Lake Lutheran Church: 125th Anniversary Observance, June 15-16, 1996. Butterfield, Minnesota, 1996.

Hale, Frederick. Swedes in Wisconsin. Madison: The Wisconsin Historical Society Press, 2002.

Harris, David A. Profiles in Injustice. Why Racial Profiling Cannot Work. New York: The New Press, 2002.

Hasselmo, Nils, ed. Perspectives on Swedish Immigration: Proceedings of the International Conference on the Swedish Heritage in the Upper Midwest, April 1-3, 1976, University of Minnesota, Duluth. Chicago: The Swedish Pioneer Historical Society, 1978.

Heilbron, W. C. Convict Life at the Minnesota State Prison Stillwater, Minnesota. Stillwater, Minnesota: Valley History Press, 1996. Reprint of 1909 edition.

Holmquist, June Drenning, ed. They Chose Minnesota: A Survey of The State's Ethnic Groups. St. Paul: Minnesota Historical Society Press, 1981.

Jacobson, N. and Gottman, J. When Men Batter Women. New York: Simon and Schuster, 1998.

Janson, Drude Krog. Saloonkeepers datter: fortaelling. Minneapolis: C. R. Rasmussens forlagsboghandel, 1892.

_____. A Saloonkeeper's Daughter. Tr. Gerald Thorson. Ed. and with an Introduction by Orm Øverland. Baltimore & London: The Johns Hopkins University Press, 2002.

Janson, Kristofer. Praeriens Saga: fortaellingar fra Amerika. Chicago: Skandinavens bogtrykkeri, 1885.

Karst, Kenneth L. Belonging to America: Equal Citizenship and the Constitution. New Haven and London: Yale University Press, 1989.

Kansas Lake Lutheran Church 1871-1971. A Century of God's Grace. Butterfield, Minnesota: Kansas Lake Lutheran Church, 1971.

Kansas Lake Lutheran Church. 125th Anniversary Observance. Butterfield, Minnesota: Kansas Lake Lutheran Church, 1996.

Klintberg, Bengt af. Svenska trollformler. Stockholm: Wahlström & Widstrand, 1965.

Knudson, Shirley R., ed. History of Watonwan County Minnesota. Dallas, Texas: Curtis Media, Inc., 1995.

Knutsson, Ivar, ed. Veinge och Tjärby genom sekler. Halmstad, Sweden: Veinge Hembygdsförening, 1986.

Koblas, John. When the Heavens Fell: The Youngers in Stillwater Prison. St. Cloud, Minnesota: North Star Press, 2002.

Lass, William E. Minnesota: A Bicentennial History. New York: W. W. Norton & Company, Inc., 1977.

Lindgren, Judith Mooney. Thirty-two Cemeteries of Douglas County, Wisconsin. Superior, Wisconsin: Judith Mooney Lindgren, 2002.

Ljungmark, Lars. Den stora utvandringen: Svensk emigration till USA 1840-1925. Stockholm: Sveriges Radio, 1965.

_____. Swedish Exodus. Tr. Kermit Westerberg. Carbondale & Edwardsville: Southern Illinois University Press, 1979.

Luecke, John C. The Chicago and Northwestern in Minnesota. Eagan, Minnesota: Grenadier Publications, 1990.

Mankato City and Blue Earth County Directory, 1904-1905. St. Paul: R. L. Polk & Co. Publishers, 1904.

Marklund, Kari, ed. NationalEncyklopedin: Ett uppslagsverk på vetenskaplig grund utarbetat på initiativ av Statens Kurlturråd. 20 vol. Illustrated. Stockholm: Bokförlaget Bra Böcker, 1989-1996.

Mattson, Hans. Reminiscences: The Story of an Emigrant. St. Paul: D. D. Merrill Company, 1892.

Meyer, Duane. The Highland Scots of North Carolina. Raleigh, North Carolina: The Carolina Charter Tercentenary Commission, 1963.

Moberg, Vilhelm. A History of the Swedish People: From Prehistory to the Renaissance. Tr. Paul Britten Austin. New York: Dorset Press, 1972.

_____. A History of the Swedish People: From Renaissance to Revolution. Tr. Paul Britten Austin. New York: Dorset Press, 1973.

_____. Den okända släkten. Stockholm: Albert Bonniers förlag, 1959.

_____. The Unknown Swedes: A Book About Swedes and America, Past and Present. Roger McKnight, tr. and ed. Foreword H. Arnold Barton. Carbondale & Edwardsville: Southern Illinois University Press, 1988. English version of Den okända släkten.

Minneapolis Pioneers and Soldiers Memorial Cemetery, 1858-1936. Minneapolis: Minneapolis Protective Cemetery Association, 1936.

1870-1920 Minnesalbum Utgifvet af Svenska Lutherska Öst Sveadahls-Församlingen i Watonwan County, Minn. med anledning af dess Femtioårs-Jubileum den 29-31 oktober 1920. Rock Island, Illinois: Augustana Book Concerns Tryckeri, 1920.

1873-1923 Minnesalbum Utgivet av Svenska Lutherska West Sveadahls-Församlinen i Watonwan County, Minn. Femtioårs-Jubileum den 24, 25 juni 1923. Rock Island, Illinois: Augustana Book Concerns Tryckeri och Bokbinderi, 1923.

Minnesota Correctional Facility — Stillwater Mission Statement 1989-1990. Stillwater, Minnesota: Minnesota Department of Corrections, 1990.

Nelson, O. M. The Swedish Element in Omaha: A Historical Record of the Cultural and Commercial Activities of Swedish-born Residents of Omaha and Their Descendants, with 500 Biographies. Omaha, 1935.

Odin, Minnesota Centennial 1899-1999: 100 Years. Odin, Minnesota: Odin Centennial Society, 1999.

Ohlmark, Åke. Spökhistorier från alla länder och tider. Stockholm: Tidens förlag, 1980.

Petri, Carl J. et al. Augustana Minnen 1866-1916: En återblick på den Femtioåriga verksamheten af Svenska Evangeliska Lutherska Augustanaförsamlingen i Minneapolis, Minn. Minneapolis: The Nygren Printing Co., 1916.

Pierson, Susan Hewitt. Pennsylvania Roots and Spreading Branches: Genealogy of Allied Lines Keller – Leckonton – Page (Barge) 1721-1980. St. James, Minnesota: Watonwan County Shoppers Guide; Blue Earth, MN: Central Graphics, 1980.

_____. Turner and Allied Ancestors. Descendants of Benjamin Turner, Mariner 1721-1985. St. James, Minnesota: County Seat Publications, [no date given].

Prison Rules, Good Time Law, Library Catalogue of the Minnesota State Prison, at Stillwater, Minnesota. Stillwater, Minnesota: The Prison Mirror, 1901.

Quackenbush, Orville F. The Development of the Correctional, Reformatory, and Penal Institutions of Minnesota: A Sociological Interpretation. Ann Arbor, Michigan: UMI Dissertation Services, 1956.

Sandklef, Albert and Salvén, Erik. Svenska gods och gårdar, del I: Halland Södra Delen. Uddevalla: Förlaget Svenska gods och gårdar, 1945.

Scott, Franklin D. Sweden: The Nation's History. Minneapolis: University of Minnesota Press, 1978.

Schoultz, Gösta von. Värmland. Stockholm: Wiksell/Gebers, 1982.

Seventy-fifth Anniversary 1871-1946, July 7-14, 1946. Butterfield, Minnesota: Kansas Lake Lutheran Church, 1946.

Skogsjö, Håkan, ed. Släktforskarnas dagbok '98. Stockholm & Göteborg: Sveriges Släktforskarförbund, 1998.

Shoemaker's Business Directory of the City of Mankato and Blue Earth County, Minn. Mankato: Jas. Shoemaker Publisher, 1888. Published yearly.

Ström, Fredrik. Folket i Simlångsdalen. Stockholm: Albert Bonniers förlag, 1903.

A Souvenir....St. James, Minnesota. Minneapolis: Wall & Haines, 1901.

Tedebrand, Lars-Göran. Värmlandsundersökningen. Karlstad, Sweden: Emigrantregistret i Karlstad. Värmlands Hembygdsförbund, 1975.

Värmland, Vallfartsmål och vildmark. Malmö: Allhems förlag, 1966.

Wishart, David T., ed. Encyclopedia of the Great Plains. Lincoln and London: University of Nebraska Press, 2004.

Yesterdays: Images of Superior & Douglas County. Superior, Wisconsin: Douglas County Historical Society, 1998.

Zust, Barbara Lois. The Meaning of INSIGHT Participation Among Women Who Have Experienced Intimate Partner Violence. Ph. d. dissertation, University of Minnesota. August, 2003.

Newspapers Cited

The Evening Telegram, Superior, WI

Madelia Times-Messenger, Madelia, MN

Mankato Herald, Mankato, MN

<u>Mankato Record</u>, Mankato, MN
<u>Mankato Revue</u>, Mankato, MN
<u>The Free Press</u>, Mankato, MN
<u>Minneapolis Journal</u>, Minneapolis, MN
<u>The Mirror</u>, Stillwater, MN
<u>The Prison Mirror</u>, Stillwater State Prison, MN
<u>Reporter</u>, Newman Grove, NE
<u>Sandstone Courier</u>, Sandstone, MN
<u>Star Tribune</u>, Minneapolis, MN
<u>St. James Courier</u>, St. James, MN
<u>St. James Herald</u>, St. James, MN
<u>The St. James Journal</u>, St. James, MN
<u>St. James Plaindealer</u>, St. James, MN
<u>The Superior Telegram</u>, Superior, WI
<u>Svenska Amerikanaren Tribunen</u>, Chicago
<u>Svenska Amerikanska Posten</u>, Minneapolis, MN
<u>Svenska Dagbladet</u>, Stockholm, Sweden
<u>Svenska Nybyggaren</u>, St. Paul, MN
<u>Watonwan County Plaindealer</u>, St. James, MN
<u>The Wells Atlas</u>, Wells, MN.

Personal Interviews and Communications

Tom Anderson, Sveadahl, MN: January 28, 2005.
Wes Beck, Sveadahl, MN: January 28, 2005.
Erik and Asta Berg, Veinge, Halland, Sweden: January 24, 2004.
Donna Beig, Tucson, AZ: March 25-26, 2005.
Carol Bratland, St. James, MN: April 20, 2002; November 29, 2003.
Shirley Moriarity Christeson, Eau Claire, WI: March 19, 2005.
Pat Henke, Fall Creek, WI: June 18, 2003; July 28, 2003; November 23, 2003.
Håkan Håkansson and Birgitta Wiman, Halmstad, Sweden: November 27, 2003; December 8, 2003.
Carl-Johan Ivarsson, Söderköping, Sweden: March 5, 2003.
Sven-Olof Johansson, Veinge, Sweden: December 3, 2003.
Inga Johansson, Snöstorp, Halland, Sweden: January 25, 2004.
Gary Johnson, Racine, WI: August 31, 2003.
Judy Klee, Temecula, CA: December 28, 2002; November 12, 2003.
Phillip Moody, Long Lake township, Watonwan County, MN: May 27, 2003.

Ragnhild Preston, Fall Creek, WI: August 30, 2003.

Reverend Evelyn Weston, East Sveadahl Lutheran Church, MN: January 28, 2005.

Unpublished Texts

Attavara I. In possession of Håkan Håkansson. Halland Genealogical Society. Halmstad, Sweden.

Alexandersson, Nils. Personer bosatta på Attavara åren 1867-1900. Halmstad, Sweden. June, 2003.

Evolution of the Blue Earth County Court House and Jail. Blue Earth County Historical Society. Mankato, Minnesota, February, 2004.

Henke, Pat. Karolina Andersdotter. Fall Creek, Wisconsin. April, 2000; updated May, 2002.

Kansas Lake Church Board Meetings 1901 to 1940 (Kansas Lake Församlings Kyrkoråds Prottokoller, år 1901 [-1940]). In possession of Kansas Lake Lutheran Church, Long Lake township, Watonwan County, Minnesota.

Kansas Lake Secretary's Book 1891-1908 (Kansas Lake Församlings Protokoller 1891 [-1908]). In possession of Kansas Lake Lutheran Church, Long Lake township, Watonwan County, Minnesota.

Kansas Lake Treasurer's Book 1892-1908 (Räkenskaps – Bock För Kansas Lake – Församling 1892 [-1908]). In possession of Kansas Lake Lutheran Church, Long Lake township, Watonwan County, Minnesota.

Protocolsbok för Westra Sweadahls Kyrkoråd / West Sveadahl Kyrkorådets [Book] 1877-1910. In possession of Dee Kleinow, Burnsville, Minnesota.

Bibliography

Photos and Illustrations

Fig. 1. A smallholder's cottage at Sterserudstorp, Värmland, such as Lars Johnson's family would have lived in. (*Author photo*)

Fig. 2. Road leading from Sterserudstorp, such as Lars and Caroline would have used. (*Author photo*)

Fig. 3. View from Attavara Farm, Halland *(Author photo)*

Fig. 4. Breared church where Andrew's Mother and Father were married in 1833. *(Author photo)*

Fig. 5. Southern Sweden, showing Halland's relation to Denmark

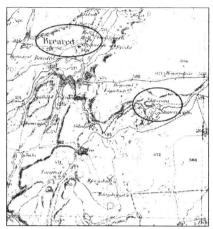

Fig. 6. Breared in relation to Lake Attavara, Halland

Fig. 7. Central Halland, showing Simlångsdalen (Breared) and Veinge Parishes

Fig. 8. Southern Värmland, Showing Kila and Bro Parishes

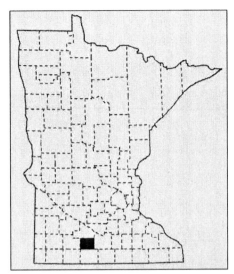

Fig. 9.Watonwan County, Minnesota

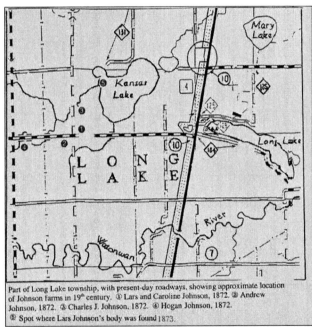

Part of Long Lake township, with present-day roadways, showing approximate location of Johnson farms in 19th century. ① Lars and Caroline Johnson, 1872. ② Andrew Johnson, 1872. ③ Charles J. Johnson, 1872. ④ Hogan Johnson, 1872. ⑤ Spot where Lars Johnson's body was found 1873.

Fig. 10. Kansas Lake

Fig. 11. Gravestone of Andrew Johnson's mother at Kansas Lake, with tender image of a lamb. *(Courtesy Ray and Dee Kleinow)*

Fig. 12. Gravesite of Andrew Johnson's father at Kansas Lake, with modern farm in the background. *(Courtesy Ray and Dee Kleinow)*

Fig. 13. Gravesite of Andrew Johnson outside of Superior, WI. *(Courtesy Donna Bieg)*

Fig. 14. The sewing box made for Caroline by Andrew
Johnson while in Stillwater Prison. *(Courtesy Pat Henke)*

Fig. 15. Andrew Johnson's
bible was his only
surviving possession.
(Courtesy Donna Bieg)

Fig. 16. Andrew and Caroline's daughter Christine at her wedding, January 26, 1893.
(Courtesy Pat Henke)

Fig. 17. Caroline, photo from 1868.
(Courtesy Pat Henke)

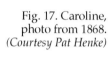

Fig. 18. Annie Johnson Barge at age 28

Fig. 19. Anna Johanna, Hogan Johnson's daughter in Sweden. *(Courtesy Håkan Håkansson and Birgitta Wiman)*

Fig. 20. Annie Johnson Barge in her old age, with her grandchildren. *(Courtesy Carol Bratland)*

Fig. 21. Andrew's son, Nels Peter, after Hinckley Fire, in Sandstone with his family. Son, Per August and wife in back row. *(Courtesy Donna Bieg)*

Fig. 22. Farm that Andrew and son Nels Peter purchased after prison. Picture is with his grandsons Aaron, Lawrence, Leo. *(Courtesy Donna Bieg)*

Fig. 23. Downtown St. James after the great blizzard of January 7, 1873. *(Courtesy Tom Anderson)*

Fig. 24. Southwest view of Kansas Lake, approximate area where Lars Johnson's body would have entered the water. *(Courtesy Tom Anderson)*

Fig. 25. Loghouse where Kansas Lake Swedish congregation was organized in 1871

Fig. 26. House where Caroline Johnson died in Madison, 1907. *(Courtesy Pat Henke)*

Fig. 27. Andrew's last home that he lived in with his late son's (Nels Peter) family. *(Courtesy Donna Bieg)*